TROUBLED LANDS

TROUBLED LANDS

The Legacy of Soviet Environmental Destruction

DJ Peterson

A RAND Research Study

WESTVIEW PRESS

BOULDER • SAN FRANCISCO • OXFORD

Copyright © 1993 by RAND

Published in 1993 in the United States of America by Westview Press, Inc., 5500 Central Avenue, Boulder, Colorado 80301-2877, and in the United Kingdom by Westview Press, 36 Lonsdale Road, Summertown, Oxford OX2 7EW

RAND books are available on a wide variety of topics. To receive a list of RAND books, write or call Distribution Services, RAND, 1700 Main Street, P.O. Box 2138, Santa Monica, California 90407-2138, (310) 393-0411, extension 6686.

Library of Congress Cataloging-in-Publication Data
Peterson, D. J.
    Troubled lands: the legacy of Soviet environmental destruction /
by D. J. Peterson.
        p.   cm.
    Includes bibliographical references and index.
    ISBN 0-8133-1673-1. — ISBN 0-8133-1674-X (pbk.)
    1. Pollution—Environmental aspects—Soviet Union.
2. Environmental policy—Soviet Union—Citizen participation.
I. Title
HC340.P55.P47   1993
363.7'00947—dc20   92-30796
                                                                                          CIP

Printed and bound in the United States of America

    The paper used in this publication meets the requirements
(∞) of the American National Standard for Permanence of Paper
    for Printed Library Materials Z39.48-1984.

10   9   8   7   6   5   4   3   2   1

Contents

Tables and Illustrations

Tables

Figures

Maps

Photographs

Foreword

Among the most disturbing revelations resulting from glasnost are widespread reports of environmental damage inflicted throughout the former Soviet Union during 70 years of communist rule. Although the reports have often been sketchy and sensationalized, what emerges is a portrait of a Soviet regime willing to sacrifice the well-being of the environment and the health of the citizenry in its quest for military and economic might.

The nuclear calamity epitomized by Chernobyl helped drag the system down. This and other environmental assaults on ancestral homelands not only fueled the fires of activism but also spurred an ethnic revival that ultimately contributed to the Soviet collapse. Now that the USSR is gone, the newly independent successor states must deal with a legacy of destruction; and as they pursue their economic goals, one wonders whether the region may not be poised for a second onslaught on nature.

In this book, DJ Peterson draws upon his travels to the capitals and provinces of the affected regions, where he interviewed officials of both the new and old governments and was given access to data heretofore unavailable. He vividly describes the overwhelming environmental problems facing the successor states: air and water pollution, degradation of land resources, and inadequate management of solid and hazardous wastes. He records and analyzes the responses of governmental actors, industry, the military, and grass-roots environmental organizations in those regions. Finally, he reflects on the roles and responsibilities of the advanced industrialized nations in mitigating problems with potentially widespread international ramifications.

Troubled Lands gives readers a wide-angle lens through which to view the struggles of newly reconstituted countries working in parallel to fundamentally redirect social and political institutions and to build stable market economies that incorporate responsible environmental policies. Beyond that, these chapters also function as case studies with important lessons for other nations around the world—the United States among them—that aspire to achieve the delicate balance between economic prosperity and environmental responsibility.

James A. Thomson
President and Chief Executive Officer
RAND
Santa Monica, California

Preface

Eco-glasnost and events in the political, economic, and environmental spheres since the late 1980s have radically altered the state of affairs in the former Soviet Union and what we in the West know about them. The material presented in this book is based primarily on recent Soviet sources and reflects the development of eco-glasnost in the post-Chernobyl era.[1] Much of the information was drawn from officially sanctioned government publications on the environment.[2] This official information was supplemented with a wide variety of evidence from regional and central newspapers, popular and academic journals, wire service reports, radio broadcasts, television reports, and personal interviews.

Chapter 1 presents an overview of the extent and means of pollution in the former Soviet Union and why it occurred as it did. Chapters 2–5 process and analyze the new data made available on air resources, water resources, land resources, and management of solid and hazardous wastes. Chapters 6 and 7 are devoted to the new efforts at environmental protection being made both by governmental institutions and non-governmental groups. Chapter 6 examines the major institutional and individual actors in contemporary environmental affairs from the top down and delves into the politics and policies of environmental protection. Chapter 7 takes advantage of the fruits of democratization to take another look at environmental politics, this time from the bottom up. Finally, Chapter 8 discusses the constraints and opportunities with which these actors will be presented as they seek to transform their economies in the post-Soviet era.

As noted here and throughout the book, environmental researchers in the former Soviet Union suffer chronic difficulties in data collection and analysis. Indeed, as the volume and sources of new information have exploded under eco-glasnost, reliability of data and testing has grown more problematic. Accordingly, I acknowledge that this book is vulnerable to the weaknesses of the source material, particularly secondary references, and thus I have noted inconsistencies and have made clarifications where possible. Being relatively new to the arena of international cooperation, officials in the former Soviet Union have not yet focused their energies on making their data collection and analysis methodologies conform with international standards and practices. To compensate as much as possible for this state of affairs, I have, when the data permit, drawn simple analogies and comparisons to conditions elsewhere in the world in an effort to give the reader a baseline for conclusions. It must be kept in mind, however, that these comparisons are but rough approximations.

In this book, measurements are provided in metric terms. The following conversion factors are provided for common equivalents:

To convert from:	*To:*	*Multiply by:*
hectares	miles, square	0.004
hectares	kilometers, square	0.01
hectares	acres	2.471
kilograms	pounds	2.679
kilometers	miles	0.621
kilometers, cubic	meters, cubic	1×10^9
kilometers, cubic	acre-feet	811,030
kilometers, square	miles, square	0.386
kilometers, square	acres	247
meters, cubic	feet, cubic	35.323
meters, cubic	gallons	264
tons, metric	tons, short	0.907

Because this book focuses exclusively on the territory of the former Soviet Union, the temptation is to view the environmental issues discussed as a uniquely Soviet phenomenon. Indeed, this view is reinforced by the statements of local commentators themselves, who, unfamiliar with affairs abroad because of decades of physical and intellectual isolation, frequently paint conditions inside the former Soviet Union as strikingly unique or severe. However, when one takes a step back and places the situation within a global context or relates it to conditions in other regions—advanced industrial or developing—what becomes eminently clear is that the challenges citizens of the new states are or will be confronting often are similar to challenges elsewhere in the world. Some conditions in the ex-Soviet republics truly are exceptional, but a preoccupation with hyperbole and exceptionalism will only blind us to their commonality with problems closer to home.

Notes

1. Two other books reflecting the fruit of glasnost are Murray Feshbach and Alfred Friendly, Jr., *Ecocide in the USSR* (New York: Basic Books, 1992); and Philip R. Pryde, *Environmental Management in the Soviet Union* (New York: Cambridge University Press, 1991).

2. Two handbooks produced by the Soviet environmental protection agency USSR Goskompriroda were *Sostoyanie prirodnoi sredy i prirodookhrannaya deyatel'nost' v SSSR v 1989 g.* (The State of the Environment and Environmental Protection in the USSR in 1989) and *Sostoyanie prirodnoi sredy v SSSR v 1988 g.* (The State of the Environment in the USSR in 1988). The Soviet statistical agency put out several reports; one used here is USSR Goskomstat, *Okhrana okruzhayushchei sredy i ratsional'noe ispol'zovanie prirodnykh resursov v SSSR* (Environmental Protection and Rational Use of Natural Resources in the USSR) (Moscow: Finansy i statistika, 1989). The author thanks Murray Feshbach, Georgetown University, Washington, D.C., for generously sharing his copy of this handbook.

Acknowledgments

Work on this book required two and one-half years and the assistance, ideas, and support of many colleagues; many, though not all, of their names appear throughout the text. I am particularly indebted to friends in the former Soviet Union who graciously shared their work, their offices, and their homes with me, especially those at Moscow's Institute of Geography and the Social-Ecological Union. Many people reviewed the manuscript in various stages of completion, helping me to refine the text: Special thanks go to John Richmond, Rebecca Ritke, Jeri O'Donnell, Cara Gilbert, Alyssa Peterson, Kristen Suokko, Craig ZumBrunnen, Ida May B. Norton, and Judith Westbury. Eric Green, a key player in Moscow's international environmental community and a close friend, deserves much more than a mention for allowing me to borrow ideas from his earlier work on Soviet environmental affairs and for offering valuable assistance—including extended lodging—which greatly facilitated much of my research in the former Soviet Union. Naturally, I assume sole liability for any misrepresentations that may exist.

Some of the material presented in this book first appeared in a series of articles published in Radio Liberty's *Report on the USSR* between 1989 and 1992. I thank Radio Free Europe/Radio Liberty Inc. for permitting me to include this material here. Grants from the RAND/UCLA Center for Soviet Studies and the Center for International Research at the University of California, Los Angeles, allowed me to travel to the former Soviet Union to conduct field research. The completion of my research for and publication of this book was made possible by the generous financial support of RAND and with the personal commitment of Vice President Wally Baer and the director of the International Policy Department, Jonathan Pollack. The professional guidance, long hours, and unalloyed enthusiasm put forth by Cindy Kumagawa of RAND's Commercial Book

Program immensely simplified and leavened the overwhelming process of putting my first book together. Rod Sato of RAND's Publications Department created the beautiful graphics presented in the text and accommodated my constant revisions. The design of the book is the work of another dear friend—Scott Ford. Again, thanks go to all. Finally, this book is dedicated to Alyssa Peterson, whose mixture of sisterly admonitions and unflagging encouragement kept me on track through the ups and downs.

DJ Peterson

TROUBLED LANDS

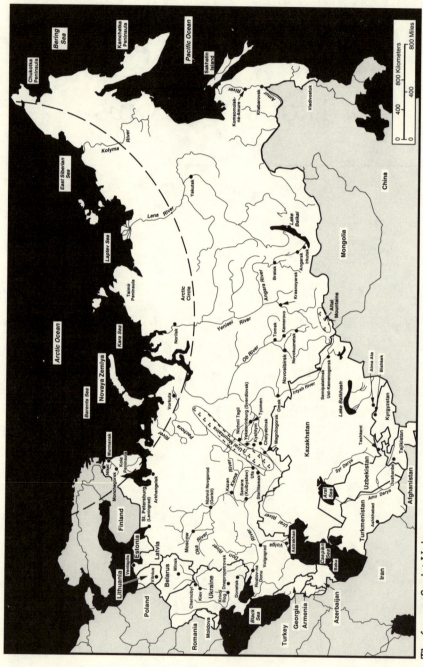

The former Soviet Union

1

Introduction

If we compare the planet with a communal apartment, we occupy the dirtiest room.
—Aleksei Yablokov,
environmental adviser to President Boris Yeltsin

For seventy years, the notion of development and progress in the Soviet Union was symbolized by the factory with its chimneys thrust into the sky, pumping out fulsome clouds of smoke. These clouds, always streaming out of the picture, evoked images of productivity and output. History has now shown that many of the achievements of the Soviet economy were never more than images. The smoke, however, was real. Cities once touted as the centers of Soviet industrial accomplishment—Magnitogorsk, Novokuznetsk, Astrakhan, Komsomolsk-on-Amur—have now been revealed (thanks to glasnost) as having terrible environmental problems. Other cities not usually associated with the Soviet heavy industrialization drive—Yerevan, Yalta, Baikalsk, Kiev—also suffer severely. "Until recently, Krivoi Rog was described as the Iron Heart of the Land of Soviets. Now it is generally admitted that this heart is chronically ailing," commented a reporter for the evening news program "Vremya."[1] "For a long time, Podolsk has been called the industrial center of the Moscow area," lamented several residents in a letter to the daily newspaper *Rabochaya tribuna* (Worker Tribune): "We do not want to be proud of this."[2]

Claiming itself to be the vanguard of socialism, the Soviet government sought unfettered, rapid economic growth and military might—a quest that befouled both air and water, impoverished the country's farms, and poisoned the land with toxic waste and radioactive fallout. For almost three-quarters of a century, the truth about what was happening to the environment remained obscured by the triumphs of Soviet development

1

and the bold righteousness of the Soviet regime. However, just as the process of glasnost and political reform initiated in the 1980s revolutionized the Soviet people's perceptions of their society, so too has it revolutionized their perceptions of their physical environment. Communism's dirty secrets are being uncovered by government officials and environmentalists alike, and each discovery adds to a list of staggering problems.

In the 1980s, air pollution levels in over one hundred cities across the former Soviet Union periodically exceeded air quality standards by a factor of ten. Fifty million citizens lived in these cities during that time. Over one-third of Moscow's population—3.5 million residents—now live with excessive air pollution. Lead, carbon monoxide, and nitrogen oxides from automobile traffic had turned the capital's Garden Ring road into the "Black Ring," noted officials at a press conference in 1989.[3]

Air quality in industrial centers such as Nizhnii Tagil and Bratsk became so severe that drivers frequently had to turn on their headlights during the day in order safely to negotiate city streets. Situated in Russia's Ural Mountains industrial region, Nizhnii Tagil is the home of the V. I. Lenin Metallurgical Combine as well as numerous enterprises related to the iron and steel industry. In the heyday of Soviet power, the combine's twenty-six furnaces churned out steel by the millions of tons. Among other goods, the combine produced one-quarter of the train rails for the Soviet Union. The Communist Party awarded medals to plant workers for their great contribution to the cause of industrialization; plant managers went on to climb the ladders of the Party and government hierarchy.

As the combine broke records for producing steel, the plant's stacks belched out pollution in great proportion—1.5 tons for every citizen of Nizhnii Tagil. "A monstrous cloud of toxic smog hangs over the city," wrote the labor daily *Trud* (Labor) in 1990. But, the paper noted, "The difficult process of reassessing the values which were sanctified for decades is under way here." Commented one worker: "Ne zhelezom yedinom zhivem" (We do not live by steel alone).[4] On the occasion of the plant's fiftieth anniversary, managers shut down an aged coking battery, but the smog did not lift. The following year, residents of the city decided to erect a monument not to the shock forces of Communist labor but to "the victims of the ecological terror."[5] "People are dying for metal," concluded *Trud*.

The situation was similarly dismal in other locations. The writer of a letter to the popular weekly magazine *Novoe vremya* (New Times) from the Baltic town of Ventspils, Latvia, described life with a local petrochemicals plant built with assistance from an American firm:

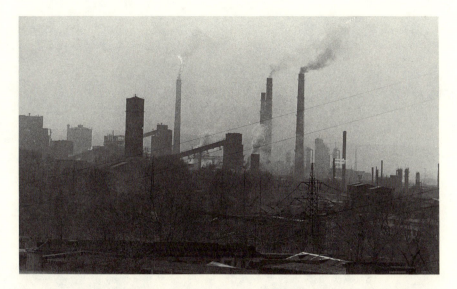

Kemerovo, center of the Kuznetsk industrial basin in central Siberia and home to enterprises producing coal, chemicals, and heavy machinery. Photo: Novosti from Sovfoto.

> Do you know that in the kindergartens of Ventspils the teachers instruct the children how to don gas masks. . . . Every resident of Ventspils has a gas mask; in case of an accident the following recommendations have been worked out: sensing a chemical smell, people must run in the direction opposite of the wind to a predetermined meeting place. But the wind usually blows from the West—we most likely will have to run into the sea.[6]

Water pollution is equally as severe as air pollution. Large and small rivers alike have been choked with sewage, petroleum products, phenols, heavy metals, and agricultural runoff. Uncontrolled dumping by the Gagarin machine-building plant in Komsomolsk-na-Amure, for example, has resulted in accumulations of zinc, chromium, and copper up to 15 times government standards in the Amur River as it flows to the Pacific Ocean. Stocks of caviar-producing sturgeon in the Volga River, the Mississippi of Russia, have plummeted, the result of severe water pollution coupled with aggressive dam building and overfishing. Once-popular resorts on the Baltic and Black Sea coasts are quiet during the summer months because untreated industrial and municipal waste has rendered the water unsafe for swimming. Interviewed by the daily newspaper *Trud*, the USSR's chief public health officer warned in 1989:

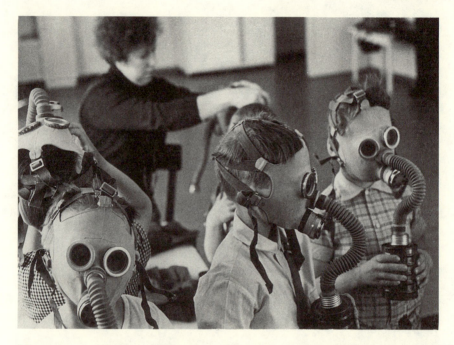

Kindergarten children in Angarsk near Lake Baikal practice donning gas masks as a drill in case of an accident at a nearby rail freight yard. Photo: TASS from Sovfoto.

"I personally would advise [holidaymakers] to put aside planned trips to the sea, and to go to some other rest spot."[7] In many regions, including large cities such as St. Petersburg, residents are advised to boil their tap water; poorly equipped and overworked treatment plants cannot remove an ever-increasing slate of contaminants.

Broad swaths of Russia and Kazakhstan have become infertile desert. To boost food supplies and compensate for the shortcomings of collective agriculture, the Soviet regime promoted the extensive mechanization of agriculture and pushed farming into fragile pasture lands in these areas. The government also supplied farmers with ample stocks of agrochemicals at virtually no cost and with minimal guidance in their use. The result was widespread soil as well as groundwater contamination. According to the Soviet government in 1989:

> The total annual load of pesticides in regions of Krasnodar Krai and in the Tajik [Republic] exceeds the national average by 3–5 times; in the Moldavian SSR it is 9–10 times, and the Armenian and the Turkmen [Republics] are 20–25 times [the national average]. In the regions of maximum pesticide

use, the incidence of illness among children less than six years old is 4.6 times higher than in areas using the least chemicals (with a predominance of skin diseases, problems of the digestive tract, lung ailments, disruption of metabolic processes, and retardation of physical development).[8]

In Central Asia, the Aral Sea is fast becoming the Aral desert. In one of humanity's greatest land-use disasters, four-fifths of the water that feeds what was the world's fourth largest lake has been diverted to support the region's cotton monoculture. As a result of fulfilling their "socialist duty" to produce cotton, however, 3 million people have had no choice but to drink water saturated with agricultural chemicals leaching into their water supplies.

Five years after the disaster at Chernobyl's reactor No. 4, there were 4 million people still living in territory tainted by radioactive fallout—2.2 million in Belarus alone. One-third of that republic's territory was contaminated, most of it agricultural land. Even where contamination was significant, the land continues to be farmed because of lack of an alternative source of income or food.[9] In Minsk, the Belarusian capital, the Red Cross frequently makes rounds of the city's stores and markets to assure that food is free of radioactivity.

But Chernobyl was not the only contributor to the list of radioactive contamination problems. More than forty years of gross negligence and bad luck in the race to build nuclear weapons resulted in contamination that, cumulatively, makes the radioactive fallout caused by the 1986 nuclear accident at Chernobyl pale in comparison. In the late 1940s and early 1950s, high-level radioactive waste from the top-secret Mayak nuclear weapons production complex in the Ural Mountains city of Chelyabinsk-40, was dumped, untreated, into a local river and then into a nearby reservoir. A 1957 explosion in a waste storage tank at Mayak subsequently spewed radioactive material across the countryside, forcing officials to wipe contaminated villages off Soviet maps. Total accumulated radiation in the region has been pegged at 1 billion curies—twenty times the contamination produced by Chernobyl. Ironically, the products of the Soviet nuclear weapons program wrought destruction not on its enemies abroad but on citizens at home. After studying these events, Thomas Cochran of the U.S. Natural Resources Defense Council concluded: "This has got to be the most polluted spot on the planet."[10]

But the contaminators were not concerned solely with military purposes. The land has been riddled with the scars of 120 nuclear explosions conducted for "peaceful purposes."[11] A product of bad science and aggressive lobbying by the nuclear weapons producers, such explosions were intended to create huge underground cavities for storage of hazardous waste, to squeeze oil deposits up to the surface, and to prospect for minerals. Many such tests failed. An explosion designed to cap a blowout at a gas well in the Pechora region of northern Russia went awry in 1980 and only worsened the leak, which eventually took six years to remedy.[12] In 1971, three explosions were conducted in northern Perm oblast (region) as part of an experiment to divert the course of a river. Instead, the project created a lake of contaminated water the local population learned about only two decades later.[13]

Several hundred miles to the north of Pechora lies Novaya Zemlya, a frozen archipelago that served as the USSR's second nuclear weapons test site. In 1991, *Komsomol'skaya pravda,* a newspaper with a reputation for probing investigation, revealed that the region also served as a dumping ground for radioactive wastes, in violation of international conventions:

> In the period 1966–1986 sailors from the Murmansk shipping line regularly deposited radioactive wastes near Novaya Zemlya. A large number of containers of radioactive waste were sunk in the bays of the northern archipelago along the Kara Sea. In one of the containers was the reactor of the atomic icebreaker *Lenin,* which was decommissioned in 1969. After being dumped, several containers remained floating. Sailors had to punch holes in them and wait until they sank. . . . Liquid radioactive wastes were released even closer: they were poured out into the western Barents Sea, right in the very same quadrants where trawlers fish.[14]

More than seventy years of industrial development have not only left a staggering list of environmental problems but also sapped the vitality and spirit of society. Commenting on the state of the famous Kuzbass coal-mining and industrial region of Siberia, Aleksei Yablokov, a prominent Russian environmentalist and adviser to Boris Yeltsin, noted:

> I visited Kemerovo recently. The situation is very alarming there. Up to 75 percent of industry in the city stands idle on windless days in order that people can breathe. People have started to leave the city quietly. If things go on like this, there will be no housing problem in the Kemerovo region in five or ten years. . . . The question arises: what is the purpose of our lives? Do we live so that a factory can fulfill and overfill its plans?[15]

During an official visit to the republics of Bashkiriya and Tatariya in Russia in 1990, Boris Yeltsin observed:

> Both regions seem to be in the worst ecological situation. And this problem, sadly, is worse than the food situation, although the food situation is thoroughly bad. . . . People are being poisoned when in Bashkiriya 460,000

tons of pollution hazardous to humans are emitted and in Tatariya 600,000 tons are emitted; that makes one million tons in one area. It's suicide![16]

As Yeltsin's statement and the reports cited here indicate, the cost of environmental degradation in terms of human health has been high, and this expense has contributed to a public health crisis the region's under-funded medical infrastructure has been ill-equipped to handle. "About twenty percent of illnesses are caused by the deteriorating state of the environment," noted two specialists in the respected weekly newspaper *Argumenty i fakty* (Arguments and Facts) in 1990.[17] Only 23 percent of Soviet children under the age of seven were determined to be "practically healthy" at the close of the 1980s, and studies indicate that the prevalence of nervous disorders, allergies, and illnesses of the in-testinal tract among children doubled from the 1970s to 1980s.[18] Unfor-tunately, it may prove impossible to ascertain the source of many of these maladies: Doctors rarely kept detailed medical records and officials frequently falsified data in order to hide this undesirable part of Soviet history.

MAPPING THE DAMAGE

To help analysts and policymakers evaluate the seriousness of envi-ronmental conditions around the country, a team of researchers led by Boris Kochurov of the Russian Academy of Science's Institute of Geogra-phy defined three states of degradation: conflict, crisis, and catastrophe. The first category, conflict, refers to areas principally affected by a form of environmental degradation that is usually reversible. Agricultural lands make up a large share of the conflict zones. Widespread overgraz-ing, intensive cultivation, and clear-cutting operations, for example, may have upset the chemical balance of the soil and contributed to erosion, desertification, and compacting of the topsoil. Such activities have caused a noticeable decline in the productivity of the land in parts of the central *chernozem* (rich black earth belt) and northern Kazakhstan (see Map 1.1). Water pollution can also contribute to problems in conflict zones, such as has happened in the Black, White, Azov, and Caspian seas, and in Lake Onega, northeast of St. Petersburg.

The second category, crisis, refers to regions in which the destructive activities of the economy have so affected the local ecosystem that, even under strict protection, its recovery would take decades or even cen-turies. In some situations, conditions are so serious that they present a health threat to people living in the area. Crisis regions include many lakes and rivers that have been choked with wastes and contaminated

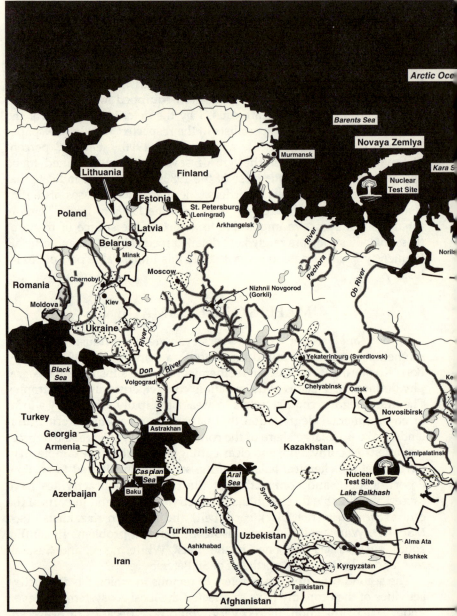

Source: Institute of Geography, Russian Academy of Sciences.

MAP 1.1. Regions of environmental degradation within the former Soviet Union

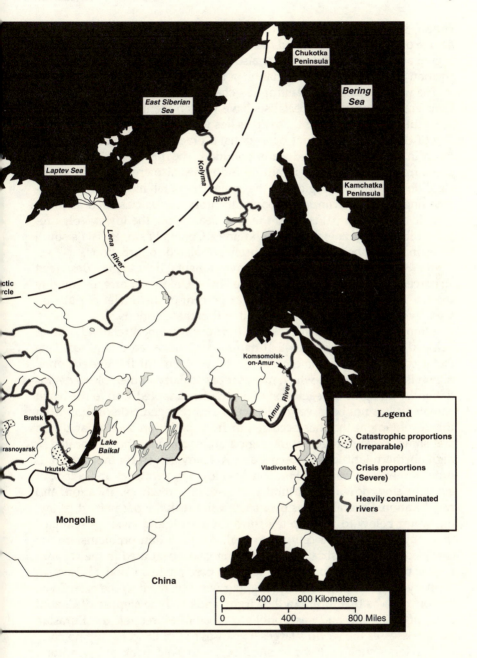

Chukotka
Peninsula

Bering
Sea

East Siberian
Sea

Laptev Sea

Kamchatka
Peninsula

Kolyma

River

Lena River

ctic
rcle

Komsomolsk-
on-Amur

Amur River

Bratsk

rasnoyarsk

Lake
Baikal

Irkutsk

Vladivostok

Mongolia

China

Legend

Catastrophic proportions
(Irreparable)

Crisis proportions
(Severe)

Heavily contaminated
rivers

0	400	800 Kilometers
0	400	800 Miles

runoff, such as Lake Baikal, Lake Ladoga (St. Petersburg's principal source of drinking water), and the Volga River. Portions of the *chernozem* region and much of Moldova are also in a crisis state caused by overcultivation and chemical contamination of the soil.

The worst category—catastrophe—characterizes regions where conditions are so severe that specialists have written them off as irreparable. The fault for the status of these areas lies with the common Soviet practice of clustering industrial operations, a practice that resulted in extraordinary levels of air and water pollution. The destruction of the landscape from mining and agricultural industries also created such severe conditions. Forty-five regions of the Soviet Union fall in this category, accounting for 3.3 percent of all Soviet territory. Areas classified as catastrophic are Karakalpakistan in the Aral Sea region, the lower Volga region, Siberia's Kuznetsk Basin, Ukraine's Donets Basin, Russia's south Urals industrial belt, and many densely populated conurbations.

In 1988, these three categories of environmental degradation described 16 percent of the entire territory of the Soviet Union—or an area roughly the size of the state of Alaska. And 26 percent of the Soviet population were living in 123 major cities located within these regions.[19]

Although much of former Soviet territory remained relatively undeveloped, Map 1.1 illustrates that nature rarely escaped unscathed. One factor contributing to the environmental problems of the undeveloped region is its geography, which makes it particularly vulnerable to degradation. Although the vegetation of Siberia has adapted well to the harsh climate, it has not been very tolerant of anthropogenic disruption from the development that has occurred or from pollution such as acid rain and snow. Because much of the region under consideration is located in high northern latitudes (Moscow and Krasnoyarsk sit on the same latitude as the south coast of Hudson Bay) low temperatures and a lack of sunlight slow down the natural processes of growth, purification, and regeneration. Several passes by a truck will break the permafrost, allowing water below to well up and turn the area into a swamp—damage that may take nature a century to heal. Air pollution problems are not confined to the industrial and urban centers concentrated in the western region; pollution produced there tends to precipitate on land, on Russian territory in particular, as the prevailing winds carry it to the east. Some topsoil, such as that found in the virgin lands and the steppes of Central Asia, often is thin and susceptible to erosion. Moreover, the Eurasian plain possesses the world's largest expanses of farmland having no natural barriers—such as trees or shrubbery—to hold back the wind and rain.[20] Intensive cultivation, overgrazing, and excessive logging thus only intensify the land's vulnerability.[21]

Given all this evidence of environmental degradation, the ultimate question that arises is this: Which areas of the former Soviet Union have remained relatively unscathed and healthy? When asked this question by a journalist, presidential adviser Aleksei Yablokov found himself at a loss for examples:

> You are the first to ask such a question. Usually, people ask about unfavorable regions, and I have become used to ticking them off. Of course, there are places barely affected by economic activity . . . one could, perhaps, include several regions of Karelia. Perhaps some regions of Belorussia, not disturbed by land improvement schemes. Probably, a part of Lithuania. It is very bad almost everywhere in Ukraine. Southern Ukraine is, in general, a zone of ecological catastrophe. The Black Sea is in a very bad state. At one time, Transcarpathia [western Ukraine] was in good condition, but heavy [air] pollution loads coming from Poland, Czechoslovakia, [and East and West Germany] have changed the picture. It is bad everywhere in Moldavia. The northern Caucasus region is heavily saturated with agricultural chemicals. Perhaps several border areas in the Caucasus have maintained their natural state. It is a catastrophe in Kalmykia and in the northern Caspian Sea region. Several desert regions may be preserved, but it is impossible to live there for other reasons. The Altai and Sayan regions are relatively clean. Several regions in eastern Siberia and the Far East have been preserved—small bits of Ussuri taiga remain there. Kamchatka has remained partly undisturbed. As you see, it's not much.[22]

THE ORIGINS OF ENVIRONMENTAL DESTRUCTION

For seven decades, the Soviet Union based its environmental protection strategy on the premise that collective ownership and central planning free of "selfish interests" would provide the "optimum solution" for protecting the environment.[23] Slogans such as "all for the good of man" reinforced a modernist and anthropocentric worldview that the USSR's boundless riches were ripe for exploitation. A preoccupation with industrial development arose, in part, from what economist Jan Winiecki has called "grandiose Marxian dreams of an economy as a single factory."[24] Big was better, huge was best, and science solved all the problems. Such a worldview was manifest in such "projects of the century" as the Great Stalin Plan for the Transformation of Nature, BAM (the Baikal-Amur Main Railway), Nikita Khrushchev's Virgin Lands Program, and the plan championed by Leonid Brezhnev to divert the flow of Siberian rivers.

In this glorious culture of transformation and modernization, tractors and cranes became the subjects of arts and letters. In a cycle of poems entitled "Bratsk Dam," Yevgenii Yevtushenko writes of mining ore in Magnitogorsk:

And trucks were charging about like beasts,
and wheelbarrows thumping, and frozen flags
were slapping with red ice.

And although the earth was like cast iron,
thousands of Sonkas were digging,
thousands of Sonkas were singing,
singing the song of the Commune.[25]

Environmental degradation, in the Soviet view, was an illness inextricably associated with bourgeois development and social and political conditions in the capitalist world. Wrote one analyst in 1980: "Like other global problems, those of ecology have a social origin, their solution largely depending on the character of the social system. . . . The socialist states and the communist parties proceed from the conviction that the socialist system offers the optimal possibilities for resolving these problems."[26] The official dogma about the infallibility of the Soviet system was so pervasive that many became blinded to reality. Said Yevgenii Velikhov, a physicist and leading member of the Soviet Academy of Sciences: "Before the Chernobyl explosion, many important specialists and political figures believed that a nuclear reactor could not explode."[27]

In line with the Communist Party and its ideology of economic growth through industrial development, the principal objective of the economic planners was to promote the speedy growth of heavy industry. Resources were channeled accordingly. A slogan popular during the initial stages of industrialization exemplifies the predatory attitude of Soviet economic planners that was to continue long afterward: "We cannot wait for favors from nature; our task is to take from her."[28] To meet the leadership's ambitious goals for industrial development, planners relied on increasing the quantity of inputs such as land, energy, and labor (i.e., *extensive* methods) rather on using resources more efficiently (i.e., *intensive* methods), thus exacerbating the strain on the environment.

One of the trademark features of the Soviet economy was its high concentration of industrial activities in a few very large enterprises that were often clustered in compact geographical regions. This concentration was encouraged by both central planners and industrial managers for several reasons. First, planners thought that the larger the size of the plant, the creater the efficiency of production. Second, weary of the high costs (manifested in uncertain delivery and the low quality of supplies) of transacting in the Soviet market, managers supported vertical integration of industry to extreme degrees. Third, industrial ministries favored large, high-visibility projects over smaller, specially targeted investments in order to move funds rapidly and meet the central planners' targets. Fourth, planners wanted to simplify the process of managing such a large economy—a priority that became progressively more important as the economy grew increasingly complex. Finally, planners sought to reduce transportation costs by locating industries close to the local natural resources they would consume.

This phenomenon of industrial concentration (both by factor and by geography) resulted in the "threading" of several ecological loads on a compact territory, giving rise to what governments have often officially declared "ecological disaster zones": pollution hot spots of exceptional intensity.[29] In addition to plaguing the traditional industrial centers of Ukraine (Donetsk, Krivoi Rog, Dnepropetrovsk), the south Urals (Chelyabinsk, Ufa, Yekaterinburg, Nizhnii Tagil, Magnitogorsk), and Siberia (Novokuznetsk, Krasnoyarsk, Kemerovo), these environmental hot spots are also found in such remote regions of the country as around Irkutsk and southern Sakhalin Island.[30] This situation is epitomized by the case of Norilsk—sulfur dioxide emissions from the Russian city's smelters exceeded total sulfur dioxide emissions for all of Italy in the 1980s.

A second feature of the Soviet economy was the USSR's propensity for allowing the industrial infrastructure to become aged and dilapidated. The distortions caused by the Soviet planning and price systems made it more profitable for firms to invest in new projects than to spend money to modernize existing plants and equipment.[31] As a result, 40 percent of the economy's physical plants had been declared "worn out" at the end of the 1980s.[32] Many industrial plants date back to the heyday of Soviet industrialization in the 1930s, when everything—human lives as well as nature—was sacrificed for the cause of Soviet economic achievement. Many factories in the Ural Mountains and Siberia were hastily moved to the region from the west during World War II, and more came from Germany after the war. More than half the blast furnaces in the Soviet Union at the time of its demise were over fifty years old; still operating were many antiquated and inefficient open-hearth furnaces.[33] A survey conducted by the Moscow city environment committee revealed that not one enterprise in the capital "complied with contemporary environmental regulations"—a result of numerous plants having been built "decades and centuries ago," noted TASS.[34] One decrepit Siberian soap factory built by a cooperative in the early 1920s was described in *Izvestiya* as "looking like a museum of the history of technology."[35] On a 1991 visit to the Rezina Production Association, a Moscow enterprise that produces rubber products, two U.S. researchers noted:

To walk around [the] production departments is to be transported back to
the last century. They are dark and dingy and the noise from the antiquated machinery can be deafening. The technology is so old—some of it
harkens back to pre–World War II days—that many of its own employees
liken it to an industrial museum. . . . We were told that when representatives of the German conglomerate, Krup, visited Rezina, they were so
amazed that machinery made in their factories in the 1920s and 1930s was
still in good working order, that they asked to buy it in order to take it back
to Germany for their museum.[36]

Because the nuts and bolts of the region's industrial infrastructure
were aged, overtaxed, and poorly maintained, reports of things breaking
down or blowing up were frequent: Trains derailed, spilling dangerous
cargoes; storage lagoons leaked, letting toxic wastes escape; and sewage
systems broke down, casting raw waste into rivers and lakes.[37] In Russia
alone up to 700 large-scale leaks occur along the nation's oil and gas
pipelines, resulting in an estimated loss of 7–20 percent—i.e. tens of millions of tons—of all oil produced.[38]

A third distinguishing feature of the Soviet economy was its great
militarization. Over the decades, the Soviet government consistently diverted a massive share of available resources to build up the nation's
large military-industrial complex as it waged a cold war with the United
States and its allies, countered perceived threats rising from China, and
projected its power into the Third World. Western estimates of the share
of the Soviet economy accounted for by the defense sector in the 1980s
range from about 15 to 25 percent and even higher; Aleksei Yablokov asserted that the real figure is on the order of 50 percent. (The rate in the
United States during the same period was about 5 percent.)

As in the West, defense-related activities proved to be some of the
most environmentally damaging—from groundwater contamination by
industrial solvents used in the aerospace industry to radioactive and
toxic contamination from unsafe storage and disposal of chemical, biological, and nuclear weapons. Playing on the Soviet regime's obsession
with national security and secrecy, the military-industrial complex ignored the most important environmental concerns and resisted interference by any proenvironmental interests. According to one estimate, the
USSR Ministry of Defense directly controlled 42 million hectares of land,
or 2 percent of Soviet territory.[39] Speaking about Murmansk, a principal
Navy port reported to be experiencing severe problems managing and
disposing of radioactive and toxic waste, the head of the Soviet environment agency commented in 1990: "We simply do not know what's going
on there."[40] Thus, the combination of widespread hazardous activity and

extreme secrecy led to catastrophic environmental disasters such as those at Chelyabinsk.

Added to the problem-producing features of the economy was the fact that the safeguards for keeping the Soviet system from producing grandiose, ill-suited, and ecologically hazardous projects in the Soviet Union's quest for industrial development were minimal at best. To win support for pet development projects, government ministries often bribed scientists by putting them on the payroll or by awarding their research institute desirable contracts. Scientists in turn did more than merely pander to developers' interests: For example, the USSR Academy of Sciences often supported big, ecologically destructive development projects (such as the St. Petersburg flood-control dam) in order to curry favor with political leaders and maintain the academy's prestige.[41] Many projects were required to undergo environmental impact assessments, but the assessment process was not stringent. At times, specialists involved in the design of a project also served on its environmental assessment panel.[42] According to one environmental authority, "[A]ll the activities largely were directed at lowering the estimated cost of construction. Other aspects simply weren't examined."[43] Cutting costs usually translated into cutting out the pollution controls.[44] Because the state was the ultimate property owner in the system, it assumed liability for environmental mishaps and thereby encouraged high-risk and hazardous development.[45] Under these conditions, Soviet endeavors such as the unique scheme to produce petroleum-based livestock feed, the use of nuclear devices for mining and excavation, and the construction of record-sized hydroelectric stations and chemical plants were approved without significant consideration of potential negative effects.

Often, a ministry would press ahead with a project before the impact assessment was conducted, thereby taking advantage of inertia in the bureaucratic process. Even if the project was found to be environmentally unsound, the fact that work already had commenced virtually ensured the project's survival. As Liya Shelest, a Russian environment official, commented about the giant Astrakhan gas complex built in the 1980s: "Even with our imperfect laws, the complex should not have been started up without the permission of the state commission [on environmental certification], but it has been running for five years. We do not have enough power to put it out of business."[46] Ultimately, if a concept was important enough to gain high-level political support, all potential opposition was effectively stifled. Even in the exceptional case of audible dissent—for example, scientists' concern about the fate of the Aral Sea when the government mounted its massive irrigation plans for Central Asia in the 1950s and 1960s—the leadership remained unswayed. "As we say, the Soviet Union is an exceptional country," proclaimed Russian Deputy Prime Minister Gennadii Fil'shin in 1990: "Exceptions were given to build a lot of polluting enterprises."[47]

The Soviet system also lacked the guide of market prices to assist its planners and project designers in their decisionmaking. As a centrally planned economy, the USSR set its prices administratively, according to political prerogatives rather than market forces. The price of a commodity therefore rarely was logically related to its actual cost of production. A thousand kilos of steel produced by the Nizhnii Tagil Metallurgical Combine grossed only 150 rubles—enough to buy just twenty kilos of apples at the local market.[48] Such a system meant that indicators of a project's viability—cost of inputs, return on investment, efficiency, and so on—were skewed. Because a large share of earnings were sent back to Moscow, local enterprises had little incentive to boost efficiency or to conserve resources. Moreover, such natural resources as land, forests, and minerals were allocated to enterprises at virtually no real cost to the user, eliminating any incentive to use them wisely. The state sold oil to its industries for about nine rubles a barrel—less than the price of a liter of vodka. Water for irrigation was provided virtually free. The end result was a perverse economy that tended to maximize the use of inputs at great cost to the environment.

Pervasive arbitrariness and lack of economic legality characterized the Soviet system rendering an economy that was not, despite official rhetoric, centrally planned, but merely centrally managed. Thus, although natural resources were in theory collectively owned (and collectively protected), the state in reality assigned extensive property rights to firms to allocate and use (and abuse) resources granted to them as long as they fulfilled the plan.[49] According to one environmental activist, enterprise managers came to approximate "czars" who controlled vast domains and who felled forests or fished out seas as they saw fit.[50] "Where natural resources are concerned, each department is interested only in using them to achieve its own goals," commented Yablokov. "Three powerful industries manage [Yakutiya territory]: diamond, gold, and coal producers. These industries behave as predators, taking no account of the natural environment and the people inhabiting this area."[51]

The Soviet regime did mount an environmental protection effort once growth in the Soviet economy began to decline and the costs of large-scale waste and environmental degradation increased. In the late 1950s, the Communist Party and government began passing a number of resolutions and laws outlining fundamental principles for protection of land, water, air, and wildlife and mandating specific conservation projects, such as those to protect Lake Baikal and improve environmental quality in Moscow. These documents set out admirable objectives, but they did little more than demonstrate the Communist Party's good intentions.

Over the years, bureaucrats toiled to encode detailed environmental regulations that were among the strictest in the world. The commitment to the environment remained solely on the books, however. The greatest obstacle to improving environmental quality proved to be the regime's development imperative. Criteria used to measure how well ministries and departments fulfilled their plans centered on quantitative indicators, such as tons of cement produced or hectares of land irrigated. As a result, managers routinely ignored quotas and guidelines for resource conservation and environmental protection. Because the leadership encouraged growth at any expense, ministries, enterprise managers, and workers understood that even flagrant disregard for environmental regulations and guidelines would be tolerated as long as the enterprise succeeded in generating its planned output. The Ministry of the Coal Industry, for example, devoted all of its resources to the production of coal; the more coal consumed by the economy, the bigger the ministry's budget, staff, and land allocations. Success for the ministry was equated with delivering a certain tonnage of coal to the state; of no concern to planners—and subsequently to managers—was how the coal was procured and what happened to the environment in the process. Issues such as controlling water pollution or restoring sites once excavation was completed ranked as minor concerns.

Another failing point of the government's effort to protect the environment was that responsibility for carrying out the government's modest environmental initiatives was divided among several ministries and state committees that often had priorities other than protecting the environment. One department was made responsible for collecting data, another for conducting the analyses, and a third for enforcement. Up to twenty-six separate state committees and ministries participated in the design and implementation of environmental regulations. In the case of Lake Baikal, over forty-five institutes affiliated with different departments and ministries conducted research on the ecology of the region. This arrangement frequently led to bureaucratic prerogatives pitting one agency against another. And in a society obsessed with secrecy, the sharing of information was anathema.

In addition, all environmental agencies were chronically underfunded. As a result, important functions such as monitoring and enforcement were delegated, without oversight, to the polluting ministries themselves. Referring to "monstrous violations" of government regulation by the fishing ministry, the Soviet environmental chief commented in 1989: "It studies [fish] resources with the assistance of its own research institutes, establishes its own fishing plan, catches the fish itself, and monitors itself."[52] As in every country, self-regulation led to abuse.

For any of the environmental regulations to have worked, the Soviet regime would have had to adopt detailed statutes enabling government agencies effectively to enforce them; it never did. Because of the low priority of environmental issues in the Soviet judicial system and the imprecise nature of Soviet environmental laws, judges frequently refused to hear such cases brought before them. Administrative approaches to environmental protection proved insufficient because enforcement agents typically were far weaker politically and financially than the polluters they were trying to control. Administrative sanctions issued by local governments could be disregarded by enterprises protected by powerful central ministries; in many cases, the local authorities themselves overlooked administrative sanctions because their informal responsibility was to ensure that local enterprises met the production quotas.

Even when the main form of punishment—monetary sanctions—was used against violators, the effects were only marginal because fines were either nominal or were picked up by the ministries; enterprises and individuals incurred virtually no material penalty for not obeying environmental regulations.[53] Money allocated to factories for the purchase of pollution abatement equipment often went unspent, and when equipment was installed, managers often refused to operate it as needed. The reason was simple: They frequently found it easier simply to continue paying fines for exceeding the emission standards than to interrupt production to install and maintain control technologies. In fact, enterprises' annual subsidies often included funds earmarked to pay fines. The result was a variation on the concept of a revolving bank account: Fines for environmental degradation went from one government pocket to another.

The net result was that environmental protection existed in name only. Noncomplying enterprises, backed by their ministries in Moscow, enjoyed privileges and rights over natural resources (including the right to pollute them) that were almost inviolable. These conditions created an incentive structure for industrial managers that supported production at the expense of public health and the environment. As two prominent economists concluded, the government's laws, decrees, and resolutions "were vague, others were simply not fulfilled; in the best of circumstances they were treated as pious wishes."[54]

Many Soviet people recognized the deplorable state of their environment, but there were no channels through which to influence the leadership's policies. The many informal environmental groups that existed were denied significant input into the political process. The idea of opposition from an independent environmental lobby threatened the official myth that the Soviet state, led by its infallible Communist Party, was capable of impartially incorporating within its policies the interests of all its citizens. The absence of any countervailing political force deprived the system of the corrective means needed to move it off its destructive path.

For seven decades, the system held. Soviet leaders congratulated themselves on pushing their country to the forefront of the world's industrial and military powers. Because success was measured in terms of output, there was much to celebrate: The USSR boasted that it was the world's largest producer of crude oil, natural gas, iron, steel, nickel, rubber, fertilizer, and tractors. Moreover, tanks, warplanes, and rockets rolled off assembly lines by the thousands. Soviet physicists designed nuclear reactors to power their cities and a fleet of submarines and icebreakers. In an extraordinary effort to overcome the challenges of nature, engineers threw dams across the strongest rivers, cut irrigation canals through the desert, and forced railway lines across the frozen tundra.

As the cases described here clearly indicate, however, many of these achievements turned out to be liabilities. The net result of the Soviet development model was an economy trapped on a treadmill of consumption and providing little output of social value: Coal was mined to produce steel, which was used to build machinery, which was used to mine coal.[55] And as the decades passed, the treadmill dragged the economy down.[56] The climb to a preeminent position in the world came at devastating cost to the environment and taxed the vigor of the economy, the people's health, and, ultimately, the legitimacy of the Soviet regime.

THE ROLE OF GLASNOST

Many observers point to the 1986 accident at Chernobyl as the precipitant of a radical change in the Soviet worldview. Some argue that Chernobyl alerted the leadership and the public to the frightening level to which the state of the USSR had deteriorated.[57] Others have linked the nuclear disaster to the Gorbachev administration's subsequent, more flexible stance in international arms control negotiations.[58] Still others believe the international community's strong reaction to the accident taught the Soviet regime about the need for openness and transparency in managing its affairs and thus led to the fateful policy of glasnost. In a 1987 article outlining the Soviet Union's proposal for a comprehensive system of international security, for example, Gorbachev wrote: "They say that one thorn of experience is worth a whole forest of instructions. For us, Chernobyl became such a thorn."[59]

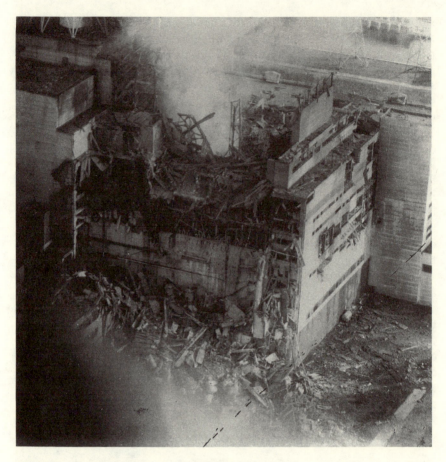

The Chernobyl No. 4 reactor smoldering shortly after it exploded on April 26, 1986. Photo: Igor' Kostin, Imago-Sygma.

The ideological constraints of the preglasnost regime had muted public discussion of environmental matters, but the new era of openness, democratization, and decentralization of authority rapidly created conditions that often encouraged political actors to emphasize the degree to which environmental quality had deteriorated. The Gorbachev regime's initiation of the policy of glasnost in 1987 was predicated on the hope that public criticism of the status quo would help motivate the leadership's reform agenda. Indeed, discussion in the media of the USSR's widespread ecological problems often pushed the limits of openness in the early years of glasnost and built public pressure for radical political and economic changes. It was not until 1989, however, that the public began to hear in graphic detail and directly from their own leaders how troubled their country was. Much of the credit for this sudden advance in eco-glasnost can be tied to the elections for and the convening of the first USSR Congress of People's Deputies. As political leaders became more outspoken, the media picked up the lead and began probing deeper into the problems.[60]

Despite the advances of glasnost, however, there still was (and the problem remains for the new republics) a serious lack of accurate information. On the issue of biodiversity, Aleksei Yablokov commented: "We lose several animal and plant species each year. What is most dangerous is that we do not know exactly how many species we are losing. Approximately 2,500 species were endemic to Lake Baikal. We have not seen 600 or 700 of these species for the past 30–40 years."[61]

This lack of information, both in baseline and time-series data, is most disturbing in the area of epidemiology. Medical workers who were poorly trained, overworked, and underpaid in the Soviet system rarely kept detailed records of their patients. Where public health conditions were extremely bad, authorities frequently banned the collection of data and the maintenance of health registries rather than face embarrassment and possible reprisals from an outraged public. "We have no statistics here because we have no tradition of keeping them," said Dr. Nikolai Kolmakov, director of the local hospital in Nikel, a Russian metallurgical town where the life expectancy is reported to be just forty-four years.[62] Referring to the fallout of Chernobyl, a physician from Mogilev, Belarus, told Radio Liberty in 1988: "A growing number of people are suffering from weakness, hair loss, and impotence. Although lab results clearly show these to be the result of radiation sickness, no mention of this will be made in the official diagnosis."[63] A physician from Dushanbe, Tajikistan, reported to Radio Liberty that radioactivity from military research and uranium mining in the region had led to "a leap in leukemia cases," prompting officials to forbid diagnoses of cancer and anemia. "In this case," the physician concluded, "perestroika precedes glasnost."[64]

Environmental agencies have moved to eliminate this shortcoming by mandating *pasportizatsiya*—the tallying of which enterprises are producing which wastes and pollutants—a process begun in the late 1980s.[65] The task will be a large one: Over 7,000 industrial enterprises, almost one-third located in Russia, had no documentation of their emissions as of the beginning of 1990.[66] And the government agencies and ministries that have collected data have not done a thorough job. Of the 117 foundries counted in a 1989 survey conducted by Moskompriroda, the Moscow city environmental agency, only 32 were previously known to officials and had been included in their statistics: "The remainder somehow are working on an illegal basis," concluded A. I. Kudin, the agency's chairman.[67] Such circumstances are likely to continue in the future: A lack of funds has forced environmental agencies to rely on self-reporting by firms, and absent is the threat of an audit.

In addition, the task of conducting accurate and comprehensive environmental observation is complicated by the lack of accurate, standardized monitoring equipment (especially automated technologies) and the rudimentary state of the information and communications systems. The region's geography doesn't help matters. Officials often must venture out to distant monitoring stations to gather samples and then transport them back to the regional office, a trip that may cover thousands of miles or require the use of a boat or helicopter. If not handled properly, samples and reagents may degrade or become contaminated, skewing the final results. As in the rest of the system, quality control is lax and poorly paid staffers are likely to cut corners. As a result of such conditions, data that have been obtained are often incomplete or inconsistent: "Currently, we obtain disturbing information only when something has gone wrong," commented Igor Gavrilov, Russia's environment minister and deputy prime minister in 1991.[68]

Finally, much of the information that is collected either is not pertinent or is published in a nonusable format. Reflecting the isolation and ideological subjectivity of past decades, methodologies do not correspond with international practice. For instance, data on the development of in-plant, closed-cycle recirculating water-supply systems are extensive, whereas data on pollutants released into waterways generally are given only in global terms of sewage released, which are sometimes broken down into partially treated and untreated. The specific types of pollutants released, as well as their rates, concentrations, and sources, remain insufficiently documented. In sharp contrast to the past, however, officials of the new republics now candidly and humbly admit that they frequently did not know what was going on inside the USSR or even their own locales, and they often are turning to the West for assistance.

Despite these serious shortcomings in the collection of environmental data, enough information was available in the system to convince both citizens and leaders alike that the state of environment in many parts of the country was alarming, if not catastrophic. This realization, in turn, led many to question the health of the Soviet Union. In a frank and emotional exchange with the country's cultural leaders in November 1990, President Gorbachev recounted a conversation with Eduard Shevardnadze during a winter walk just prior to Gorbachev's promotion to the General Secretaryship in March 1985. They were comparing observations on the state of the Union, and Shevardnadze turned to Gorbachev, concluding, "It had all gone rotten." Noting his justification for launching perestroika, Gorbachev commented five years later: "Everything was indeed rotten to the core, and it is the people who are suffering most. That a vast country with such intellectual potential, with such attachment to and love for the land, with such resources . . . should be in such a condition!"[69] Thus, the destruction of nature had come to serve as a solemn metaphor for the decline of a nation.

Notes

1. Central Television, "Vremya," September 3, 1990, as translated in FBIS-SOV-90-174, p. 40.

2. *Rabochaya tribuna,* February 11, 1990, p. 1.

3. TASS, September 20, 1989.

4. *Trud,* July 18, 1990, p. 2.

5. *Komsomol'skaya pravda,* March 22, 1991, p. 1.

6. *Novoe vremya,* No. 49, 1990, p. 3.

7. *Trud,* July 25, 1989, p. 3.

8. USSR State Committee for the Protection of Nature (hereafter abbreviated USSR Goskompriroda), *Sostoyanie prirodnoi sredy v SSSR v 1988 g.* (Moscow: VINITI, 1989), pp. 131–132.

9. Of the roughly 70,000 square kilometers of Belarusian territory that received radioactive fallout, 3,000 square kilometers (about 4 percent of the total) were taken out of cultivation. *Sovetskaya Belorussiya,* June 19, 1990, p. 1. See also a summary of the report of the USSR Gosplan expert commission on the accident in "Chernobyl'skaya avariya—velichaishaya katastropha zemli," *Energiya: Ekonomika, tekhnika, ekologiya,* No. 7, 1990.

10. *New York Times,* August 16, 1990, p. 3.

11. Testimony of First Deputy Chair of USSR Council of Ministers Vladilen Nikitin before USSR Supreme Soviet, Radio Moscow, March 28, 1990.

12. *Argumenty i fakty,* No. 2, 1990, p. 7.

13. *Rabochaya tribuna,* November 11, 1990, p. 4; Radio Moscow, April 22, 1990.

14. *Komsomol'skaya pravda,* September 28, 1991, p. 1. See also *Izvestiya,* October 29, 1991, pp. 1, 7; *Pravda,* December 7, 1991, p. 4; Matthew J. Sagers, "Nuclear Waste Illegally Dumped at Sea Off Novaya Zemlya," *Soviet Geography,* December 1991, pp. 706–707.

15. Olga Papkova, "Putting a Fish Near a Goldfish Bowl," *New Times,* No. 33, 1988, p. 39.

16. Central Television, "Vremya," August 8, 1990.

17. *Argumenty i fakty,* No. 15, 1990, p. 1. The data were collected by the All-Union Central Research Institute for Occupational Safety. Presumably alluding to the same data, A. I. Kudin, chairman of the Moscow City Committee for the Protection of Nature, said in late 1989 that "one-fifth of all Muscovites' illnesses are related to the state of the environment." *Vechernyaya Moskva,* December 23, 1989, p. 2.

18. See, for example, USSR Goskompriroda, *Sostoyanie . . . v 1988 g.*, p. 132. The study of children's health was conducted by the Institute of Hygiene and Illness Prevention Among Children and Adolescents.

19. Boris I. Kochurov, "Na puti k sozdaniyu ekologicheskoi karty SSSR," *Priroda*, No. 8, 1989, pp. 10–17.

20. Lester R. Brown and John E. Young, "Feeding the World in the Nineties," in Lester E. Brown et al., *State of the World 1990* (New York: Norton, 1990), p. 74.

21. For more on the relationship of geography to nature in the USSR, see Charles E. Ziegler, *Environmental Policy in the USSR* (Amherst: University of Massachusetts Press, 1987), ch. 1.

22. Vladislav Larin, "Opasnoe neponimanie," *Energiya: Ekonomika, tekhnika, ekologiya*, No. 4, 1990, p. 3.

23. V. Granov, "The Ideological Struggle and Ecological Problems," *International Affairs*, No. 12, 1980, p. 93.

24. Jan Winiecki, "Large Industrial Enterprises in Soviet-Type Economies: The Ruling Stratum's Main Rent-Seeking Area," *Communist Economies*, Vol. 1, No. 4, 1989, p. 365.

25. Yevgenii Yevtushenko, *Bratsk Station and Other New Poems*, trans. Tina Tupikina-Glaessner, Geoffrey Dutton, and Igor Mezhakoff-Koriakin (New York: Anchor Books, 1967), p. 64. Sonka is a seventeen-year-old who leaves her village to work in the ore pits of Magnitogorsk. For a compelling discussion of the linkage between ideology, culture, and the environment, see Douglas R. Weiner, *Models of Nature: Ecology, Conservation, and Cultural Revolution in Soviet Russia* (Bloomington: Indiana University Press, 1988).

26. Granov, "Ideological Struggle," p. 87, cited in Eric Green, *Ecology and Perestroika* (Washington, DC: American Committee on U.S.-Soviet Relations, 1990), p. 51.

27. Yevgenii Velikhov, "Chernobyl Remains on Our Mind," in *Voices of Glasnost: Interviews with Gorbachev's Reformers*, Stephen Cohen and Katrina Vanden Heuvel, eds. (New York: W. W. Norton, 1989), p. 162.

28. Green, *Ecology and Perestroika*, p. 1.

29. A. T. Khrushchev, *Geografiya promyshlennosti SSSR* (Moscow: Vysshaya shkola, 1990), p. 37.

30. For more on threading and problems associated with the distribution of Soviet industry, refer to S. B. Lavrov, "Regional and Environmental Problems of the USSR: A Synopsis of Views from the Soviet Parliament," *Soviet Geography*, September 1990.

31. Alec Nove, "The Investment Process in the USSR," *Bericht des Bundesinstituts für ostwissenshafliche und internationale studien*, No. 53, 1989, p. 13.

32. Khrushchev, *Geographiya promyshlennosti SSSR* , p. 9.

33. V. N. Bol'shakov and O. F. Sadykov, "Kontseptsiya formirovaniya regional'noi sistemy ekologicheskoi bezopasnosti (na primere Urala)," *Vestnik Akademii Nauk SSSR*, No. 11, 1988, p. 97. Likewise, much of the pollution control equipment simply is worn out; half of installed air pollution controls were over ten years old in 1987. USSR Goskomstat, *Okhrana okruzhayushchei sredy*, p. 89.

34. TASS, September 6, 1991.

35. *Izvestiya*, July 16, 1989, p. 2.

36. Michael Burawoy and Kathryn Hendley, "Strategies of Adaptation: A Soviet Enterprise Under Perestroika and Privatization," University of California, Berkeley-Duke University (Durham, NC) Occasional Papers on the Second Economy in the USSR, No. 29, June 1991, p. 6.

37. In its annual review of the state of the nation's economy, the Soviet government reported that 2,000 accidents having "a serious negative effect" on the nation's land, water, and air were recorded by the government in 1989. *Izvestiya*, January 28, 1990, p. 3.

38. Aleksei Yablokov, "Zayavlenie dlya pressy," *Tsentr Obshchestvennoi Informatsii po Atomnoi Energii Informatsionnyi Byulleten'*," No. 3, 1992, p. 5.

39. *Pravda*, January 11, 1991, p. 3. Not included in this figure is territory controlled by thousands of defense-related industries.

40. *Sovetskaya kul'tura*, No. 31, 1990, p. 3.

41. *Izvestiya*, August 7, 1990, p. 3.

42. In the case of the Siberian river diversion plan, G. V. Voropaev, director of the USSR Academy of Sciences Institute of Water Problems, served as the head of the USSR Gosplan commission that reviewed the viability of the project; his institute played a key role in the plan's development. See N. F. Glazovskii, "Malen'kie khitrosti bol'shikh proektov," *Nash sovremennik*, No. 1, 1987, p. 122; and Robert G. Darst, Jr., "Environmentalism in the USSR: The Opposition to the River Diversion Projects," *Soviet Economy*, July–September 1988, p. 236.

43. Petr I. Poletaev, "Vosstanovit' garmoniyu prirody i cheloveka," *Zdorov'e*, No. 6, 1989, p. 1. Such a narrow focus, notes Poletaev, a deputy chairman at USSR Goskompriroda, was in line with the phrase repeated often at the time: "The economy must be economical."

44. In a speech to the First USSR Congress of People's Deputies, Mikhail Gorbachev noted: "We, in order to lessen the cost of construction, continue to support projects that are unfit from the perspective of ecological safety." Gorbachev went on to recount a story he heard from a deputy from Komsomolsk-na-Amure: In order to ameliorate a furniture shortage plaguing the Far East, the central government spent $20 million to import machinery for a new furniture factory there; but the government did not buy the associated pollution control equipment. "Who needs such economizing?" Gorbachev asked. "In Komsomolsk-na-Amure, demonstrations already are being held on account of this." See *Pervyi s"ezd narodnykh deputatov SSSR: Stenograficheskii otchet*, Vol. 1 (Moscow: Izdatel'stvo Verkhovnogo Soveta SSSR, 1989), pp. 444–445.

45. Roland N. McKean, "Products Liability: Implications of Some Changing Property Rights," *Quarterly Journal of Economics*, Vol. 84, No. 4, 1970.

46. Liya Shelest, first deputy chair of RSFSR Goskompriroda, presentation at conference on Democratic Federalism and Environmental Crisis in the Republics of the Former Soviet Union, Moscow, August 1991.

47. Mike Edwards, "Siberia: In from the Cold," *National Geographic*, March 1990, p. 27. For more on the subject, see Philip R. Pryde, "The Soviet Approach to Environmental Impact Analysis," in Fred Singleton, ed., *Environmental Problems in the Soviet Union and Eastern Europe* (Boulder, CO: Lynne Rienner, 1987). As

Darst, *Environmentalism in the USSR*, points out, grandiose and ecologically ill-suited projects have been pursued elsewhere, namely the water management schemes in the western United States. How the Soviet and U.S. processes have differed is in the opportunities for open, independent, and critical assessment—the relative democracy of each decision process.

48. *Trud*, July 18, 1990, p. 2.

49. See, for example, Joseph S. Berliner, *Factory and Manager in the USSR* (Cambridge: Harvard University Press, 1957); David Granick, *Management of the Industrial Firm in the USSR* (New York: Columbia University Press, 1954); John H. Moore, "Agency Costs, Technological Change, and Soviet Central Planning," *Journal of Law and Economics*, Vol. 24, October 1981, pp. 189–215.

50. DJ Peterson, "Property Rights and the Environment in Centrally and Post Centrally Planned Economies: The Case of the Soviet Chemicals Industry," unpublished manuscript, May 1992. The term "tsar" was used by Andrei Ivanov-Smolenskii, coordinator for conservation programs, USSR Social-Ecological Union, to describe the manager of a fishing enterprise located in the Arctic port of Dikson. Personal communication, Los Angeles, October 1991.

51. Aleksei Yablokov, Presentation at conference on Democratic Federalism and Environmental Crisis in the Republics of the Former Soviet Union, Moscow, August 1991.

52. Mikhail Dubrovskii, "Zashchita Vorontsova," *Poisk*, No. 28, 1989, p. 4.

53. In 1989, for example, the government brought 479,000 individuals to "administrative accountability" and fined them a total of 11.4 million rubles—an average of less than 24 rubles per person. USSR Goskomstat, *Press-vypusk*, No. 226, June 7, 1990.

54. Konstantin G. Gofman and Nikolai P. Fedorenko, "Ekonomicheskaya zashchita prirody," *Kommunist*, No. 5, 1989, p. 31, cited in Green, *Ecology and Perestroika*, p. 5.

55. This observation was made by Andrei Piontkowskii, a chief researcher at the USSR Academy of Science Institute of Systems Studies and consultant to reformist parliamentarians, during a presentation at the Council on Environmental Quality, Washington, D.C., August 1990.

56. Wrote one Soviet researcher, "More and more resources are going towards maintaining or slowing the decline in output of [natural resources], not increasing it." Forty percent of all capital investment went to the energy sector in 1986 in that year, energy development claimed 65 percent of Soviet pipe production, 20 percent of all other steel output, 15 percent of copper and aluminum production, and about the same share of cement and machinery output. A. Arbatov, "Problemy obespecheniya ekonomiki SSSR mineral'nym syr'yem," *Voprosy ekonomiki*, No. 1, 1987, p. 34.

57. See, for example, Philip R. Pryde, *Environmental Management in the Soviet Union* (New York: Cambridge University Press, 1991), chs. 1 and 3.

58. William C. Potter, "Soviet Decisionmaking for Chernobyl: An Analysis of System Performance and Policy Change," report submitted to the National Council for Soviet and East European Research, December 1989, p. 83.

59. See Gorbachev's speech "Reality and Guarantees for a Secure World," *Pravda*, September 17, 1987, as translated in *International Affairs*, No. 11, 1987, p. 8.

60. Melissa Dawson, "Politics and the Press in the Soviet Union: The Press as a Fourth Estate in a Centralized System," unpublished manuscript presented at Trilateral Graduate Student Conference on the Post-Soviet Era, Santa Monica, CA, May 1992.

61. Aleksei Yablokov, presentation at conference on Democratic Federalism and Environmental Crisis in the Republics of the Former Soviet Union, Moscow, August 1991.

62. *Guardian*, January 11, 1991.

63. Radio Liberty, Soviet Area audience and opinion research, *Soviet Background Notes: Unevaluated Comments by Recent Emigrants*, SBN 5-88, December 1988, p. 4.

64. Radio Liberty, Soviet Area audience and opinion research, *Soviet Background Notes: Unevaluated Comments by Recent Emigrants*, SBN 2-88, April 1988, p. 5.

65. In its 1990 long-range environmental program, USSR Goskompriroda called for air pollution inspections of all cities and industrial sites in the Soviet Union by 2005. See "Gosudarstvennaya programma okhrany okruzhayushchei sredy . . . ," *Ekonomika i zhizn'*, No. 41, 1990, insert page 5.

66. *Zelenyi mir*, No. 1, 1990, p. 3. In 1990, Nikolai Vorontsov, the head of the Soviet environmental agency, estimated there were a total of 2.2 million "polluting enterprises and industrial objects" in the USSR. Novosti Press Agency, October 5, 1990.

67. *Vechernyaya Moskva*, December 23, 1989, p. 2.

68. Igor Gavrilov presentation at conference on Democratic Federalism and Environmental Crisis in the Republics of the Former Soviet Union, Moscow, August 1991.

69. *Izvestiya*, December 1, 1990, p. 4.

2

The Air

You are lucky, a breeze is blowing today. It is still possible to breathe.
—Chemical industry worker interviewed by a *Pravda*
journalist visiting the Bashkir city of Sterlitamak

On July 21, 1989, severe smog in Siberia's third largest city of Omsk forced the local government to declare a state of emergency. A heat wave had exacerbated air pollution problems created by oil refineries, tire factories, chemical plants, and other industrial enterprises crammed into the city of 1.1 million residents. To combat the smog, the city government ordered factories to reduce output and limited the use of private automobiles to daytime hours.[1] In August 1989, "Vremya," the evening news television program, carried the following report from the city of Sterlitamak in the Bashkir republic of Russia:

> Immense chimneys belching out clouds of smoke into the sky and a blue-grey pall of poisonous smog creeping over the horizon—thus the second [largest] city of Bashkiriya . . . where 270,000 people live, awakens. The Ministry of the Chemical Industry and the Ministry of the Petrochemical Industry have so crammed Sterlitamak with enterprises that they annually discharge 200,000 tons of harmful waste. The citizens have to pay the highest price possible for this large-scale chemical industry: their health. . . . Discharge of the most harmful wastes occurs, as a rule, at night. Drivers of trolley buses who work early in the morning are the first to breathe the fumes. It is they who issued an ultimatum to the executive committee of the city soviet: If the ecological situation in the city did not improve by the beginning of August, then trolley bus traffic would be stopped. This is the main form of public transport in Sterlitamak.[2]

One year later, Boris Yeltsin visited the city as part of a major tour of Siberia; he met a populace angry over a recent accident at the Kaustik chemical plant that resulted in the release of poisonous gases. Summing up his travels, Yeltsin concluded: "I have been travelling through Tatariya and Bashkiriya for a week now, but until [here], I had not received such a grim impression, especially after visiting Kaustik. My impression was depressing, simply sickening."[3]

According to the Soviet environmental protection agency, air pollution ranked highest on the list of environmental problems that faced the Soviet Union. On the eve of the collapse of the USSR, the country produced roughly the same volume of air pollution as the United States, despite its lower economic output. Meanwhile, the high concentration of industry focused the environmental and public health impact of air pollution in urban regions, resulting in citizens living in many industrial areas suffering some of the worst air pollution in the world. Minimal pollution controls on industry and automobiles have prevented citizens of the former Soviet Union from enjoying the improvement in air quality that U.S. residents have enjoyed with the imposition of tighter emission controls since the 1960s. On a visit to California, one Kazakh environmentalist summed up the situation in her hometown: "Los Angeles's pollution is *nothing* in comparison to Alma-Ata's."[4]

THE VOLUME OF ATMOSPHERIC EMISSIONS

In 1980, the Soviet meteorological service, Goskomgidromet, began collecting data on the output of atmospheric emissions classified into two broad categories: stationary sources (i.e., industrial enterprises, power plants, and heating plants) and transport. Determination of the former was made possible by a nationwide inventory of air pollution sources in urban and industrial regions conducted that year. The figures for exhaust fumes from vehicles were estimated using data on the consumption of motor fuel and on traffic loads in urban regions.[5]

According to this methodology, 58.5 million tons of toxic substances were discharged into the atmosphere from over 3,000 sources in 1989.[6] The single greatest polluters that year were the USSR Ministry of Ferrous and Nonferrous Metallurgy[7] and the USSR Ministry of Power Engineering and Electrification; their plants produced one-half of all air pollution from stationary sources. Other major polluters at the all-Union (Soviet-wide) level were the oil and chemical industries, accounting for 9 and 7 percent of emissions, respectively (see Table 2.1). By republic, Russia accounted for more than 60 percent of emissions from stationary sources (see Figure 2.1).

Automobiles contributed another 35.5 million tons of air pollution, bringing the total for 1989 to 94 million tons. However, this figure should

TABLE 2.1   Crude weights of atmospheric emissions by selected all-Union industries, 1989

	Metric Tons (in thousands)	Percent of Total	Percent Change from 1986
Total stationary sources	58,508	100	−12.0
Power engineering and electrification	14,517	24.8	−16.5
Ferrous and nonferrous metallurgy	15,348	26.2	−12.9
Oil industry	5,209	8.9	+9.0
Chemical and petrochemical industry	4,183	7.1	−19.2
Gas industry	2,628	4.5	+12.4
Construction materials industry	2,091	3.6	−48.7
Forestry industry	1,286	2.2	−15.5
Fertilizer industry	556	1.0	−26.1
Other sectors	12,690	21.7	−1.2

Source: USSR Goskompriroda, *Sostoyanie prirodnoi sredy i prirodookhrannaya deyatel'nost' v SSSR v 1989 godu* (Moscow: Institut Molodezhi, 1990), p. 13.

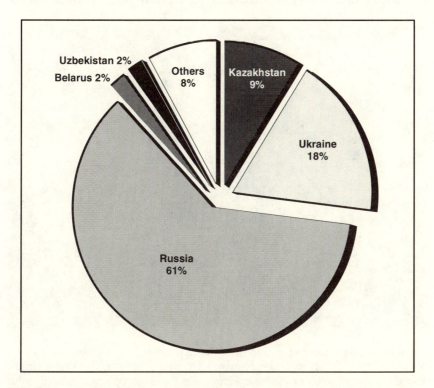

FIGURE 2.1   Atmospheric emissions from stationary sources by republic, 1989

not be considered the sum of pollution for several reasons. First, as mentioned before, the data for transportation are for urban areas only. Second, this figure excludes other sources of pollution such as diesel locomotives, boats, and airplanes. Third, the counting of stationary sources does not include other sources, such as waste landfills and evaporation ponds. Finally, the data do not account for malfunctioning or leaking equipment, accidents, and unregistered pollution sources; these are crucial factors, given the fact that enterprises traditionally have reported their emissions to the government but because officials lacked the resources to audit the data, underreporting was probable.

A breakdown of atmospheric emissions from transport and stationary sources for major cities (including the capitals of the fifteen former Union republics) in 1987 is presented in Table 2.2. The table should not, however, be interpreted as a complete list of the cities with the greatest emissions; it also indicates the relatively small share of transport-based pollution in the Soviet Union compared with other cities around the world.

One characteristic of many former Soviet cities is the high concentration of pollution from industrial sources. The city with the record emis-

Pollution from a smelter of the Norilsk Mining-Metallurgical Combine drifts over the Arctic city. Taken together, Norilsk's factories represent the single largest stationary source of air pollution in Russia and the largest point source of sulfur dioxide emissions in the world. Photo: DJ Peterson.

TABLE 2.2   Atmospheric pollution emissions for selected cities in 1987

City	Total (1000s of metric tons)	Source of Emissions (percent) Transport	Stationary
Alma-Ata (Kazakhstan)	213	77	23
Angarsk (Russia)	482	3	97
Arkhangelsk (Russia)	116	28	72
Ashkhabad (Turkmenistan)	46	87	13
Baku (Azerbaijan)	788	38	62
Bishkek (Kyrgyzstan)	163	46	54
Chelyabinsk (Russia)	534	16	84
Dnepropetrovsk (Ukraine)	444	28	72
Donetsk (Ukraine)	328	41	59
Dushanbe (Tajikistan)	114	67	33
Irkutsk (Russia)	152	41	59
Kiev (Ukraine)	327	71	29
Kishinev (Moldova)	133	68	32
Krasnoyarsk (Russia)	400	27	73
Krivoi Rog (Ukraine)	1,369	6	94
Magnitogorsk (Russia)	900	3	97
Minsk (Belarus)	235	53	47
Moscow (Russia)	1,211	70	30
Nizhnii Tagil (Russia)	712	4	96
Norilsk (Russia)	2,426	1	99
Novokuznetsk (Russia)	949	6	94
Riga (Latvia)	138	71	29
St. Petersburg (Russia)	626	59	41
Sterlitamak (Russia)	201	9	91
Tallinn (Estonia)	108	62	38
Tashkent (Uzbekistan)	362	86	14
Tbilisi (Georgia)	312	87	13
Temirtau (Kazakhstan)	1,018	2	98
Ufa (Russia)	475	27	73
Vilnius (Lithuania)	97	62	38
Volgograd (Russia)	396	29	71
Yerevan (Armenia)	248	71	29
Munich[a]	213	27	73
Mexico City	5,027	80	20
São Paulo	2,110	86	14
Athens[b]	394	59	41
London[c]	1,200	86	14
Los Angeles[d]	3,391	87	13

[a] 1974/1975
[b] 1976
[c] 1978
[d] 1982

Sources: USSR Goskomstat, *Okhrana okruzhayushchei sredy i ratsional'noe ispol'zovanie prirodnykh resursov v SSSR* (Moscow: Finansy i statistika, 1989), pp. 22–27; Asif Faiz, *Automotive Air Pollution: An Overview* (Washington, DC: World Bank, 1990), cited in World Resources Institute, *World Resources 1992–93* (New York: Oxford University Press, 1992), p. 196.

sions was Norilsk, a Stalin-era industrial boomtown located 200 miles
above the Arctic Circle in central Siberia. In 1991, the volume of pollutants pumped by local metal smelters into the air over the city amounted
to 2.5 million tons—roughly half the volume of air pollution of Mexico
City although Norilsk has only 1 percent the number of inhabitants and a
similar fraction of automobiles.[8] Industries based on the mining of oil
shale and phosphorites clustered in the Narva region of northeast Estonia accounted for over one-half of stationary source emissions in the republic and produced more sulfur dioxide than all of Sweden in the late
1980s.[9] According to the Soviet statistical agency, the area around the
southern Ural Mountains, which includes cities such as Yekaterinburg,
Ufa, Chelyabinsk, Sterlitamak, and Magnitogorsk, is the industrial region
in the former Soviet Union with the highest emissions per unit of area.[10]

Regionwide, stationary sources accounted for 62 percent of all air
pollution in 1989, but the balance between air pollution from stationary
sources and transport varied greatly by city. In many cases, a city's pollution problem derives from a single plant or industry. In Norilsk, for
example, the principal source of pollution is the city's copper, cobalt, and
nickel smelters run by the Norilsk Mining and Metallurgical Combine. In
total, stationary sources account for over 99 percent of the city's air pollution. In many cities, such as Ashkhabad, Kishinev, and Vilnius, motor
vehicles are the dominant air pollution source. Generally, the larger,
wealthier cities (state capitals, for example) suffer more from automobiles. In the late 1980s, Moscow counted 800,000 trucks and automobiles
and suffered concomitant air pollution problems; in 1987, motor vehicles
generated 73 percent of the total air pollution.[11]

In comparison, the United States produced about 127 million tons of
air pollutants in 1988, making the volume of the two countries' emissions
approximately equal. As can be seen in Table 2.3, stationary sources generated the same volume of air pollution in the Soviet Union as in the
United States, despite the fact that the Soviet economy before the
breakup of the USSR was generally estimated to measure one-fourth to
one-half that of the United States. Soviet performance compared with
that of the United States was even worse in the transportation sector.
Motor vehicles serve as an example. In the United States, automobiles
emitted 70 million tons of pollution in 1988.[12] Although U.S. motor vehicles overall produced about 85 percent more toxic fumes by volume
than those in the Soviet Union, their numbers were far greater: In the
United States, there were approximately twelve times as many privately
owned automobiles as in the Soviet Union.[13] In terms of usage, U.S.
trucks hauled more than twice as much freight as their Soviet counterparts, and U.S. buses 17 percent more passengers.[14]

TABLE 2.3 Air pollutant emissions from stationary sources, 1987 (in millions of metric tons)

Substance	USA[a]	USSR
Particulates	4.3	13.7
Sulfur oxides	19.8	16.8
Nitrogen oxides	11.4	4.5
Carbon monoxide	12.3	14.0
Volatile organic compounds	9.4	8.4
Lead (thousands of tons)	2.5	6.3[b]
Total	57.2	57.4

[a] 1988

[b] 1989

Sources: USSR Goskompriroda, *Sostoyanie prirodnoi sredy i prirodookhrannaya deyatel'nost' v SSSR v 1989 godu* (Moscow: Institut Molodezhi, 1990), p. 12; US Bureau of the Census, *Statistical Abstract of the United States: 1991* (Washington, DC: Government Printing Office, 1991), p. 209.

CIA estimates of Soviet gross national product can be used as a crude yardstick to determine that the Soviet economy produced roughly $26,000 of output for every ton of air pollutants in 1988. The corresponding figure for the United States was about 50 percent higher—$38,000. In addition to stricter emissions controls in the United States, another factor contributing to the discrepancy is the greater presence of heavy industry in the economy of the former Soviet Union and of service industries in the U.S. economy. In 1987, for example, the Soviet Union produced 80 percent more steel, 85 percent more fertilizer, and twice as much cement and generated about the same quantity of primary energy as did the United States.[15]

Because of the size of the Soviet economy, its emphasis on heavy industry, and its relative inefficiency, the region plays a major role in global environmental issues. In 1989, the Soviet Union was responsible for the emission of over 1 billion tons of carbon into the atmosphere—18 percent of the world's carbon emissions resulting from energy production that year. The USSR was second only to the United States, which produced 22 percent.[16] In terms of total global greenhouse gas emissions (including chlorofluorocarbons and methane), the USSR accounted for about 13.5 percent of global output in 1989—the second largest share—although unaccounted leaks from natural gas pipelines could make the share larger. According to the World Resources Institute, the USSR ranked number 14 in per capita emissions behind other industrialized nations such as the United States (6), Canada (9), and Czechoslovakia (13).[17] In 1986, the Soviet Union accounted for 9.5 percent of global chlorofluorocarbon production, slightly less than the share produced by Japan.[18]

AMBIENT AIR QUALITY IN THE SOVIET UNION

The Soviet meteorological service began monitoring air quality in the mid-1960s and by 1988 had checked the air for 80 substances in 534 cities. Under the Soviet regime, cities with a population of over 100,000 were assigned at least one monitoring station, with Moscow having the largest number (twenty-three). According to a standard methodology, each station sampled the air for at least eight substances over a twenty-minute period, and most conducted these tests three to four times a day. The observations were averaged over various time intervals and compared with established norms.[19] Standards for individual pollutants in the atmosphere were expressed in terms of maximum permissible concentrations (*predel'no dopustimaya kontsentratsiya* in Russian, or PDK) tolerated for human health. These standards were established by the USSR Ministry of Health and were derived from the minimum concentration of a substance that demonstrated an observable physiological effect. This principle was in line with methodologies for determining air pollution standards in the United States and other Western countries, and it produced standards that according to one observer were "very strict."[20]

The basic conclusion from local reporting is that no major city in the former Soviet Union escaped air pollution problems. In 1989, all major cities failed to comply with standards for suspended particulate matter, nitrogen dioxide, ammonia, and phenol. The most problematic pollutants nationwide were carbon disulfide, formaldehyde, and benzopyrene (a carcinogenic substance found in coal tar); concentrations of these compounds exceeded norms everywhere by a factor of 2 to 4.[21] Given the uneven nature of Soviet development, air quality and the specific types of pollutants vary greatly by location, and some unfortunate cities have fared worse than average. For example, in 1989 the mean daily concentration of particulates in the Russian oil- and gas-producing city of Nizhnevartovsk was six times PDK. Mean daily formaldehyde concentrations in the Russian city of Lipetsk averaged almost tem times PDK. And in the Siberian city of Bratsk, home to one of the world's largest aluminum smelters, mean daily concentrations of benzopyrene measured 17 times PDK.[22] See Table 2.4 for an official list of those cities with the worst problems with specific pollutants.

In 1989 and 1990, about 130 Soviet cities being monitored for air pollution were included on the "black list"—that is, there were periods when

TABLE 2.4 Major air pollutants and cities with the highest mean annual concentrations, 1989

Pollutant	City (Republic)	Factor by Which Standard Exceeded
Dust	Kutaisi (Georgia)	8.5
	Nizhnevartovsk (Russia)	6.0
	Ararat (Armenia)	5.4
Soot	Aleksandrovsk-Sakhalinskii (Russia)	5.2
Sulfur dioxide	Karabash (Russia)	5.4
Carbon monoxide	Yerevan (Armenia)	2.0
	Zestafoni (Georgia)	1.6
	Tbilisi (Georgia)	1.4
Nitrogen dioxide	Yerevan (Armenia)	3.8
	Zyryanovsk (Kazakhstan)	3.6
Ozone	Bekabad (Uzbekistan)	2.8
	Yerevan (Armenia)	2.5
	Alma-Ata (Kazakhstan)	2.4
Phenol	Dzerzhinsk (Ukraine)	5.3
	Norilsk (Russia)	3.5
Chlorine	Yavan (Tajikistan)	1.6
	Sumgait (Azerbaijan)	1.4
Formaldehyde	Lipetsk (Russia)	9.8
	Groznyi (Russia)	7.8
	Severodonetsk (Ukraine)	7.1
	Odessa (Ukraine)	7.1
Ammonia	Dneprodzerzhinsk (Ukraine)	5.1
	Andizhan (Uzbekistan)	4.5
	Rustavi (Georgia)	3.7
Benzopyrene	Zima (Russia)	22.2
	Ussuriisk (Russia)	18.9
	Bratsk (Russia)	17.0

Source: USSR Goskompriroda, Sostoyanie prirodnoi sredy i prirodookhrannaya deyatel'nost' v SSSR v 1989 godu (Moscow: Institut Molodezhi, 1990), pp. 45–46.

the concentration of a single pollutant exceeded PDK by at least 10 times[23]—an increase from the 103 cities reported in 1988.[24] Nationwide, 3,300 such violations were reported in 1990. Often pollution levels reached 50 or more times above health norms.[25] Air pollution affected every corner of the USSR; according to a 1989 statement by the Uzbek environment agency, "There is not one industrial center nor large settlement in the republic in which the air quality complies with health norms."[26]

The "black list" has often been cited by commentators and politicians to demonstrate the seriousness of the air pollution problem.[27] Counting the number of cities that exceed pollution norms, however, does not adequately convey the impact of air pollution on the environment and public health. On the one hand, readings by a monitoring station measure pollution at one locus and therefore may be affected by relative proximity to a polluter; pollution may disperse before reaching populated areas; and high readings may be registered as the result of unusually large or transient discharges or because of prevailing weather conditions. On the other hand, measurements based on peak emissions do not reflect ambient concentration over extended periods of time, the toxicity of a single pollutant, or the effect of a "bouquet" of combined pollutants.

To have a better measure, scientists at USSR Goskompriroda, in conjunction with specialists from Goskomgidromet and the USSR Ministry of Health, developed the Index of Atmospheric Pollution (*Indeks zagryazneniya atmosfera*, or IZA). According to this subjective measure, the concentration of the five most problematic pollutants in a city was tabulated by taking their concentrations, weighted according to their relative levels of toxicity, and aggregated to yield an index of air pollution. Using this system, scientists arrived at a list of 73 cities—which in 1989 included about 32 million inhabitants, or over 10 percent of the Soviet population[28]—deemed "especially dangerous for living."[29] Table 2.5 identifies the 30 cities that scored the worst over the period 1985–1989 and lists the problem pollutants and their sources.

Drawing comparisons with the West is difficult given incompatible methodologies for measuring air quality. However, Soviet air pollution standards compare roughly to those in the West, and it is not surprising that over 100 Soviet cities failed to meet air quality standards at least once yearly in the late 1980s and early 1990s. By way of comparison, 52 metropolitan areas in the United States exceeded the norm for low-level ozone concentrations for at least one day in 1989; the Los Angeles area exceeded that standard for 122 days.[30] Milan exceeded World Health Organization norms for sulfur dioxide for an average of 66 days per year in the early 1980s, and Beijing exceeded norms for suspended particulate matter for an average of 272 days annually.[31] What is unusual is the number of Soviet cities that experienced periodic episodes above norms

TABLE 2.5 Thirty-five cities with the worst air quality and its derivation, 1985–1989

City (Republic)	Problem[a]	Source
Alma-Ata (Kazakhstan)	BP, F, dust	power plants, automobiles
Almalyk (Uzbekistan)	BP, ammonia, dust	fertilizers, nonferrous metallurgy
Bishkek (Kyrgyzstan)	BP, F, dust, NO2	power plants, automobiles
Bratsk (Russia)	BP, methylmercaptan, carbon bisulfide	nonferrous metallurgy, paper, power plants
Chardzhou (Turkmenistan)	BP, hydrogen fluoride, dust	fertilizers, automobiles, power plants
Chelyabinsk (Russia)	BP, F, sulfur dioxide	iron and steel, power plants
Dneprodzerzhinsk (Ukraine)	BP, F, ammonia, dust, NO2	fertilizers, steel, construction materials
Donetsk (Ukraine)	BP, NO2, dust, phenol	iron and steel, coal
Dushanbe (Tajikistan)	BP, F, nitric oxide	construction materials, power plants, railways
Dzhambul (Kazakhstan)	BP, dust, hydrogen fluoride, ammonia	fertilizers, power plants
Fergana (Uzbekistan)	BP, F, NO2, dust	petrochemicals, fertilizers, power plants
Groznyi (Russia)	F, BP, NO2, phenol	petrochemicals
Kemerovo (Russia)	BP, F, ammonia, NO2	fertilizers, chemicals, iron and steel
Kommunarsk (Ukraine)	BP, NO2, dust	iron and steel
Komsomolsk-on-Amur (Russia)	BP, lead, F, dust	electronics, iron and steel, power plants, petrochemicals
Krasnoyarsk (Russia)	BP, dust, NO2, F, carbon disulfide	chemicals, nonferrous metallurgy, construction materials, automobiles
Magnitogorsk (Russia)	BP, carbon disulfide, NO2	iron and steel
Mariupol (Ukraine)	BP, F, hydrogen fluoride, ammonia	iron and steel
Nizhnii Tagil (Russia)	BP, F, phenol, dust	iron and steel
Novokuznetsk (Russia)	BP, F, dust, hydrogen fluoride	iron and steel, nonferrous metallurgy, coal, power plants
Odessa (Ukraine)	BP, F, hydrogen fluoride, phenol	metal casting, fertilizers, automobiles
Osh (Kyrgyzstan)	BP, dust, NO2	power plants, construction materials, industrial boilers
Perm (Russia)	BP, F, hydrogen fluoride	petrochemicals
Rustavi (Georgia)	BP, dust, ammonia, phenol	construction materials, iron and steel, fertilizers
Samara (Russia)	F, hydrogen fluoride, BP	petrochemicals, electronics
Ust-Kamenogorsk (Kazakhstan)	lead, BP, F, sulfur dioxide	nonferrous metallurgy, power plants
Yerevan (Armenia)	BP, chloroprene, NO2, ozone	chemicals, power plants, automobiles
Zaporozhye (Ukraine)	BP, NO2, phenol, F	iron and steel, nonferrous metallurgy
Zestafoni (Georgia)	manganese dioxide, BP	iron and steel
Zyryanovsk (Kazakhstan)	BP, dust, NO2	nonferrous metallurgy

[a]BP = benzopyrene; F = formaldehyde; NO2 = nitrogen dioxide.

Source: USSR Goskompriroda, *Sostoyanie prirodnoi sredy i prirodookhrannaya deyatel'nost' v SSSR v 1989 godu* (Moscow: Institut Molodezhi, 1990), pp. 47–48.

by a factor of 10 or more and, as indicated in Table 2.4, the number that chronically exceeded norms by a factor of 2 to 3 times or more.

In contrast, most infractions of air quality standards in the Los Angeles area, the region with the worst overall pollution in the United States, are relatively minor; in the late 1980s, episodic pollution levels rarely reached twice the federal norm. Comparisons with other regions of the world may be more appropriate. In the early 1980s, mean annual sulfur dioxide levels in Milan, the worst performer monitored by the United Nations, exceeded UN guidelines 3 times; Seoul and Rio de Janeiro were not far behind. Shen-yang, New Delhi, Beijing, and Calcutta exceeded UN guidelines for particulates 3 to 4 times, Kuwait 6 times.[32]

THE FALLOUT FROM AIR POLLUTION

According to the Soviet environmental agency, "extensive studies" based on public health data established "a clear relationship between the level of air pollution and population morbidity."[33] Numerous reports in the specialist and popular media have linked air pollution with the public's health—as does this report from Moscow's evening newspaper *Vechernyaya Moskva:*

> Increased air pollution manifests itself in an increase of lung illnesses. Thus, the incidence of bronchial asthma, acute bronchitis, conjunctivitis, pharyngitis, tonsillitis, and chronic otitis is 40–60 percent higher in raions (districts) with increased air pollution. Children living in houses along the Garden Ring Road . . . experience six times the incidence of ear, throat, and nose infections and three times the incidence of bronchitis as children living, for example, around Filevskii Park.[34]

Three large chemical plants are crowded in the southern Kazakhstan city of Dzhambul; one of the plants, Khimprom, spewed out over 10,000 tons of toxic gases alone in 1989.[35] In response to rising concern about air pollution in Dzhambul, *Leninskaya smena* (Leninist Youth), a regional paper, carried the following report from Kazakh health authorities:

> Spontaneous abortions in the polluted zone . . . surrounding the plants . . . occur 12.5 times as frequently as the average, the rate of premature births is 5.4 times as high as the average, and the rate of infertility is 3.8 times as high. People in the zone are 13.5 times as likely to seek medical treatment for acute respiratory diseases, and 13.5 times as likely to seek treatment for chronic pharyngitis and laryngitis. The inhabitants of these neighborhoods are 7 times as likely to suffer from bronchial pneumonia. . . . We shall see if

this distressing news provides the momentum for immediate measures for the ecological recovery of the city.[36]

Nine-tenths of the residents of Nikel, along the remote Russian-Norwegian border, suffer from serious respiratory ailments, among other maladies, according to the estimates of local doctors.[37] Moscow Radio likened living in the city to sitting on death row.[38] Such allegations of a linkage between air quality and public health problems are, however, difficult to substantiate given the poor state of local medical data and confounding factors, such as the high rate of cigarette smoking. On the other hand, the linkages between certain air pollution problems and environmental quality are less problematic to establish.

Three massive smelters producing refined nickel, copper, and cobalt on Russia's Kola Peninsula—at Nikel, Zapolyarnyi, and Monchegorsk—discharged a collective estimated 1 million tons of pollutants, 700,000 tons of it sulfur dioxide—twice as much sulfur as emitted in all of Finland.[39] The fallout of sulfur and heavy metals has eradicated flora and fauna for hundreds of miles. Nikel and Zapolyarnyi are located close to the Finnish-Russian border; thus a large share of their air pollution crosses the border and damages the forests across northern Scandinavia. In Lapland, the pollution has reduced the forest to a lunar landscape, in the appraisal of one Finnish diplomat.[40] The situation on the Kola Peninsula is not unique: Industrial pollution from Norilsk, the south Urals, the Kuznetsk Basin, Krasnoyarsk, and the Angara Basin has damaged adjacent forest and tundra lands. Across the former USSR, air pollution has seriously affected 10,000 square kilometers of forest.[41]

According to researchers at the USSR Academy of Sciences Economics Institute, the cost, in pre–price reform values, of correcting the environmental damage caused by the emission of one ton of pollutants ranged from 150 to 180 rubles.[42] With atmospheric emissions averaging about 100 million tons in the late 1980s, that would yield a total bill of 15–18 billion rubles. Other sources pegged the cost to remedy air pollution damage at 13–16 billion rubles a year.[43]

To minimize damage to the landscape and public health in the immediate vicinity of industrial sites, engineers built tall stacks to send fumes high into the atmosphere where they could be dispersed more widely. This may lessen environmental damage locally, but the potential for damage far from the source of the pollution increases. When they linger in the atmosphere, sulfur and nitrogen, for example, are converted into acids that then precipitate back to earth in the form of rain and snow. The potential impact of long-range atmospheric pollution is important to conditions in the former Soviet Union, because the region's environment is particularly susceptible to degradation due to the lower productivity of its ecosystems, particularly in the tundra and taiga of the north. As a result of climatic conditions and geography, almost all of the forestry stock is classified as low- and medium-yield and, therefore, more sensitive to pollution.

In 1980, Goskomgidromet began operating a nationwide network of almost 1,000 stations to measure the level of pollutants in the snow cover. Another 300 stations monitored pollution in precipitation. Using the data collected from this network, Soviet scientists estimated in the late 1980s that 13.8 million tons of sulfur were deposited on the continental Soviet Union every year. About 1.1 million tons of sulfur annually fell on the Black, Caspian, and Aral seas, and 300,000 tons fell on the Arctic Ocean.[44] The Soviet Union's geographical location and the prevailing weather patterns put the region in the position of a net importer of air pollution; over one-fifth of the supply of atmospheric sulfur in the Soviet Union (about 4 million tons annually) came from transboundary sources, largely from neighboring states in Eastern Europe.[45] In the region immediately adjacent to the western boundaries of Belarus and Ukraine, incoming sulfur reached 30–40 percent of deposits.[46] In contrast, transboundary exports of atmospheric sulfur from the Soviet Union amounted to about 1.6 million tons per year.[47]

Although the volume of pollution in the atmosphere over the Soviet Union was high in the late 1980s, the acidity of the precipitation has exceeded established environmental norms on only a relatively small part of Soviet territory. Elevated levels of acidity in the soil (a pH less than 5.0) have been registered in relatively confined regions along the western borders of Ukraine and Belarus and downwind from large cities and industrial centers; these include the northwest region of Russia (St. Petersburg and northward through Karelia), western and central Ukraine, Tula and Kalinin oblasts, the Vorkuta Basin, and the eastern Urals, including Yekaterinburg and Tyumen. Moderately acidic conditions (pH of 5.0–5.5) have been registered on the Kola Peninsula and along the coasts of the Kara and Laptev seas. (See Map 2.1.)

TRENDS IN EMISSIONS AND AIR QUALITY

In 1988, the USSR State Committee for the Protection of Nature announced that in the cities monitored using the IZA system, overall air quality had been improving steadily. Whereas the average city registered pollution in excess of four the times the maximum permissible concentration in 1974, the average in 1988 was down to half that.[48] During the second half of the 1980s, ambient concentrations of particulates decreased by 12 percent, and sulfur compounds were reduced by up to 25 percent. Even greater decreases were registered for less common but potentially more harmful compounds like ammonia (13 percent), hydrogen sulfide (48 percent), hydrogen fluoride (14 percent), and phenol (14 percent). Concentrations of lead and formaldehyde, however, remained unchanged.[49]

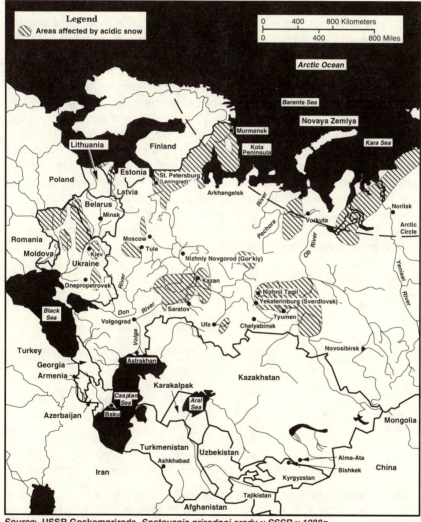

Source: USSR Goskompriroda, *Sostoyanie prirodnoi sredy v SSSR v 1988g.* (Moscow: VINITI, 1989), p. 23.

MAP 2.1 Regions with acidic snow cover (pH less than 5.5), 1988

This improvement was possible because the total volume of pollutants being released into the atmosphere from monitored sources in the Soviet Union decreased by about 18 percent during the 1980s, despite an increase in economic output. Between 1980 and 1990, the volume of pollutants emitted from stationary sources in the Soviet Union declined by over 23 percent (see Table 2.6). A modest 8 percent decrease in emissions from motor vehicles during the same period yielded a decrease in total emissions of 18 percent (see Figure 2.2). In comparison, total emissions in the United States decreased by about 17 percent between 1980 and 1988.[50] Despite the reported decrease in overall emissions from the transport sector, ambient concentrations of carbon monoxide and lead remained constant, and nitrogen dioxide and nitric oxide levels increased by 12 and 8 percent, respectively, during the second half of the 1980s.[51]

Interestingly, the decrease in automobile emissions occurred despite a rapid expansion of the transport sector. In the early 1970s, the Soviet Union reported to the World Health Organization that motor vehicle fumes (from trucks, buses, and automobiles) accounted for 13.1 percent of all toxic pollutants produced.[52] Thereafter, this sector expanded dramatically: Between 1970 and 1988, the trucking industry increased by about 225 percent, and use of buses similarly.[53] Meanwhile, a 16-fold increase in sales of automobiles for private use[54] brought the number of privately held automobiles to 16 million vehicles by 1990.[55] Thus, the share of air pollution emitted nationwide by the transport sector increased to 34 percent in 1980 and 39 percent in 1990.

TABLE 2.6 Atmospheric emissions, 1980–1990 (million tons)

		Source of Emissions		Percent of Total	
	Total	Stationary	Transport	Stationary	Transport
1980	110.8	72.8	38.0	66	34
1985	105.0	68.3	36.7	65	35
1986	103.6	66.5	37.1	64	36
1987	100.5	64.3	36.2	64	36
1988	97.5	61.7	35.8	63	37
1989	94.0	58.5	35.5	62	38
1990	90.7	55.7	35.0[a]	61	39

[a] Estimate.

Sources: USSR Goskomstat, *Okhrana okruzhayushchei sredy i ratsional'noe ispol'zovanie prirodnykh resursov v SSSR* (Moscow: Finansy i statistika, 1989), p. 7; USSR Goskompriroda, *Sostoyanie prirodnoi sredy i prirodookhrannaya deyatel'nost' v SSSR v 1989 godu* (Moscow: Institut Molodezhi, 1990), p. 20; *Ekonomika i zhizn'*, No. 35, 1991, p. 6.

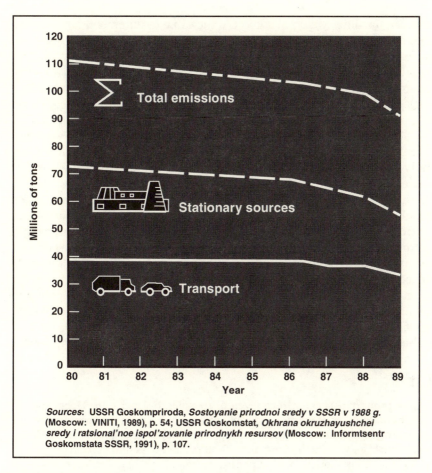

FIGURE 2.2 Air pollution emissions, 1980–1989

AIR POLLUTION CONTROL EFFORTS

The decrease in emissions in the Soviet Union was the result of an effort initiated by the government in the 1970s to improve urban air quality. In conjunction with the USSR Ministry of Health, the USSR State Committee for Hydrometeorology developed standards of maximum permissible emissions (*predel'no dopustimyi vybros* in Russian, PDV) and temporarily permissible emissions limits for over 200 hazardous pollutants. A Soviet law, which took effect in 1981, required all new enterprises or enterprises that renovated or modernized their production processes to ensure that emissions complied with the established norms.

Existing facilities were not subject to the same requirement, but were expected to control their emissions at least to some extent.

To attain these goals, the government allocated 2.15 billion rubles for capital investment in measures to reduce air pollution from stationary sources between 1981 and 1989. This effort, however, was hampered by a lack of adequate and readily available technology and by reluctance on the part of the ministries to sacrifice output in favor of pollution control. As a result, a significant portion of the government's money went unspent every year, and government targets for pollution reduction regularly were unmet. Between 1985 and 1989, outlays for capital investments increased 78 percent, yet the portion of funds unspent every year during this period increased from about 10 percent to almost 25 percent.[56] As a result, the installation of pollution control equipment did not keep pace with the construction of new industry, not to mention the demands of retrofitting established enterprises. Between 1985 and 1988, the share of pollution sources outfitted with pollution control equipment fell from 47 percent to 40 percent.[57]

In February 1990, during a major speech on environmental policy to the Ukrainian Supreme Soviet, V. A. Masol, the chairman of the Ukrainian Council of Ministers, noted the small fraction of the republic's enterprises fitted with air pollution control equipment, pointing out that even in cases where it was installed, such equipment did not always work as designed:

> The primary reason for [high levels of air pollution] is that the technological processes are imperfect and the outfitting of industrial enterprises with treatment equipment is unsatisfactory. Thus, in power engineering and the chemical and coal industries, only 30–40 percent of pollution sources have treatment installations, and in petrochemicals, 20 percent. No less damage is done by the low efficiency of the treatment equipment [installed]. The Ukrainian State Committee for the Protection of Nature checked the status of gas and dust scrubbers at the Voroshilovgrad and Krivoi Rog [power plants]. Practically all of them were in disrepair or worked at very low efficiency. Unfortunately, such examples are not isolated. They attest to the low level of production expertise and discipline. Of course, fines are being levied on the individuals guilty of these gross violations. But, in the end, they can in no way compensate for the damage done to the environment and people's health.[58]

The performance of pollution control equipment installed on factories has been very poor, especially when compared with Western control technologies. In 1989, overall efficiency of Soviet-built technology was rated at 78 percent. The process efficiency equipment to scrub down flue gases in specific was pegged at just 31 percent; for heat and power plants, the single greatest polluting sector, the rate was a mere 1.2 percent in 1989.[59]

Two factors account for the poor performance of Soviet air pollution controls. First was the low quality of Soviet technology installed. According to *Business in the USSR*, the best available Soviet air pollution control technologies for the chemical industry were at least twenty years behind world standards.[60] Scrubbers at the Nikel plant could remove only 10 percent of sulfur emissions; Western technology on the same plant would be able to trap an estimated 85 percent or more of the pollution.[61] A large share of equipment was either outdated or worn out. Control technologies on plants in Narva, Estonia, for instance, were built in the 1950s.[62] According to USSR Goskompriroda, the low quality of Soviet scrubbers and filters resulted in an extra 9 million tons of pollutants (about 15 percent of total annual emissions from stationary sources) being emitted every year.[63]

Second, the poor manner in which pollution controls were operated contributed to pollution problems. In 1987, the Soviet government conducted a survey of the effectiveness of 61,300 air pollution control installations at enterprises across the country. The results were remarkable: One-fifth of the equipment tested operated at less than its designed capacity.[64] The chief reasons for such poor performance were many: Plant managers refused to halt production in order to perform necessary maintenance and repairs; spare parts were in short supply; personnel were poorly trained in proper operation of the equipment; and technologies were installed for tasks they were not designed to handle. In some cases, filters were simply turned off—usually at night when local residents could not see the effect.[65] A scientist at the Kazakh Academy of Sciences reported his observation of air pollution controls at the fertilizer plants in Dzhambul:

> [Smokestack] filters never work 100 percent of the time. They are often disabled and they are often simply disconnected, since they consume a lot of electricity. Energy is constantly in short supply, and the deficit is ever increasing. In spite of the growing attention to ecological questions, filters continue to be disconnected at night and at the end of the month and the quarter, when the equipment runs at maximum capacity in order to fulfill the plan. On average, filters were not used 15–20 percent of the time.[66]

According to USSR Goskompriroda, the failure of Soviet air pollution devices to perform at their designed capacities resulted in 7 million more tons of pollutants (11 percent of emissions) unnecessarily being sent into the atmosphere in 1987.[67] Given all of these problems, only 40 percent of

Soviet enterprises were in compliance with emissions norms as of the beginning of 1991.[68]

In addition to its effort to combat pollution from stationary sources, the Soviet government mandated that automobile factories take measures to reduce vehicle emissions. These efforts were stymied, however, as auto plant managers, focused on fulfilling their output quotas, were able to avoid many of the government's edicts. Through the early 1990s, cars continued to be produced without catalytic converters and basics like electronic ignition and exhaust-gas recirculation. Once on the road, many cars did not meet the government's modest emissions standards; in 1989, almost 10 percent of all cars tested for compliance failed.[69] Under a strict monitoring program called "Clean Air" implemented in Moscow in the mid-1980s, 50 percent of automobiles were found to have

Truck driver undergoing roadside inspection for automobile emissions. In the 1980s, Moscow tightened testing in order to reduce air pollution from an estimated 800,000 vehicles in the capital. Photo: TASS, from Sovfoto.

above-norm emissions in 1987; by the following year, the rate had been reduced to 20 percent.[70]

Given problems with Soviet air pollution control efforts, the decrease in emissions achieved during the 1980s was not attributable solely to the modest accomplishments of Soviet pollution control technology. As discussed in Chapter 7, another factor was officials' increasing tendency to shut down "objects having especially great environmental impact."[71] A large proportion of the reduction also can be attributed to a dramatic shift in the country's energy balance away from a heavy reliance on oil and coal in favor of increased consumption of natural gas. The impact of the shift in the region's fuel balance was most significant in terms of sulfur emissions because only a few electric power stations (the principal source of sulfur emissions) were outfitted with sulfur-scrubbing technology as of the early 1990s.[72]

Between 1980 and 1989, for example, the consumption of natural gas by the Soviet economy increased by 91 percent; the use of coal and oil fell slightly.[73] Accordingly, the sharp drop in emissions from the electric power industry noted in Table 2.1 was effected largely through the wide-scale conversion of power plants from burning high-sulfur bunker oil to natural gas.[74] In 1985, one-third of electricity was generated using natural gas, compared with 20 percent the decade before.[75] Moreover, the rapid expansion of centralized urban steam-supply systems (fired largely by natural gas) replaced reliance on in-house boilers, many of which were fueled with oil and coal.[76] By 1985, natural gas accounted for four-fifths of the fuel burned for heat and power in Moscow, contributing to a 60 percent reduction of particulate emissions and a 39 percent cut in sulfur dioxide emissions from 1975 levels,[77] which helped to bring the capital into compliance with air quality standards for these compounds.[78] The Soviet government's gasification program also extended to motor vehicles under a pilot program begun in 1983. By 1989, over 100,000 general-purpose trucks on the roads were natural-gas powered—about 1.4 percent of the fleet.[79]

Unlike the situation in the United States and other advanced industrialized nations, energy demand and, concomitantly, carbon emissions grew steadily in the USSR throughout the 1970s and 1980s as domestic price controls eliminated the economic imperative for firms to increase efficiency after the energy price shocks of the 1970s. Without the dramatic shift in favor of natural gas, which has a significantly lower carbon content, the USSR's contribution of greenhouse gases could have been far worse.

EMISSIONS TRENDS IN THE FUTURE

During 1990 and 1991, emissions from stationary sources dropped by over 10 percent from 1989 levels—a significant increase over the rate of improvement registered in the mid-1980s. This turn for the better was not attributed to wild success in the government's antipollution program but to the rapid deterioration in the state of the economy (in 1991 alone GNP was estimated to have fallen 17 percent) and in the oil refining, iron and steel, and cement industries in particular.[80] That emissions did not drop even more in accordance with the overall economy may have been because enterprise managers, under such severe economic pressures, were more likely than before to ignore environmental concerns.

Finally, the breakdown of the Soviet economy has produced good news in terms of global climate change. According to Christopher Flavin of the WorldWatch Institute, carbon emissions from the Soviet Union decreased by 4 percent in 1990 and were estimated to decrease another 5 percent in 1991, largely because of the decline in economic output. By 1995, the drop in carbon emissions may reach 30 percent, thereby contributing to a 5 percent decline in global carbon output.[81]

Notes

1. Radio Moscow, July 23, 1989; TASS, August 2, 1989.

2. Central Television, "Vremya," August 10, 1989.

3. *Pravda*, August 14, 1990, p. 2.

4. Hamida Yernazarov, staff assistant, Kazakh Ecological Fund, personal communication, Los Angeles, April 1992.

5. G. L. Gromyko, ed., *Sotsial'no-ekonomicheskaya statistika* (Moscow: Izdatel'stvo Moskovskogo Universiteta, 1989), pp. 106–108.

6. USSR Goskompriroda, *Sostoyanie prirodnoi sredy i prirodookhrannaya deyatel'nost' v SSSR v 1989 godu* (Moscow: Institut Molodezhi, 1990), p. 13.

7. This "superministry" was created in 1989 as a result of an amalgamation of the former ministries of ferrous metallurgy and nonferrous metallurgy; in 1988 they were responsible for 17 percent and 10 percent, respectively, of total stationary emissions. USSR Goskompriroda, *Sostoyanie prirodnoi sredy v SSSR v 1988 g.* (Moscow: VINITI, 1989), p. 55.

8. Asif Faiz, *Automotive Air Pollution: An Overview* (Washington, DC: World Bank, 1990), cited in World Resources Institute, *World Resources 1992-1993* (New York: Oxford University Press, 1992), p. 196.

9. USSR Goskompriroda, *Sostoyanie . . . v 1989 godu*, p. 234; Friends of the Earth, cited in *Svenska Dagbladet*, July 29, 1989, p. 3, translated in FBIS–SOV–89–161, p. 52.

10. USSR Goskomstat, cited in S. B. Lavrov, "Regional and Environmental Problems of the USSR: A Synopsis of Views from the Soviet Parliament," *Soviet Geography*, September 1990, p. 498.

11. *Vechernyaya Moskva*, December 23, 1989, p. 2. The figure of 800,000 motor vehicles was cited by A. I. Kudin, chair of Moskompriroda, the city's environmental protection agency. Another source estimates the number of vehicles at almost 1 million, a figure that includes 680,000 Moscow-registered automobiles and 300,000 from out of town. Fatei Shipunov, "Smog nad Moskvoi," *Moskva*, No. 4, 1989, p. 164.

12. U.S. Bureau of the Census, *Statistical Abstract of the United States: 1991* (Washington, DC: Government Printing Office, 1991), p. 209. This comparison is based on data for emissions of five principal air pollutants: carbon monoxide, sulfur dioxide, nitrogen oxides, volatile organic compounds, and particulates. In 1988, these substances accounted for about 98 percent of all emissions in the Soviet Union. USSR Goskompriroda, *Sostoyanie . . . v 1988 g.*, p. 55.

13. USSR Goskomstat, *Sotsial'noe razvitie i uroven' zhizni naseleniya SSSR* (Moscow: Finansy i statistika, 1989), p. 122; U.S. Bureau of the Census, *Statistical Abstract of the United States: 1990* (Washington, DC: Government Printing Office, 1990), p. 603. Given America's greater reliance on the automobile, the difference in gasoline consumption and miles-per-vehicle driven in the United States and the former USSR is even greater, but a lack of Soviet data on vehicle travel prevents an exact comparison.

14. U.S. Bureau of the Census, *Statistical Abstract, 1990*, p. 589; USSR Goskomstat, *Narodnoe khozyaistvo SSSR v 1988 g.* (Moscow: Finansy i statistika, 1989), pp. 572, 579. Comparisons are made in terms of ton-kilometers for trucks and passenger-kilometers for bus transport.

15. Central Intelligence Agency, *Handbook of Economic Statistics, 1989* (Washington, DC: Government Printing Office, 1989), pp. 24, 63–68. The figures are for Soviet GNP and U.S. GDP and are calculated using purchasing-power equivalents.

16. William Chandler, ed., *Carbon Emissions Control Strategies: Executive Summary* (Washington, DC: Conservation Foundation, 1990), pp. 3–4. This figure is based on 1986 worldwide carbon emissions of 5.6 billion tons produced from the burning of fossil fuels, which accounts for about three-quarters of all carbon emissions caused by human activity.

17. Estimates are by the International Panel on Climate Change and World Resources Institute, cited in *World Resources, 1992–1993*, pp. 208, 210.

18. USSR Goskompriroda, *Sostoyanie . . . v 1988 g.*, p. 33. For comparison, production in the United States and the European Community amounted to 30 and 45 percent of global output, respectively.

19. *Trud*, July 5, 1989, p. 1; USSR Goskompriroda, *Sostoyanie . . . v 1988 g.*, pp. 5–6.

20. Charles E. Ziegler, *Environmental Policy in the USSR* (Amherst: University of Massachusetts Press, 1987), p. 105.

21. USSR Goskompriroda, *Sostoyanie . . . v 1989 godu*, p. 40.

22. Ibid., pp. 45–46.

23. *Ekonomika i zhizn'*, No. 5, 1991, p. 11.

24. USSR Goskompriroda, *Sostoyanie . . . v 1988 g.*, p. 14.

25. *Ekonomika i zhizn'*, No. 5, 1991, p. 11. In 1988, 16 Soviet cities reported peak levels of various pollutants at more than 50 times the permitted maximum. USSR Goskompriroda, *Sostoyanie . . . v 1988 g.*, p. 14.

26. *Pravda vostoka*, November 21, 1989, p. 3.

27. See, for example, the speech made by Mikhail Gorbachev to the First Congress of People's Deputies, *Pervyi s"ezd narodnykh deputatov SSSR: Stenograficheskii otchet*, Vol. 1 (Moscow: Izdatel'stvo Verkhovnogo Soveta SSSR, 1989), pp. 444–445.

28. USSR Goskompriroda, *Sostoyanie . . . v 1989 godu*, pp. 48–50.

29. *Ekonomika i zhizn'*, No. 4, 1989, p. 18.

30. U.S. Bureau of the Census, *Statistical Abstract, 1991*, p. 210.

31. Hilary F. French, *Clearing the Air: A Global Agenda*, WorldWatch Institute, Paper No. 94, Washington DC, January 1990, pp. 10–11.

32. United Nations Environment Programme, *Environmental Data Report* (Oxford: Blackwell, 1989), pp. 14–15.

33. USSR Goskompriroda, *Sostoyanie . . . v 1988 g.*, p. 129. Since the late 1980s, Soviet media accounts have been replete with reports of elevated illness rates in localities with severe pollution problems, although such stories usually fail to establish a causal linkage.

34. *Vechernyaya Moskva*, February 17, 1990.

35. USSR Goskompriroda, *Sostoyanie . . . v 1989 godu*, p. 196.

36. *Leninskaya smena*, April 13, 1991, p. 1, as translated in JPRS–TEN–91–014, pp. 86–87.

37. *Guardian*, January 11, 1991; Radio Moscow, September 13, 1991.

38. Radio Moscow, September 13, 1991.

39. *Aftenposten*, April 27, 1991, p. 12, translated in JPRS–TEN–91–012, pp. 77–78.

40. *Wall Street Journal* (European ed.), October 24, 1989.

41. *Ekonomika i zhizn'*, No. 41, 1990, insert page 1.

42. *Argumenty i fakty*, No. 15, 1990, p. 1.

43. See comments by Nikolai Vorontsov in USSR Goskompriroda, *Sostoyanie . . . v 1989 godu*, p. 8; and V. A. Shirokov, "Pochemy 'ne rabotaet' zakon ob atmosfernogo vozdukha?" *Energiya: Ekonomika, tekhnika, ekologiya*, No. 11, 1988, p. 29.

44. V. N. Vasilenko et al., "Zagryaznenie territorii SSSR vypedaniyami sery i azota," *Meteorologiya i gidrologiya*, No. 8, 1988, Allerton Press translation, pp. 49–56.

45. Ibid. p. 32. Anthropogenic emissions from the USSR were pegged at 11.8 million tons per year. Another 2.1 million tons of sulfur come from the upper troposphere or natural sources, bringing the total atmospheric supply to 17.9 million tons annually.

46. USSR Goskompriroda, *Sostoyanie . . . v 1988 g.*, p. 25.

47. Vasilenko et al., "Zagryaznenie," pp. 49–56. The breakdown for trans-boundary emissions is as follows: Precipitation over the Arctic Ocean, 300,000

tons; transport across the western boundary, 600,000 tons; transport across the southern and eastern boundaries, 200,000 tons. Releases into the upper troposphere total 500,000 tons. As previously mentioned, another 1.1 million tons of sulfur fell on the Black, Caspian, and Aral seas annually; the two former instances may be considered in part transboundary emissions.

48. USSR Goskompriroda, *Sostoyanie . . . v 1988 g.*, p. 12.

49. USSR Goskompriroda, *Sostoyanie . . . v 1989 godu*, p. 42.

50. U.S. Bureau of the Census, *Statistical Abstract, 1991*, p. 209.

51. USSR Goskompriroda, *Sostoyanie . . . v 1989 godu*, p. 42.

52. Cited in Victor L. Mote, "Air Pollution in the USSR," in Ivan Volgyes, ed., *Environmental Deterioration in the Soviet Union and Eastern Europe* (New York: Praeger, 1974), p. 38.

53. During the period 1970–1988, turnover in general-use trucking increased from 64.2 billion to 143.4 billion ton-kilometers, and bus use increased from 202 billion to 480 million passenger-kilometers. USSR Goskomstat, *Narodnoe khozyaistvo SSSR v 1988 g.*, pp. 557, 568.

54. Ibid., p. 117.

55. *Za rulem*, No. 1, 1991, p. 7.

56. USSR Goskompriroda, *Sostoyanie . . . v 1988 g.*, p. 138; *Vestnik statistiki*, No. 11, 1988, p. 56; USSR Goskomstat, *Press-vypusk*, No. 226, June 7, 1990.

57. USSR Goskomstat, *Narodnoe khozyaistvo SSSR v 1988 g.*, pp. 249; USSR Goskomstat, *Okhrana okruzhayushchei sredy i ratsional'noe ispol'zovanie prirodnykh resursov v SSSR* (Moscow: Finansy i statistika, 1989), pp. 86–87.

58. *Pravda Ukrainy*, February 17, 1990.

59. USSR Goskompriroda, *Sostoyanie . . . v 1989 godu*, p. 13. The gas-scrubbing efficiencies of control technologies in the natural gas and coal industries were 4.8 and 0.6 percent, respectively.

60. "Questions for Puzzle Enthusiasts" (no author), *Business in the USSR*, October 1990, p. 39.

61. *Guardian*, January 11, 1991.

62. K. K. Rebane, "Severo-vostok Estonii: Bolevaya tochka sostoyaniya okruzhayushchei sredy," *Izvestiya Akademii Nauk SSSR*, No. 11, 1988, p. 87.

63. *Vestnik statistiki*, No. 11, 1988, p. 57.

64. USSR Goskomstat, *Sbornik statisticheskikh materialov, 1988* (Moscow: Finansyi statistika, 1989), pp. 278–280.

65. V. G. Glushkova, "Vazhnye napravleniya ekologicheskoi situatsii v Moskve," in E. M. Pospenov et al., eds., *Problemy uluchsheniya ekologicheskoi situatsii i ratsional'nogo prirodopol'zovaniya v Moskovskom regione* (Moscow: Moskovskii filial Geograficheskogo obshchestva SSSR, 1989), p. 71.

66. Leonid Liubomirskii, "Another Look at the Reliability of Official Soviet Pollution Control Statistics," *Environmental Policy Review*, Vol. 5, No. 1, January 1991, p. 34.

67. USSR Goskomstat, *Sbornik statisticheskikh materialov*, pp. 278–280; USSR Goskomstat, *Okhrana okruzhayushchei sredy*, p. 89.

68. *Vestnik statistiki*, No. 11, 1991, p. 65.

69. *Za rulem*, No. 1, 1991, p. 7. Of those cars that failed their emissions test, about one-half reportedly had their registration revoked.

70. Glushkova, "Vazhnye," p. 72.

71. *Vestnik statistiki*, No. 11, 1991, p. 63.

72. R. Caron Cooper, "Former Soviet Republics and Transboundary Pollution: SO₂," paper presented at Trilateral Graduate Student Conference on the Post-Soviet Era, RAND, Los Angeles, May 1992, p. 17.

73. "Soviet Energy Situation Update for 1989," *PlanEcon Report*, Nos. 9–10, 1990, p. 7.

74. The reduced reliance on oil has been especially significant because the oil supplied to electric plants has a sulfur content of 2.5 percent or higher in contrast to the 0.5 percent content of oil consumed in Japan and the United States. I. A. Glebov et al., "Ekologiya: Nasha obshchaya trevoga i zabota," *Elektricheskie stantsii*, No. 9, 1989, p. 3; Yu. K Semenov, "O sostoyanii elektroenergetiki, i problemakh energoobespecheniya na perspektivy i sotsial'noi zashchish-chennosti trydyashchikhsya otrasli," *Elektricheskie stantsii*, No. 3, 1991, p. 7.

75. A. A. Troitskii, ed., *Energetika SSSR v 1986–1990 godakh* (Moscow: Energoatomizdat, 1987), p. 13. By comparison, the U.S. share of electricity generated using natural gas declined over the 1980s, to about 10 percent. U.S. Bureau of the Census, *Statistical Abstract, 1990*, p. 573. For more on the shift in the energy balance of Soviet power stations, see Matthew Sagers, "News Notes," *Soviet Geography*, No. 3, 1990, pp. 227–231.

76. A. A. Bekker, " Sostoyanie i tendentsii ismeneniya zagryazneniya atmos-fernoggo vozdukha v Moskve," in Pospenov et al., eds., *Problemy uluchsheniya ekologicheskoi situatsii*, p. 55. Between 1980 and 1985 alone, generation of heat in centralized systems increased by over 18 percent. Troitskii, *Energetika*, p. 12.

77. Bekker, "Sostoyanie i tendentsii," p. 56.

78. USSR Goskompriroda, *Sostoyanie . . . v 1989 godu*, p. 88.

79. USSR Goskomstat, *Okhrana okruzhayushchei sredy*, p. 90. Original plans called for a total of 500,000 gas-powered vehicles by 1990. For an early review of the USSR's gas-powered motor vehicle program, see *Ekonomicheskaya gazeta*, No. 41, 1987, p. 17.

80. *Ekonomika i zhizn'*, No. 6, 1991, p. 13. See also *Vestnik statistiki*, No. 11, 1991, p. 63.

81. *New York Times*, December 8, 1991, p. 17. Christopher Flavin, vice-president, WorldWatch Institute, personal communication, Los Angeles, January 1992.

3

The Water

Don't spit into the well water—you'll need to drink it later.
—Russian proverb

There is no water in this city, spread along the largest river in Europe. What a joke.
—Television newscast reporting on contaminated drinking
water in the Russian city of Volgograd

The Soviet Union faced two major problems with water resources, one natural, one humanmade. Although the Eurasian region is blessed with ample amounts of rain and snow feeding its great rivers and lakes, the bulk of its water resources are located in relatively undeveloped regions of Siberia—in the basins of rivers that carry the water north and even farther away from the areas where it is needed most. Three-quarters of the region's population and 70 percent of its industry enjoy ready access to only 16 percent of total available water resources. Seasonal variations exacerbate the distribution problem as meltwater combines with heavy rainfalls in spring and early summer to cause flooding. Autumn and winter in Eurasia tend to be dry, with runoff stopping completely during the long winter freeze. The region is also noted for great variations in precipitation from year to year, rendering agricultural output unpredictable. To overcome these challenges of nature, engineers dammed, diked, drained, and diverted water resources in an effort to work the Soviet Union into a single hydrographic network.

Where and when water was available, resources were squandered through poor allocation, misuse, and severe pollution. According to a 1990 government survey of 10,000 citizens living in ecologically depressed regions, water pollution was the problem that troubled people the most.[1] Given the fact that many bodies of water cross the borders of

newly independent states, the Soviet legacy of these two issues—the distribution and degradation of water resources—could prove to be one of
the most contentious environmental problems of the post-Soviet era.

WATER DIVERSIONS AND WATER USE

In 1988, a total of more than 80,000 enterprises, associations, farms,
and urban water utilities drew off 365 cubic kilometers (365 billion cubic
meters) of water, about 8 percent of the annual renewable supply. (The
term *water withdrawal* means water physically abstracted, the majority of
which returns to the water table.) In 1987, water withdrawals in the Soviet Union equaled about 3.3 cubic meters of water per person per day.
For comparison, following are the rates in other countries during the
same time period: Bulgaria, 2.3 cubic meters of water per person per day;
Hungary, 1.9; Czechoslovakia, 0.9; and the United States, 6.4.[2] Water
withdrawals by economic sector are presented in Table 3.1; included for
comparison are data for the United States.

The volume of water used by the economy was actually much greater,
but the Soviet government expended hundreds of millions of rubles annually during the 1970s and 1980s to develop recirculating supply systems. Between 1980 and 1988, the volume of water recycled by industry
increased 42 percent, reaching 72 percent of all water used. In turn, water
use dipped slightly during this period, while the economy grew.[3] Despite these efforts, however, water usage remained inefficient by interna-

TABLE 3.1 Water withdrawals for the national economy in the Soviet Union and
the United States

	Soviet Union (1988)		United States[a] (1985)	
Purpose	Cubic Kilometers	Percentage of Total	Cubic Kilometers	Percentage of Total
Industry[b]	140.2	38.4	289.8	52.6
Irrigation	194.5	53.3	189.3	34.3
Public supply	24.5	6.7	55.1	10.0
Other	5.7	1.6	17.0	3.1
Total	364.9	100.0	551.2	100.0

[a]Includes salt and fresh water.

[b]Includes water used by the agroindustrial complex for purposes other than irrigation
and water used by power plants.

Sources: USSR Goskompriroda, *Sostoyanie prirodnoi sredy v SSSR v 1988 g.* (Moscow:
VINITI, 1989), p. 43; U.S. Bureau of the Census, *Statistical Abstract of the United States: 1989*
(Washington, DC: Government Printing Office, 1989), p. 198.

tional standards. To produce one ton of steel, the average Soviet factory required 270 cubic meters of water; the average in West Germany was 180 cubic meters.[4] To produce one ton of pulp, the Baikal Pulp and Paper Combine (an efficient plant, by Soviet standards) used 375 tons of water and discharged 231 kilograms of mineral salts (sodium sulfate) in its effluent. The corresponding figures for pulp production in the United States were 250 tons and 64 kilograms, respectively.[5] The more water used to produce a measure of output, the greater the resources that must be expended to ensure its purity before returning it to the environment.

A second concern related to the issue of water use and efficiency is water consumption—the volume of water abstracted but not returned ultimately to the local water table. Although improvements such as recirculating water supply systems improved the efficiency of water use, the economy continued to consume a large volume of water. Of the total amount of water withdrawn in 1988, 182 cubic kilometers, or 50 percent, was irretrievably lost.[6] The U.S. economy withdrew significantly more water from the environment, but a much larger proportion was returned; in 1985, water consumption was 127 cubic kilometers, or just 23 percent of withdrawals.[7]

Heavy water consumption, not use, frequently led to environmentally disruptive decreases in the levels of many rivers and lakes. By the 1980s, water flows throughout the Soviet Union were reduced by 2.5 percent, and in the southern regions of the country by an average of about 14 percent.[8] Water consumption has deprived the Volga of 5 percent of its historic flows, flows in the Dnieper have been reduced by 19 percent, and supplies of water feeding the basins of the rivers Don and Kuban have been reduced by one-third. Even in water-rich Siberia, the Tom, Ishim, and Chulym rivers have been in "a strained condition," according to USSR Goskompriroda.[9] The agricultural sector traditionally has consumed the most water; in parched regions under extensive irrigation, such as Central Asia and Kazakhstan, on average one-quarter of the annual supplies of water are not returned to the local water table.[10] The Aral Sea is an extreme case: Consumption of water drawn from the Amu Darya and Syr Darya rivers, which feed the Aral Sea, is almost complete. What water still flows in those rivers is largely agricultural runoff laden with fertilizer and pesticides; in some years, water from neither river has reached the Aral Sea.

One reason efficiency remained low and consumption high is that water often was diverted unintentionally. Fourteen percent of the water pumped out of ground- and surface-water resources in 1988 (50.6 cubic kilometers) was lost in transmission between source and end user—a volume equivalent to sacrificing almost all the water that flows down the

Dnieper River in a year. Ninety-two percent of all water lost in the national economy occurred in the agricultural sector from irrigation systems that often were crudely constructed and poorly maintained.[11]

For a region of great seasonal and geographical disparities in the distribution of water, the expansion of irrigation systems has played a central role in boosting agricultural output. In the 1970s and 1980s, the area of land under irrigation doubled to include a total of 21 million hectares.[12] By the late 1980s, almost one-third of all agricultural production, in terms of ruble value, came from irrigated land; grown on irrigated land were all cotton and rice produced in the Soviet Union, three-quarters of the vegetables, half the fruit, and 30 percent of the corn.[13] The benefits of irrigation, however, have cost the environment dearly. In the haste to boost irrigation, the Ministry of Land Reclamation and Water Resources frequently dug channels directly in the soil or sand, often without adequate lining or covering. More than half of irrigation systems consist of simple unlined furrows, and as a result, seepage has averaged almost 20 percent.[14] In Georgia, 78 percent of all channels are unlined and uncovered, and water losses in the republic are as high as 40–60 percent.[15] Of the 180,000 kilometers of irrigation canals in Central Asia, 15,000—only 8 percent—have linings.[16] Seepage from the Karakum Canal (for which water has been diverted from its course into the Aral Sea) has inundated the Turkmenistan capital of Ashkhabad; to prevent flooding, the authorities have had to drill 150 wells to pump the water out of the city.[17] Sergei Zalygin, who is not only one of Russia's foremost literary figures and environmentalists but also a water resources engineer, has estimated that 25 million hectares of land not intended for irrigation are virtually swamped by misdirected water supplies.[18]

Although the total area of irrigated land and the volume of water used in the entire former Soviet Union have been roughly comparable to figures for the United States, the distribution of available resources has been very uneven, and the distribution and application have been ineffective and often damaging. In addition to spawning leaks, Soviet irrigation networks frequently have no means with which to regulate the water supply. Of the 7,000 sources feeding the irrigation systems of Georgia, only 18 percent are metered.[19] About 40 percent of irrigated land (7.7 million hectares in 1988) has been equipped with more water-efficient sprinkler systems; the remaining 60 percent is watered using simple furrows.[20] Sprinkler systems are used almost universally in the Baltic states, Ukraine, Belarus, and Moldova (regions with only small irrigation systems), but they are largely absent elsewhere. Turkmenistan and Uzbekistan, two of the republics with the largest share of irrigated land, have scarcely a sprinkler system between them.[21] High-efficiency sprinkler systems and slow-drip technologies have not been exploited.[22] In the end, according to Zalygin, a mere 20–30 percent of water withdrawn ultimately reaches the crops for which it is intended.[23]

A U.S. researcher, Michael Rozengurt, has pointed out that crops in Central Asia and Kazakhstan may receive between 4 and 6 times the amount of water they require.[24] Half of the 2.3 million hectares of farmland in Ukraine are reported to be overwatered.[25] According to a study by the Soviet statistical agency, of the farms surveyed that had established norms for irrigation, 44 percent were found to be applying too much water to their crops to the extent of a total of 100 million cubic meters.[26] Overwatering encourages erosion, and 10 percent of all irrigated land already has been affected.[27] In addition, excessive irrigation promotes the leaching of nutrients, minerals, and agricultural chemicals, which eventually contaminate ground and surface water resources. Finally, the swamping of irrigated land in southern regions has promoted the return of malaria, a disease Soviet authorities had considered eradicated.[28]

Just as it rapidly developed irrigation systems, the Soviet government aggressively expanded its network of hydroelectric power stations in order to meet the economy's growing demand for electricity following World War II. Dam building was a pet project of Lenin's and evolved into a grand effort. Under the "Great Volga" scheme initiated under Stalin, the Volga River (often referred to as the "main street of Russia") and its tributaries were dammed up with 34 large and small hydroelectric power stations.[29] In the 1950s, thousands of aspiring young Communists answered the call of the Komsomol, the Leninist youth league, and flocked to the wilds of Siberia to help build the Bratsk dam. Great pride was exhibited in the construction of the world's tallest dam—Tajikistan's Nurek and the most powerful hydroelectric station, then the Krasnoyarsk. At the close of the 1980s, there were about 210 large- or medium-sized hydroelectric stations in the Soviet Union.[30]

The government's hydroelectric program claimed 62,000 square kilometers of land in the former Soviet Union—an area equal in size to West Virginia—a result, in part, of numerous dams being built in lowlands.[31] Before the dam-building program, it took one month for water to travel the course of the Volga; by the 1980s, the trip had been slowed to a year and a half.[32] "The Volga has virtually ceased to be a river," laments Aleksei Yablokov. "[I]t has become a chain of reservoirs."[33] In 1988, the Soviet environmental agency reported that the USSR Ministry of Land Reclamation and Water Resources and the USSR Ministry of Power Engineering and Electrification—the dams' builders—did not ensure the proper preparation of lands inundated by the reservoirs. As a result,

Siberia's Bratsk, Krasnoyarsk, and Ust-Ilimsk reservoirs had accumulated 3.6 million cubic meters of wood debris. The subsequent decay of the wood raised the concentration of phenols to as much as 10 times established norms.[34] Because lowlands surrounding the reservoirs were not stabilized or protected, they became subject to flooding and erosion, which eventually fills the reservoirs with silt, diminishing their capacity and useful lifetime.

Hydroelectric stations accounted for almost one-fifth of Soviet generating capacity and produced 13.5 percent of the electricity consumed, roughly the same share as the nuclear power industry.[35] Because many regions have suffered chronic energy shortages, energy managers are often forced to rely on hydroelectric power to cover gaps in supply, especially when demand peaks during the winter heating season. Water stocks are thus depleted during the winter and can only be replenished in the spring, when rivers rise with melting snow and heavy rainfall. The resulting cycle, which runs counter to the natural cycle of heavy spring flow and low winter flow, has wrought havoc with the aquatic systems of the rivers downstream; reproduction and migration patterns of fish have been disturbed. Planners expected winter flows to double along the Volga south of Volgograd because of the operation of the massive Volga-Kamsk hydroelectric power station. Power shortages in the region have forced the plant to work overtime, and flows during the winter are actually three or more times their natural level.[36]

Many dams in the Soviet Union were constructed without fish ladders, and those that do exist are ineffective. Commenting on the performance of fish ladders at the Volgograd hydroelectric power station, which was completed in 1958, Vladimir I. Luk'yanenko, a laboratory director at the USSR Academy of Science Institute of Inland Waters Biology, wrote:

> Regrettably, this is the only apparatus [along the Volga] that allows something "to pass." But only "something." The effectiveness of its operation is extraordinarily low—on the order of thousandths of a percent of the number of spawning sturgeon . . . that reach the dam. However, in actuality, the passing of even this infinitesimal portion of these reproducers has been nullified as a result of the subsequent construction of the Saratov (Balakovo) hydroelectric station and the rise of the Saratov reservoir, the hydrological regime of which is not compatible with the natural reproduction pattern of the passing fish. It is true that in the dam of this hydroelectric station a fish ladder has been built, but its performance is of a symbolic nature.[37]

In addition to obstructing migration routes, the dams have inundated valuable wetlands above but allowed those below to dry out, particularly during the spawning season in spring. Damming the Volga has reduced the spawning grounds for some species of sturgeon from an estimated 3,000–4,000 hectares to only 400 hectares—all located in the one remaining zone of relatively undisturbed riverbed between Volgograd and the river delta on the Caspian. Spawning grounds for beluga have been decimated completely. The construction and operation of the Tsimlyansk and Nevinnomyssk dams on the rivers Don and Kuban also have disrupted reproduction cycles and have completely destroyed the spawning grounds of beluga and 80 percent of the spawning grounds for other species of sturgeon.[38]

In 1990, however, the spring floods returned to the lower Volga after more than 20 years' absence. Fearing a complete and irreversible loss of aquatic life in the lower reaches of the river, concerned citizens in the "tens of thousands," with the backing of the RSFSR State Committee for the Protection of Nature, convinced both the Volgograd and Astrakhan oblast soviets to change the operating cycle of the Volgograd hydroelectric station—not a trivial demand. To make the change possible, the USSR Ministry of Power and the Russian Ministry of Land Reclamation and Water Resources agreed, after months of negotiation, to reduce electricity demand during peak hours and days by 20 percent; a 10 percent reduction was expected to be achieved through economies, and the remainder by rescheduling operations of local industries to the weekends.[39]

WATER RESOURCES MANAGEMENT POLICY RECONSIDERED

The vast schemes to harness water resources epitomized one of the core tenets of Soviet development: to overcome the imperfections of nature and to tame it for the benefit of society. As illustrated in the preceding section, projects often were praised more for their daring and scale than for their practicality or effectiveness. Ultimately, ecological concerns were eclipsed by planners' and engineers' ambitions. Such preoccupations resulted in projects that were designed and approved based on "concepts lacking reliable methodological foundations," according to one Soviet specialist.[40]

One of the most important factors influencing the direction of water resources development was the absence of market-based prices. Despite large capital investments made by the state to build dams and irrigation networks, water was supplied to industrial consumers at virtually no cost and to farms for free, leading to its widespread abuse by both industry and agriculture. Similarly, the absence of market pricing of electric power hampered decisionmaking with regard to the development and operation of hydroelectric facilities. Many Soviet officials recognized the need to raise the price of water and electricity, but their efforts were repeatedly stymied.[41]

The problems in the management of water resources also could be tied to the narrow institutional interests of the principal government agencies involved—the most important being the Ministry of Reclamation and Water Resources. To maintain its large budget and staff, the agency, with the help of in-house research institutes, continually advocated new projects, regardless of their merit. The environmental effects of such projects largely were irrelevant. Although reorganized several times over the 1980s, the ministry remained concerned solely with moving water— the more the better. Issues such as water quality or agricultural output were not its concern.

This cavalier approach to economics and the environment eventually caught up with the ministry. In August 1986, a nascent environmental movement won its first major victory when the government elected to scrap grandiose plans to divert water from the Russian north down to the Aral and Caspian seas. In addition to reversing the flow of the Irtysh River, the project entailed construction of a 2,200-kilometer navigable channel, dubbed "Sibaral," across the Kazakh steppe. This "project of the century" had been in the planning stage since the 1950s, and over 120 agencies were involved in its elaboration and assessment.[42] Opposing the project was an alliance of environmentalists like engineer/writer Sergei Zalygin and Russian nationalists such as writers Valentin Rasputin and Vladimir Soloukhin.

The reappraisal of the water diversion also turned on economic factors as the Gorbachev administration sought to reverse traditional Soviet policy of channeling investment into lengthy and costly new development projects. During the Tenth Five-Year Plan (1976–1981), for example, the overall cost of improving a hectare of land in Ukraine increased by over 20 percent, but agricultural productivity increased by just 8.6 percent.[43] Across the country, the area of new land coming under irrigation each year fell throughout the 1970s and 1980s; between 1986 and 1988, new capacity dropped by over a third.[44] Commissioning of new hydroelectric plants also slowed by 50 percent over this period.[45] In March 1990, an expert commission of the USSR State Planning Committee recommended canceling the nine-year-old Volga-Don-2 canal project.[46] The 65-kilometer canal, then under construction for five years at a cost of billions of rubles, was to divert water from the Volga north of Volgograd toward the Don, which had been depleted by withdrawals for other uses. The commission instead recommended the refurbishing of existing irrigation systems at lesser cost.

In the wake of the Sibaral decision, opposition to development projects exploded all across the Soviet Union. A constellation of similar economic, environmental, and ethnic considerations led the all-Union and republican governments to vote to cancel or postpone work on the Danube-Dnieper and Volga-Chogray canals as well as the Daugavpils, Rogun, Turukhansk, and Katun hydroelectric projects.

The increasing cost of bringing new marginal lands under irrigation and damming more remote rivers will limit even the smallest of projects in the future, as the newly independent regions move their economies to market relations and governments are faced with hard budget constraints. Nevertheless, many water industry officials remain undaunted by the new challenges to their prerogatives.

WATER POLLUTION AND POLLUTION CONTROL

In terms of fiscal outlays, improved water quality and water conservation were the highest environmental priorities of the Soviet regime; between 1976 and 1988, the government allocated over 22 billion rubles for such purposes—approximately 75 percent of all spending on environmental protection.[47] Total wastewater treatment capacity in the USSR increased by 53 percent between 1980 and 1988. In 1980, 78 percent of cities and 47 percent of towns were served with some level of centralized sewerage; by 1988, the levels were 87 percent and 53 percent, respectively. Significant improvements in wastewater treatment were achieved in the Ukrainian city of Odessa, for example: Between 1985 and 1988, the municipality halved its emissions of untreated sewage into the Black Sea.[48]

Overall, however, the quantity of effluent generated increased more than fourfold during the 1970s and 1980s, and one estimate was that effluent production would increase by another 150 percent by the year 2000.[49] Despite the investments in improved treatment, capacity remained small, and most communities relied on only primary, mechanical systems.[50] Over one-quarter of treatment systems surveyed at the end of the 1980s were overtaxed, and one-fifth operated with worn-out or outdated technology.[51] In Tallinn, the capital of Estonia, wastewater treatment equipment was forced to handle 10 times its designed capacity.[52] The result is that such systems release incompletely treated or raw sewage directly into the environment. In the provincial capital of Yaroslavl, an extremely overworked sewage treatment system spewed into the Volga River effluent containing organic compounds 5 times over the permitted maximum. In addition, the system released nitrogen and petrochemical compounds at a rate 20 to 40 times the permitted maximum, and concentrations of other pollutants reached more than 100 times the permitted maximum. In 1985, the city was forbidden to connect any more apartment blocks or enterprises to the sewage system until the plant's capacity had been expanded. The city ignored the order and offered the government assurances that new treatment capacity would come on line shortly; by 1988, it was apparent that it would not be ready before the mid-1990s.[53]

In 1989, one-third of all enterprises and utilities did not comply with wastewater standards.[54] In Moscow, 2,800 industrial enterprises were hooked up to the city's sewer system, but the wastes from over nine-tenths of them did not meet government norms.[55] In St. Petersburg, only 30 percent of the effluent flowing into the Neva River from this city of over 5 million inhabitants underwent any treatment at all.[56] As a result, each city spewed over 1 billion cubic meters of poorly treated sewage into their rivers in 1990.[57] At the end of the Soviet period, many cities still did not have even primary sewage treatment facilities—for example, Kaunas (1990 population 430,000) in Lithuania and the Russian port city of Murmansk (472,000). In Latvia, only 2 of 29 cities had wastewater treatment systems; the capital Riga (917,000) was able to treat less than 10 percent of its wastes according to norm.[58] Baku (1.8 million), the capital of Azerbaijan, also was equipped with only the most rudimentary system, and an upgrade was a decade behind schedule.

In 1988, urban sewage systems across the Soviet Union discharged 2.2 million cubic meters of raw and 10.7 million cubic meters of insufficiently treated sewage into the nation's waterways.[59] The republics with the most overtaxed municipal sewage treatment systems were Tajikistan, Belarus, Ukraine, Latvia, and Lithuania.[60] In addition, many industrial plants released untreated or improperly treated effluent directly into the environment—200 industrial enterprises were not connected to the St. Petersburg sewer system as of 1990[61]—bringing the total volume of effluent that did not meet sanitary norms to 32.6 million cubic meters in 1989, more than the annual throughput of the river Don. Between 1986 and 1989, the share of effluent adequately treated decreased sharply from 60 to 25 percent, a function of stricter treatment standards as well as deteriorating performance.[62] Even without this change in targets, the actual performance of treatment plants worsened, resulting in a 14 percent increase in pollutant emissions between 1988 and 1989.

Russia accounted for the major share of water pollution. In 1989, treatment facilities in the federation could process adequately just one-tenth of the wastewater produced, resulting in the release of 27.1 million cubic meters of raw or partially treated sewage into the environment—83 percent of the Soviet total. Ukraine accounted for about 9 percent of improperly treated wastewater emissions in the Soviet Union.[63] A breakdown of performance by republic is provided in Table 3.2. Table 3.3 indicates the types of contaminants released into the environment with wastewater.

Table 3.4 shows the destination of waterborne pollution. As it indicates, the region's topography tends to retain pollutants, mitigating the opportunity for nature to dilute and process pollution. Over 20 percent of former Soviet territory is composed of closed or nearly closed hydrological systems: Pollution from the Volga Basin collects in the northern Caspian Sea, and pollutants from the rivers Don and Kuban aggregate in the sea of Azov. Contaminants from the Danube, Dniester, South Bug, and Dnieper rivers are released into the northern Black Sea. A similar

TABLE 3.2 Performance of wastewater treatment as reported by republic, 1989

	Total Volume of Wastewater Requiring Treatment (millions of cubic meters)	Percent Treated in Compliance with Norm	Percent Treated but Not Complying with Norm	Percent Remaining Untreated
USSR average	43,564	25	51	24
Armenia	557	55	1	44
Azerbaijan	597	51	12	37
Belarus	994	93	7	0
Estonia	517	52	37	10
Georgia	626	49	9	42
Kazakhstan	591	43	48	9
Kyrgyzstan	180	78	17	6
Latvia	367	30	39	31
Lithuania	450	25	47	28
Moldova	298	37	48	39
Russia	30,633	11	61	28
Tajikistan	286	62	35	3
Turkmenistan	na[a]	na	na	na
Ukraine	6,706	57	36	7
Uzbekistan	762	65	8	27

[a]Not available.

Source: USSR Goskompriroda, *Sostoyanie prirodnoi sredy i prirodookhrannaya deyatel'nost' v SSSR v 1989 godu* (Moscow: Institut Molodezhi, 1990), p. 99.

TABLE 3.3 Compounds released into surface waters, 1989
(metric tons)

Petroleum products	74,000
Suspended solids	2,236,000
Sulfates	20,953,000
Chlorides	19,189,000
Phosphates	65,689
Nitrates	240,056
Phenols	925
Surfactants	15,726
Copper	1,002
Iron	37, 435
Zinc	2,367
Nickel	915
Chromium	967
Mercury	1,978

Source: USSR Goskompriroda, *Sostoyanie prirodnoi sredy i prirodookhrannaya deyatel'nost' v SSSR v 1989 godu* (Moscow: Institut Molodezhi, 1990), p. 99.

situation exists with Lake Balkash in Kazakhstan, Lake Issyk-kul in Kyrgyzstan, and the Aral Sea.[64]

Remedial construction lagged far behind government targets as water pollution control projects were plagued by material shortages and bottlenecks. Essential materials and equipment proved difficult to procure, given the low priority and undeveloped nature of environmental protection industries. A lack of hard currency precluded the option of importing foreign technology. As a result, wastewater treatment facilities and enterprises were forced to build a large share of their own equipment. On a tour of Moscow's Kuryanovo wastewater treatment facility, for example, the plant's chief engineer, Fedor Dainenko, proudly pointed to huge agitators he had personally designed, adding that his enterprise built equipment for other facilities. Labor also was in short supply, particularly the specialists needed to elaborate the plans for the projects. The completion rate of planned treatment facilities averaged under 60 percent in 1988 (see Table 3.5). Some republics fared much worse: Plan fulfillment in 1988 for Kazakhstan was 1 percent, Azerbaijan 2 percent, and Georgia 12 percent.[65]

Installing water pollution control equipment was only one challenge; making it work properly was another. The quality of the latest Soviet wastewater treatment technology, when it could be procured, was not a significant obstacle. According to Soviet sources, the process efficiency of effluent treatment systems installed in the late 1970s was roughly equal

TABLE 3.4 Destination of untreated and partially treated effluent discharges, 1990

	Cubic Meters (millions)		Percent
Total USSR	33,564		100.0
Caspian Sea	12,458		37.1
Volga River		11,050[a]	
Kura River		371	
Other		1,037	
Sea of Azov	4,956		14.8
Don River		1,565	
Kuban River		1,704	
Other		1,687	
Baltic Sea	3,646		10.9
Neva River		1,592	
Lake Ladoga		390	
Other		1,664	
Yenisei River	3,160		9.4
Ob River	3,044		9.1
Black Sea	2,722		8.1
Dnieper River		1,945	
Other		777	
North Dvina River	839		2.5
Aral Sea	550		1.6
Syr Darya		276	
Amu Darya		75	
Other		199	
Amur River	543		1.6
Lake Baikal	192		0.6
Selenga River		81	
Other		111	
Lena River	143		0.4
Other	1,311		3.9

[a]Of the total volume of polluted effluents entering the Volga River basin, 4,700 million cubic meters are derived from the Oka River basin and 2,200 million cubic meters are from the Kama River basin.

Source: USSR Goskomstat, *Okhrana okruzhayushchei sredy i ratsional'noe ispol'zovanie prirodnykh resursov* (Moscow: Informtsentr Goskomstata SSSR, 1991), pp. 76–77, 93.

to that in the United States, able to deal with about 90 percent of organic material and 10–40 percent of inorganic substances.[66] Rather, much of the problem lay in the application of available technology. This factor cannot be overemphasized with respect to the Soviet Union. Water purification systems tended to break down frequently because of poor construction, improper maintenance, and operator error. At industrial enter-

TABLE 3.5 Performance of water pollution control programs by ministry at all-Union level, 1988

	Discharges of Improperly Treated Effluent		Treatment Capacity Installed	
Ministry	Volume (thousands of cubic meters)	Percentage Untreated	Plant Treatment Capacity (thousands of cubic meters per day)	Percentage of Planned Capacity
Total USSR	28,434	28	5,196	59
Timber	2,718	15	185	79
Ferrous metallurgy	1,324	23	1,017	90
Petroleum refining and petrochemicals	1,251	16	742	105
Mineral fertilizer	1,104	30	207	74
Power engineering and electrification	1,097	69	48	41
Chemicals	959	27	25	13
Nonferrous metallurgy	629	38	98	83
Coal	574	25	102	45
Pharmaceuticals and microbiology	185	20	57	49
Construction materials	56	25	na	na
Other	18,537	29	2,714	na

[a]Not available.

Source: USSR Goskompriroda, Sostoyanie prirodnoi sredy v SSSR v 1988 g. (Moscow: VINITI, 1989), pp. 56–57, 142–143.

prises, plant managers accorded environmental protection a low priority because the consequences of not fulfilling the plan or contracts were more grave than those for violating environmental norms. Management, therefore, was disinclined to halt production in order to construct, maintain, and repair pollution control equipment. The poor state of effluent treatment equipment was confirmed in a 1989 survey conducted by USSR Goskomstat: Urban systems were found to be working at 79 percent efficiency—in other words, 21 percent of effluent passing through the system was not being treated as specified. Treatment of industrial effluent fared much worse; only 42 percent of treated effluent was properly processed. The sectors that performed worst were pharmaceuticals (7 percent properly processed), coal (11 percent), light industry (29 percent), and timber and paper (38 percent).[67]

Goskomstat gave several reasons for this poor performance. First, many systems were overtaxed. In a quarter of the installations surveyed, the volume of effluent to be processed was too large, and almost a third of the systems were not suitably equipped to handle the types of effluent present. Second, a fifth of the equipment surveyed was worn out, much of it being more than twenty years old. To compound the problem, little money was spent on maintenance: in 1988, less than 500 million rubles were allocated for capital repairs of water pollution control equipment— a tenth the amount of money appropriated for investment in new water purification facilities.[68] Third, in 10 percent of the cases surveyed, the necessary equipment was missing or simply turned off. Finally, lack of essential treatment agents was a problem at 2 percent of the sites investigated. USSR Goskomstat concluded that "a significant number of enterprises" were plagued by two or more such problems simultaneously.

In consequence, breakdowns and malfunctions in sewage treatment facilities occurred frequently, according to media reports and personal interviews. On June 6 and 16, 1989, two releases of untreated sewage into the Oka River (a tributary of the Volga) occurred at the wastewater treatment plant in Orel, a provincial center 350 kilometers south of Moscow. On June 26, the river again was polluted when sludge from an overfilled holding tank flowed into the river. Despite widespread fish kills and complaints from citizens, local officials refused to acknowledge the accident or to warn the public of high bacteria levels in the river. On July 2, a fire at a pump substation forced the sewage plant to be shut down for two days; the result was the discharge of 150,000 cubic meters of untreated effluent into the Oka. Damage was assessed at 1.1 million rubles, and the river was closed to recreation in several neighboring oblasts. On January 22, 1990, a sewage collector in the same city burst because of settling ground and released another 40,000 cubic meters of waste into the Oka.[69]

In January 1990, workers at the Khimvolokno Production Association in Gomel oblast, Belarus, addressed an open letter published by *Pravda Ukrainy* to their comrades at the Slavyansk Chemical Production Association in Donetsk oblast, Ukraine. The Khimvolokno workers noted that in 1989 their enterprise was scheduled to receive from Slavyansk 13,000 tons of soda ash with which to treat their effluent, but only a third was delivered. "Not having received the soda," the workers wrote, "our shop has been forced to dump untreated, aggressive industrial discharges into the Berezina River—a tributary of the Dnieper." They added that they regretted their "barbaric pollution" of a region already reeling from the Chernobyl accident, noting that their work collective had suffered the wrath of local environmental groups and had incurred fines of 89,000 rubles for the poisoning of fish.[70]

The previously mentioned Goskomstat study of wastewater treatment performance was concerned only with whether installed technology worked as intended; it did not investigate whether the processed effluent actually complied with government standards. As already illustrated, many urban authorities have either no treatment capacity or only primary effluent treatment systems, and even if all the effluent treatment equipment operated as well as it was intended to, the quality of installed technology is such that not all of the processed effluent would comply with existing environmental standards. If performance is to be improved, more modern technology and much greater sums of money are required—two things in short supply in the environmental budgets of the newly independent republics.

Unfortunately, the story and the data related here are not complete. First, data on water pollutants count only effluent passing through sewer mains. A factory that released its effluent (treated or untreated) directly into a local lake, for example, would not be included in the statistics. Underreporting due to this situation is most likely in the less developed regions of the former Soviet Union, most importantly, the Central Asian republics. This, in turn, would make the data reported in Table 3.1, for instance, look much less favorable. Second, in addition to the three categories of wastewater previously mentioned (treated, partially treated, and untreated), statisticians identify a fourth class of wastewater: water not polluted during use and that is released directly into the environment. An example is cooling water. Actually, such water often is contaminated in the process, due to equipment malfunctions, although it is not considered as such.[71] Third, figures for the output of tainted effluent do not include those for drainage systems for collecting storm runoff. In urban areas, storm runoff contains significant amounts of contaminants, such as petroleum products that accumulate on roads; in most cases, water from urban storm drains is not treated before being released or percolating down to the water table. Likewise, soil contamination, for example, in and around industrial sites can reach the water table. Fourth, illegal discharges as a result of accidents and malfunctions in treatment equipment are not included in the statistics.

Finally, officials are under great pressure to underreport. Sergei Pomogaev, co-chair of Delta, a St. Petersburg environmental group, described the situation in his city thus: When firms are hooked up to the city sewer authority, Vodokanal, they often underreport their emissions to avoid paying excessive fees. Vodokanal officials, on the other hand, often lack the resources to audit polluters, yet are faced with extra treatment burdens for which they are ultimately responsible. Moreover, Vodokanal relies on fees to cover half of its budget. Both sides strike a deal: Industries agree to report a certain volume of emissions for which they pay a fee, and Vodokanal and its officials are assured a steady income. "It's the greatest mafia ring" in town, Pomogaev concludes.[72]

Agriculture, by virtue of its nature and scale, has presented an equally great if not greater pollution threat than that from industry or urban utilities. Agricultural runoff, which totaled an estimated 40 billion cubic meters in 1990,[73] often contains significant quantities of pesticides and fertilizers. Another problem has been poor storage facilities for agrochemicals that allow their contents to leach into the water table. The agricultural component of water pollution in Ukraine reportedly amounted to 45–48 percent in the 1980s.[74] One geographer estimated that 10–20 percent of the contaminants entering Lake Ladoga came from the region's agricultural operations, most notably 210 livestock farms located along major tributaries of the lake.[75] The extensive cutting of trees for timber denuded the land of cover in many regions, reducing the capacity of the soil to hold water and making it more susceptible to erosion. Irrigation exacerbated the leaching process, yet less than 2 percent of irrigation water was reclaimed to reduce surface water contamination.[76] The result has been the washing of a significant proportion of the topsoil down rivers and into lakes and coastal waters. Along with topsoil, erosion washes pesticides, fertilizers, salts, and organic matter, such as manure, which contains nitrites. One-third of the pesticides and fertilizers used leaches into the soil and water table; in the Russian Federation the rate of loss averages 40 percent, and in the central *chernozem* region and Tatarstan losses are as high as 50 percent.[77] In Ukraine alone, about 2.75 million tons of nitrogenous compounds, phosphates, and calcium enter the republic's waterways every year.[78]

Although comprehensive data have not been published on the subject, groundwater contamination has become a major threat in many areas. As of the beginning of 1990, the USSR Ministry of Geology had discovered over 750 incidences of groundwater contamination across the Soviet Union, almost half of which had occurred as a result of toxics leaching into the soil from industrial waste stored on enterprise grounds. Serious cases of groundwater contamination have been discovered around the Ukrainian industrial cities of Krivoi Rog, Lisichansk, and northern Crimea as well as in the vicinity of Russia's Magnitogorsk.[79] The Astrakhan gas condensation complex, located in the vulnerable Volga delta, discharges effluent in such a polluted state that it must be diverted into huge evaporation ponds. The contaminants, nevertheless, have found their way into the ground. As a result, use of the land and water within a 25-kilometer radius of the plant has been prohibited.[80]

Thermal pollution from nuclear power plants also has had a serious effect on water resources. In 1989, *Sovetskaya Rossiya* published an article painting a dismal portrait of two lakes near the Tver (Kalinin) nuclear power station, located northwest of Moscow. Water from the lakes is used to cool the plant's two reactors; since the inauguration of the second generating block in 1986, the ambient temperature of the lakes has risen several degrees, thus killing off much of the native flora and fauna and altering the local climate. In winter, the lakes no longer freeze over, instead enveloping the surrounding region in a blanket of fog. In the words of the newspaper, the lakes are facing imminent catastrophe: If the situation is not reversed, they will become "lifeless, dirty, stinking puddles with deadly consequences for nature, people, and incidentally Kalinin nuclear power station itself." In 1988, the high temperature of the incoming water for cooling forced a reduction in the plant's energy output. To make matters worse, two more generating blocks are under construction.[81] Similar problems have been reported at Lake Druksiai, which serves the Ignalina nuclear power station in Lithuania.[82]

WATER QUALITY

Water quality standards were established for about 2,500 different substances in the Soviet Union[83] and, like those regarding air quality, were strict.[84] Strict standards did not ensure compliance, however. As one scientist, K. S. Losev, commented, they should not have remained "just a scientific achievement" but should have been translated into guidelines, regulations, and laws that provided for the attainment of these standards.[85] Instead, the setting of strict standards largely was an academic exercise; that industrial ministries and other powerful authorities permitted such standards to be set at all attested to the fact that there was little intention to enforce them.

The Soviet government did not begin systematic monitoring of water quality until 1975.[86] The conclusion from the testing of thousands of locations was that there remained few bodies of water not seriously tainted by economic development. Table 3.6 illustrates that few major river systems complied with basic water quality criteria. The data in the table are presented for rough comparison only, as these figures are annual averages and specific locations are not provided. For many rivers, conditions are likely to be much worse downstream from industrial and urban development. According to expert assessment, the most seriously polluted rivers were the Dniester, Danube, Don, and West Bug; also heavily pol-

Officials in Norilsk check a factory's cooling system for signs of contamination. Photo: DJ Peterson.

luted were the Volga, Kuban, Pechora, Yenisei, Lena, lower Amur, the rivers of Sakhalin Island, and rivers and lakes of the Kola Peninsula.[87] Common pollutants such as petroleum products, phenols, nitrogen compounds, heavy metals, organic substances, and sulfates in many waterways often exceeded the maximum by a factor of 10 and sometimes by a factor of 100.[88] In Estonia, 40 percent of lakes were declared to be in "unsatisfactory condition."[89]

Industrial wastes pour into the Ob from its headwaters on the Mongolian border from the mining and industrial regions of eastern Kazakhstan and the Kuznetsk Basin, the industrial centers of Chelyabinsk and Yekaterinburg, and the oil- and gas-producing region of Tyumen. In the winter of 1989–1990, vast sections of the Ob failed for the first time to freeze over: "Even Siberian frosts cannot freeze the hundreds of millions of cubic liters of polluted water annually discharged into the river," the Novosti Press Agency observed.[90]

TABLE 3.6 Mean annual concentration of pollutants for selected major rivers, 1990 (milligrams/liter)

River	Biological Oxygen Demand[a]	Oil and Petroleum Products	Phenols	Surfactants
Amu Darya	1.18	0.09	0.005	0.05
Amur	2.20	0.01	0.003	0.03
Angara	1.45	0.14	0.001	na[b]
Danube	3.13[c]	0.41	0.005	na
Daugava	2.16	0.06	0.003	0.03
Dnieper	3.11	0.04	0.003	na
Dniester	3.04	0.11	0.001	0.02
Don[d]	3.55	0.11	0.002	0.04
Irtysh	2.52	0.51	0.006	na
Kama	2.07	0.10	0.004	0.02[e]
Kuban	2.36	0.31	0.001	0.01
Lena	2.07	0.08	0.002	0.02
Neva[c]	1.90	0.09	0.000	0.00
Ob	2.93	0.54	0.006	0.01
Oka[c]	3.30	0.20	0.000	0.40
North Donets	4.01	0.23	0.006	na
North Dvina	2.46	0.03	0.000	0.01
Selenga[d]	1.47	0.09	0.000	na
South Bug	6.31	0.02	0.000	0.01
Syr Darya	1.75	0.04	0.002	0.02
Tobol	2.84	0.38	na	0.03
Tom	2.36	0.46	0.004	na
Ural	2.58	0.08	0.001[e]	na
Volga	2.24	0.21	0.002	0.04
West Bug	7.01	0.07[c]	0.003	0.08
Yenisei	na	0.41	0.005	na
Soviet Standard	3.00	0.05	0.001	0.1

[a] Biological Oxygen Demand is a measure of the quantity of suspended or dissolved organic matter.
[b]Not available.
[c]1987.
[d]1989.
[e]1985.
Source: USSR Goskomstat, *Okhrana okruzhayushchei sredy i ratsional'noe ispol'zovanie prirodnykh resursov* (Moscow: Informtsentr Goskomstata SSSR, 1991), pp. 102–103, 106.

As shown in Table 3.4, over 11 billion cubic meters of raw or partially treated municipal and industrial wastes were discharged into the Volga River in 1990—almost one third of all such documented wastes released into the environment in the Soviet Union.[91] Over 90 percent of the wastewater discharged into the Volga from Saratov oblast, Kalmykia, and Tatarstan did not meet government standards in the late 1980s.[92] As a result, ambient concentrations of phenols and petroleum products exceeded permitted norms by 8 to 9 times, and nitrogen and copper compounds were 3 to 4 times above norm. In the lower reaches of the river, the concentration of copper rose to as much as 15 times permitted limits.[93] The impoundment of the Volga by the extensive network of dams exacerbated problems by slowing down the river's flow and increasing the retention time of pollutants by between 8 and 10 times.[94] Fertilizers collected by the dams promoted algal blooms, which, combined with accumulation of silt, have choked the reservoirs.

Half of all coastal regions monitored by the Soviet government were classified as "polluted, very polluted, or extremely polluted." Included are the Azov, Caspian, and Black seas. Major pollutants include phenols, detergents, and heavy metals. High concentrations of petroleum products (primarily from offshore oil and gas extraction and shipping) were registered virtually everywhere: In the Baltic and White seas, concentrations were an average of 1.5–2.0 times the maximum permissible concentration; in sections of the Sea of Okhotsk, they reached 6 times the maximum. An estimate by UNESCO, the United Nations scientific branch, pegged the Baltic as the world's dirtiest sea; the Baltic's largest sources of pollution are the rivers feeding the Gulf of Riga. Jurmala, located on the southern coast of the gulf, once was one of the region's premier resorts, but beaches there have been closed repeatedly because of high levels of fecal coliform bacteria and other pollutants. Overworked sewage systems in resort and industrial regions on the Black Sea coast have forced medical authorities to ban swimming at beaches there too. In the waters around Yalta, the concentration of detergents doubled in the period from 1987 to 1988 and reached levels twice the sanitary norm. The bacteria count at beaches on the northeastern shores of the Black Sea often exceeded norms by a factor of up to 200.[95]

Ninety percent of the Black Sea has been declared dead. Every year, 7,600 tons of copper, 900 tons of petroleum products, 600 tons of lead, and 200 tons of detergents (to name just a few pollutants) flow into the Black Sea from municipal sewage systems alone. Extensive industrial development (particularly of ferrous metallurgy and chemicals) along the tributaries of the Black Sea and on its periphery are one problem. The

Dnieper, for instance, passes through the Ukrainian industrial heart-
land—cities like Kremenchug, Dnepropetrovsk, and Zaporozhye—pick-
ing up contaminants before emptying into the Black Sea east of Odessa,
another major industrial center (see Map 3.1). These sources, combined
with extensive naval operations, make the area in and around Odessa the
most polluted part of the Black Sea. In 1988, concentrations of phenols
were more than 30 times greater than the permitted sanitary norms, and
levels of detergents were as much as 52 times the norm.[96] The Black Sea
also suffers from severe pollution in the vicinities of Russia's Krasnodar
region, which includes the port of Novorossiisk and the resort of Sochi,
and of the Georgian industrial port cities of Batumi and Sukhumi.

The principal threat to sea life, however, is a stratum of dissolved hydrogen sulfide welling up from the sea bottom—an anoxic environment
in which sea life cannot survive. Since 1935, the rate of ascent of the upper limits of the hydrogen sulfide layer has increased from 3 centimeters
to 2 meters per year. Though the presence of hydrogen sulfide is a natural result of the currents present in the Black Sea and the fact that the
basin is almost totally landlocked, the increase in hydrogen sulfide has
been accelerated by the large volume of organic materials dumped into
the Black Sea. Every year, 5,000 tons of nitrogen and phosphorous compounds are released into its basin from municipal sewage systems; in es-
tuarine zones, agricultural runoff has caused the concentration of these
compounds to surge to 30 to 50 times their levels in the 1960s.[97]

In a sense, the sea has been fertilized by the untreated sewage and
agricultural runoff. The sewage provides ample bacteria, which multiply
rapidly in the fertile waters during the long warm summers, depleting
the dissolved oxygen. Concomitantly, the enriched waters promote algal
blooms. When the algae die, they sink to the bottom, where they decom-
pose slowly, thereby producing more hydrogen sulfide. Experts predict
that at the present rate, the upper limit of the anoxic layer, now at a
depth of 80 meters, will reach the surface in forty years. Others give the
Black Sea just ten to fifteen more years of life.[98]

THE IMPACT ON FISHERIES

One simple measure of the effect of the discharge of effluent,
damming, and desiccation of waterways is the state of the region's fisheries. Vladimir Luk'yanenko reports that in the period 1965–1980, 1,348
large-scale fish kills occurred in the Caspian Sea as a result of pollution
incidents. During the 1980s, the number of such fish kills increased dramatically, totaling almost 500 in 1986–1987 alone. Between 1948 and 1983

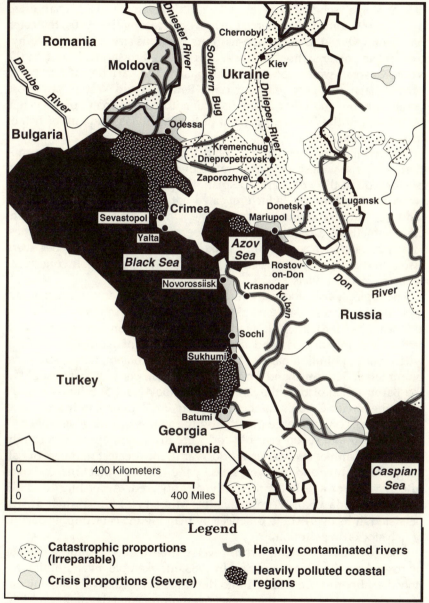

Legend

- Catastrophic proportions (Irreparable)
- Crisis proportions (Severe)
- Heavily contaminated rivers
- Heavily polluted coastal regions

Source: Institute of Geography, Russian Academy of Sciences.

MAP 3.1 Environmental degradation in the Black Sea region, late 1980s

the annual fish catch from inland lakes and rivers decreased from 1 million tons to just 200,000 tons.[99] Before the initiation in the 1930s of the "Great Volga" scheme to develop the river's resources, fishers harvested over 600,000 tons of commercial fish every year; by the 1980s, the catch had been reduced to about one-tenth its previous size. Operation of hydroelectric power stations on the Volga reduced the annual catch in the Volga-Caspian watershed by 41,000 tons.[100] The varieties of fish being caught have also changed over time: Before World War II, sturgeon, perch, salmon, and other prime fish constituted 80 percent of the catch; by the end of the 1980s, 80 percent of the catch was made up of fish of low commercial value.[101]

Reports indicate that many of the fish caught are not fit for consumption. After the widespread appearance of disease among the population of sturgeon in the Volga and Caspian, the government commissioned a two-year study in 1988, which revealed not only disease in the muscles, kidneys, and reproductive organs of the fish but concentrations of pesticides sometimes exceeding maximum permissible levels by 2 to 5 times. Heavy metals, such as cadmium, nickel, mercury, lead, and copper, were also found at levels "far exceeding the maximum permissible concentrations for food products."[102]

The region's fish stocks are threatened not just by environmental factors but also by the aggressive policies of the fishing industry. In the late 1980s, the Soviet fish catch averaged over 11 million tons annually—a rate second only to Japan and achieved at the cost of overfishing.[103] Even where water pollution has not been a serious problem, fish stocks have plummeted. Between 3 and 4 million tons of fish per year were caught in the Barents Sea; of this, the Soviet Union took 1.0–1.5 million tons. By 1988, the Soviet Union's catch was a mere 250,000 tons, indicating that the sea was "on the verge of ruin" in the words of one geographer.[104] Whereas six- and seven-year-old cod were the largest age cohort caught in the years immediately after World War II, the greatest numbers of fish caught were three and four years old by the 1970s. By that time, cod over fifteen years of age had practically disappeared. According to USSR Goskompriroda chair Vorontsov, the Ministry of the Fish Industry persisted in its overfishing practices by blaming the catastrophic decline of fish stocks on pollution.[105]

The government attempted to reverse the trend of declining catches by restocking threatened species. In 1988, for example, over 1 billion fry (mostly salmon) were released into the wild. Their survival rate, not surprisingly, was low, given the impact of environmental degradation.[106]

TO DRINK OR NOT TO DRINK THE WATER?

In July 1989, the citizens of Bryansk were warned to boil water before drinking it; after a heavy rainstorm, the city's water had become contaminated with "harmful substances" that could not be removed effectively.[107] One of the causes of the contamination was the dumping of waste by local farms and enterprises, which had turned the Desna River into "a gutter." No explanation of how the contaminants had found their way into the water supply was offered in the media. In January 1990, bottlenecks in the rail transport system delayed the shipment of antibacterial agents necessary for the treatment of water for public supply destined for Tallinn, Riga, and St. Petersburg. In Tallinn, stocks had dwindled to that sufficient for two days, and residents faced the possibility of having to boil drinking water.[108] The protozoan parasite *Giardia*, which causes severe gastrointestinal distress, is endemic to the tap water of St. Petersburg and other major cities. Drinking water drawn from the Volga and its tributaries in Ryazan, Tver (formerly Kalinin), and Volgograd oblasts failed to meet public health standards even after treatment, the weekly journal *Glasnost'* reported in 1990.[109]

Such anecdotes attest to the fact that despite the high level of urbanization and industrialization achieved in the Soviet regime, the government ultimately could not ensure its citizens a reliably safe supply of drinking water. In the advanced industrial countries, water utilities have been able to spend significant resources on procuring clean water supplies while relying on new technologies to counter increasing water pollution. Constrained resources, government priorities, and limited technology precluded these options in the Soviet Union. As a result, environmental degradation and deterioration of drinking water are closely related. Most cities, like Bryansk, draw their drinking water from rivers and lakes subject to pollution: "There are already numerous unavoidable instances where [communities] are forced to use river water, the level of chemical and biological contamination of which resembles wastewater," wrote researchers in a 1991 article in the *Bulletin of the USSR Academy of Sciences.*[110] Then they must treat it as best they can. As a result of these problems and the publicity surrounding them, almost three-quarters of the population surveyed in late 1990 expressed concern about the quality of their drinking water.[111]

In 1988, the Soviet government conducted almost 4.5 million tests of the public water supply. According to official data, over one-tenth of the samples tested for bacteria content did not meet government health standards; in the republics of Azerbaijan, Turkmenistan, and Tajikistan, the failure rate was more than 20 percent.[112] The USSR Academy of Sciences reported that almost one-half of Soviet cities equipped with running water surveyed failed government tests for bacteria content, adding that high bacteria levels were responsible for the USSR's high rates of enteric illness and hepatitis.[113]

Of water samples tested for their chemical content, 18.4 percent nationwide failed to meet standards (see Table 3.7). Latvia had the worst record—one-third of all samples failed. Not far behind were Belarus, Turkmenistan, Azerbaijan, and Uzbekistan.[114] Health officials in Tatarstan have reported that of samples drawn from the water supply, 27 percent did not meet biological standards, and 31 percent failed tests for chemical indicators.[115]

Moscow enjoyed the reputation of having the best-quality drinking water in the former Soviet Union, but in the late 1980s, persistent rumors suggested otherwise. A series of reports in the media investigating these rumors and their potential implications for public health only served to increase people's apprehension further.[116] When asked about the quality of Moscow's drinking water sources, an oblast official responded: "There is nothing to be happy about." Despite the designation of sanitary buffers, many of the city's reservoirs were subject to considerable pollution from the surrounding territory, particularly livestock farms.[117]

TABLE 3.7 Reported noncompliance with drinking water standards in municipal water supply systems by republic, 1988 (percentages)

	Chemical Indicators	Bacteriological Indicators
USSR average	18.4	11.3
Armenia	5.3	10.9
Azerbaijan	31.4	21.8
Belarus	29.5	9.0
Estonia	12.2	13.6
Georgia	7.9	14.7
Kazakhstan	12.7	7.4
Kyrgyzstan	3.7	14.1
Latvia	33.4	8.1
Lithuania	22.3	5.1
Moldova	14.5	8.6
Russia	20.5	11.7
Tajikistan	21.5	21.7
Turkmenistan	27.5	23.4
Ukraine	13.1	9.9
Uzbekistan	25.9	14.7

Source: USSR Goskomstat, *Okhrana okruzhayushchei sredy i ratsional'noe ispol'zovanie prirodnykh resursov v SSSR* (Moscow: Finansy i statistika, 1989), p. 36.

In autumn 1989, the weekly *Nedelya* featured an article about Moscow's tap water with "To Drink or Not to Drink?" as the provocative title. It contended that Moscow's drinking water fell within the norms for public health, but noted that the city did not test for many toxic substances such as cadmium, chromium, and nickel.[118] Responding to the concern and denying any cover-up, Valerii Saikin, then mayor, announced at a meeting of the city council: "There are no secrets. The water in Moscow conforms with government standards." A *Pravda* reporter inquired into the matter and found the reality was quite different: The mayor was being truthful, admitted Aleksandr Lopatin, an official at the city's public health department, "not because there is no secrecy, but because there is nothing about which to be secretive. There is no data." Lopatin tersely explained why: "There is no equipment, no procedures, no reagents, [and] of course no hard currency with which all of this could be purchased abroad."[119]

The plight of the Bashkirian capital of Ufa provides a clear—if extreme—example of the pollution threatening the public. In April 1990, over half of the city's 1.1 million residents were forced to go without running water for a fortnight because the municipal water system became contaminated with phenol. Rapidly melting snow from the previous month had brought with it this highly toxic compound, which had accumulated in the soil surrounding a petrochemical plant located at the edge of the city. The phenol leached into the soil initially as the result of "gross violations of production discipline" by plant personnel, according to a government commission that investigated the accident.[120] The phenol made its way into the Belaya River and then downstream to where the city's water is drawn off. At the height of the crisis, the concentration of phenol in the city's drinking water exceeded sanitary norms by 500,000 times.[121] On August 23, a new unit producing phenol acetone at the Ufa alcohol works exploded and sent out a plume of burning toxic gases, which necessitated the hospitalization of 110 people. According to TASS, "a blend of various chemical mixtures was washed by the foam of dozens of fire engines from the territory of the plant into the river Ufimka." Again, the water supply of two-thirds of the city's residents was shut off.[122] The following February, *Komsomol'skaya pravda* reported that the city was in a state of shock: Water samples tested during the phenol crisis the previous spring had revealed that "frightening quantities" of dioxins had been discovered in drinking water several days after the government had announced that the city's water supply was safe.[123]

The data presented here pertain only to the public water supply. Aside from the question of accuracy, evidence suggests that the problem of contaminated drinking water is far worse than officially reported.[124]

According to USSR Goskomstat, 15 percent of small towns and cities in the Soviet Union did not have running water at all in 1988[125] and therefore were subject to the uncertain quality of local ground- and surface-water supplies. Five million rural inhabitants of Uzbekistan did not have running water at the close of the 1980s, a problem so serious that the republic's president, Islom Karimov, signed a special decree in July 1990 ordering that the capacity of municipal water systems installed be quadrupled.[126] In many regions of Turkmenistan, such as Tashauz oblast along the lower reaches of the Amu Darya, up to 90 percent of inhabitants are forced to drink water from irrigation canals and ditches that often carry pesticide- and fertilizer-laden runoff.[127] In Tashauz, the bacteria count in the drinking water exceeded health standards by a factor of 10 times, reports revealed in 1990. Further, 70 percent of the population was reportedly ill, and the infant mortality rate had soared past 1 in every 10 live births, as the people were forced to drink the poisoned water.[128]

As the water supply in the former Soviet Union has become more contaminated with industrial, municipal, and agricultural pollution, it also has become more difficult and costly to purify. Unlike the United States, the Soviet government never expended significant resources to counter the rising impact of environmental degradation on drinking water supplies by building more sophisticated purification systems or by piping water from distant, albeit more pristine, sources. Now, the financial resources to effect an improvement have become even scarcer as the Soviet successor states slash public investment and confront the rigors of economic reform and upheaval. The disruption of traditional supply lines as a result of economic collapse and rising barriers to trade has further impaired the functioning of the region's shaky wastewater and drinking water treatment facilities. Unlike the sharp decrease in atmospheric emissions registered as a result of the economic downturn in 1991, the rate of water pollution remained unchanged.[129] In 1991, the Russian government reported substantially higher rates of dysentery and intestinal illnesses; in Siberia's Tom River basin, health officials reported sharp increases in gastroenteritis, hepatitis A, and bacterial dysentery as a result of maintenance problems in water purification systems.[130]

THE CASE OF LAKE BAIKAL

Unlike elsewhere, citizens of Irkutsk like to point out that it is still possible to drink the water from Lake Baikal directly, even though the lake has been threatened by industrial and agricultural development for over thirty years. Though Baikal now competes for attention with the catastrophes at Chernobyl and the Aral Sea, the damage to Baikal has been quite minimal in comparison. Nevertheless, its cultural and scientific value makes whatever damage the lake has sustained quite alarming and painful. Indeed, the fate of Baikal epitomizes the struggle to combat water pollution elsewhere.

Lake Baikal covers 31,500 square kilometers, making it larger than Belgium or the state of Maryland. It is fed by 336 rivers (the Selenga River flowing out of Mongolia provides over one-half of the inflow) covering a watershed area of 600,000 square kilometers, equivalent to the size of France or Ukraine. Baikal is the deepest continental body of water in the world (1,620 meters), making it the world's largest fresh-water lake. The lake is so large, in fact, that it accounts for about 80 percent of the reserve of surface fresh water in the former Soviet Union, or 20 percent of the entire world's reserve. Formed 25 million years ago, Lake Baikal is also the oldest fresh-water lake in the world. As a result of these conditions, more than two-thirds of the 2,400 different plants and animals living in the lake are found nowhere else in the world.

Baikal (see Map 3.2) is threatened by three types of pollution: industrial and municipal emissions, agricultural runoff, and airborne pollution. First, and most directly, it is affected by direct dumping of wastes from industrial plants and urban sewerage systems. There are three principal sources of direct water pollution in Baikal: the Baikal Pulp and Paper Combine (Russia's largest paper plant), the city of Ulan-Ude (located upstream from the lake on the Selenga River), and the Selenginsk Pulp and Cardboard Combine. In 1988, they were responsible for 40 percent, 30 percent, and 6 percent, respectively, of the polluted wastewater dumped into the Baikal basin.[131] Because of problems with the sewage system in Ulan-Ude, the city dumps almost 500 tons of nitrates into the water—70 percent of all nitrates entering the basin.[132] Baikal Pulp and Paper, the largest single polluter, emitted 32 million cubic meters of wastewater directly into Baikal in 1987.[133] The water near the plant registers above-norm levels of sulfates, chlorides, and suspended particles, and a 20-square-kilometer tract of lake bottom has been fouled.[134] In addition to these polluters, there are 100 smaller enterprises and settlements located around the lake that have no wastewater treatment capacity at all.[135] As a result, Baikal is threatened by large quantities of phenols, petroleum-based substances, detergents, suspended particulates, and other substances.

Second, the lake is affected by erosion and runoff from surrounding lands that have been denuded by agriculture, logging operations, and a high rate of tree loss due to illness. One researcher estimated that 60–70

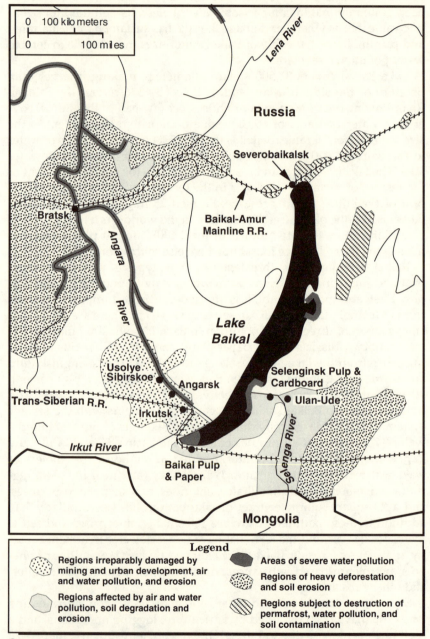

Legend

Regions irreparably damaged by mining and urban development, air and water pollution, and erosion

Areas of severe water pollution

Regions affected by air and water pollution, soil degradation and erosion

Regions of heavy deforestation and soil erosion

Regions subject to destruction of permafrost, water pollution, and soil contamination

Source: Institute of Geography, Russian Academy of Sciences.

MAP 3.2 Environmental degradation in Lake Baikal region, late 1980s

percent of all pollution of Lake Baikal comes from agricultural sources; there are almost 700 agricultural and forestry enterprises located in the Baikal Basin.[136] In the post-World War II era, the Soviet government facilitated the rapid exploitation of the region's agricultural and forest resources with the expansion of traffic along the Trans-Siberian Railway to the south of Lake Baikal, and construction of the Baikal-Amur Mainline Railroad to the north. Although farmers in the vicinity of Lake Baikal heeded the laws of nature in the past with respect to their crops and livestock, the demands of central planners under Soviet rule changed farming practices in the region. As a result, the soil has tended to become compacted and prone to erosion because of overgrazing and the cultivation of pastureland.

Finally, Baikal has been threatened by large amounts of airborne pollutants passing over the lake. Although one does not usually associate air pollution with the eastern Siberia region, Lake Baikal suffers it acutely. Industrial plants situated along the Angara River to the west of Baikal churn out aluminum, wood and paper products, and chemicals. Cities such as Irkutsk, Angarsk, Usolye-Sibirskoe, Shelekhov, and Bratsk suffer high concentrations of formaldehyde, benzopyrene, nitrogen oxides, and particulates as well as other pollutants and ranked on the Soviet government's league table of cities with the worst air pollution in 1989. Industries in Angarsk, one of which is a large chemical plant relocated from Germany in the 1940s as part of war reparations, discharged over 430,000 tons of harmful airborne pollutants in 1988—38 percent more than industries in the city of Moscow.[137] These pollutants are then blown over the lake and its watershed by the prevailing winds. The interaction of these air- and waterborne forces has multiplied the negative effect on the region's ecosystem, which the forces of nature then concentrate on the lake.

In recognition of the lake's cultural and scientific significance, four joint Communist Party/government resolutions were passed between 1969 and 1987 to clean up and to protect Baikal.[138] The first three proved to be little more than statements of good intentions by the leadership, but the last was hailed by many environmentalists as a significant step forward. In the resolution, the government mandated the development of a long-range integrated plan for the development and protection of the entire Baikal Basin. It called for 162 projects to clean up the local environment between 1987 and 1995. These included the retooling of Baikal Pulp and Paper into an environmentally safe plant for producing furniture and the transferral of the pulp mill to a new location downstream. In the meantime, immediate measures were ordered to clean up the factory's wastes. The resolution also created a series of water protection zones in the regions adjacent to the lake that provided strict limits on, and in some areas prohibition of, development. Finally, a commission was appointed to oversee implementation of the resolution.

There have been some encouraging signs. In 1987, the Gusinoozerskii regional power plant located upstream on the Selenga River inaugurated a recirculating cooling system, which contributed in large measure to a 60 percent reduction in the total amount of wastewater being emitted into the Baikal Basin.[139] In 1988, production of pulp at Baikal Pulp and Paper was scaled back slightly, and the heavily polluting yeast operation was shut down, leading to a 17 percent decrease in the total volume of wastes emitted into the lake. As a result, biological indicators in the lake near the plant showed an improvement. Measures taken to rework the transport system in the region include a ban on the transport of timber by floating rafts and a reduction in shipping by 30 percent. Commercial logging operations in the vicinity immediately around the lake have been banned since 1988, and the number of forest fires in the region has been reduced.[140]

Nevertheless, other developments have shown that the environmentalists' successes have turned out to be Pyrrhic victories. The total volume of wastewater (most of which already met sanitary norms) being dumped into the Baikal Basin decreased and the volume of wastes being properly treated increased in the late 1980s, but the volume of untreated waste increased rapidly (see Table 3.8). Furthermore, although the concentration of pollutants in the immediate vicinity around Baikal Pulp and Paper fell, the levels of suspended particles, petroleum-based substances, and nitrogen compounds increased in other areas of the lake.[141] One of the most ominous signals that the lake was in trouble was the

TABLE 3.8 Volume of improperly treated and untreated wastewater released in Lake Baikal watershed (millions of cubic meters)

	Improperly Treated	Untreated
1985	124	0
1986	66	0
1987[a]	104	3
1988	184	7
1989	183	15
1990	180	12

[a]Some of the increase after 1986 is attributable to a tightening of standards.

Sources: USSR Goskomstat, *Okhrana okruzhayushchei sredy i ratsional'noe ispol'zovanie prirodnykh resursov v SSSR* (Moscow: Finansy i statistika, 1989), p. 133; USSR Goskomstat, *Okhrana okruzhayushchei sredy i ratsional'noe ispol'zovanie prirodnykh resursov* (Moscow: Informtsentr Goskomstata SSSR, 1991), p. 220.

mass death of 6,000–7,000 of the lake's unique fresh-water seals in 1987 and 1988 from a mysterious virus.[142]

The retooling and transferral of Baikal Pulp and Paper originally was scheduled to take five years and be completed in 1993. After two years, only 15 million of the total 3 billion rubles allocated to the project had been spent, and workers had managed only to clear the site for the new plant at Ust-Ilimsk, down the Angara River.[143] The plant's management tried to sidestep the decree calling for the plant's closure by undertaking a crash program to build a pipeline that would divert wastewater away from the lake to the Irkut River, which releases into the Angara downstream. Only after strong public resistance was the pipeline abandoned.[144] Nevertheless, by late 1991, environmentalists doubted whether officials would be able to close the paper operation as planned, because the Russian economy faced severe paper shortages and unemployment: "There is a lot of concern that the factory won't close on schedule," said Vera Shlenova, an official of the Russian Society for the Protection of Nature. "After all, people are more worried about bread than about air or water."[145]

Notes

1. *Pravitel'stvennyi vestnik*, No. 24, 1991, p. 10.

2. USSR Goskomstat, *Okhrana okruzhayushchei sredy i ratsional'noe ispol'zovanie prirodnykh resursov v SSSR* (Moscow: Finansy i statistika, 1989), p. 63; U.S. Bureau of the Census, *Statistical Abstract of the United States: 1989* (Washington, DC: Government Printing Office, 1989), p. 198. The U.S. figure is for 1985.

3 . USSR Goskomstat, *Okhrana okruzhayushchei sredy*, p. 62.

4. V. P Kukhar', "Nekotorye aktual'nye ekologicheskie problemy Ukrainskoi SSR," *Vestnik Akademii Nauk SSSR*, No. 11, 1988, p. 110.

5. V. V. Vorob'yev, "Problems of Lake Baikal in the Current Period," *Geografiya i prirodnye resursy*, No. 3, 1988, translated in *Soviet Geography*, No. 1, 1989, p. 40.

6. USSR Goskompriroda, *Sostoyanie prirodnoi sredy v SSSR v 1988 g.* (Moscow: VINITI, 1989), p. 47.

7. U.S. Bureau of the Census, *Statistical Abstract, 1989*, p. 98.

8. B. Babich et al., "Okhrana i ratsional'noe ispol'zovanie vodnykh resursov—krupnaya ekonomicheskaya problema," *Planovoe khozyaistvo*, No. 8, 1980, p. 97.

9. *Pravda*, August 11, 1989, p. 2; USSR Goskomstat, *Okhrana okruzhayushchei sredy*, p. 66; USSR Goskompriroda, *Sostoyanie . . . v 1988 g.*, p. 42.

10. Michael A. Rozengurt, *Water Policy Mismanagement in the Southern USSR: The Ecological and Economical Impact*, report to the National Council for Soviet and East European Studies, November 1989, p. 55.

11. USSR Goskomstat, *Okhrana okruzhayushchei sredy*, pp. 70–71.

12. USSR Goskomstat, *Narodnoe khozyaistvo SSSR v 1989 g.*, (Moscow: Finansy i statistika, 1990), p. 456; USSR Goskomstat, *Narodnoe khozyaistvo SSSR v 1970 g.* (Moscow: Finansy i statistika, 1971), p. 347.

13. USSR Goskomstat, *Sel'skoe khozyaistvo SSSR* (Moscow: Finansy i statistika, 1988), p. 213; V. Ivashchenko, "Intensifikatsiya zemledeliya—osnovnoi put' realizatsii prodovol'stvennoi programmy," *Planovoe khozyaistvo*, No. 8, 1986, p. 107. The share of agricultural production grown on irrigated land reached a peak in 1985 of 33.3 percent of the total. By 1987, the proportion had dropped to 31.9 percent, equal to the level of the late 1970s.

14. USSR Goskomstat, *Sbornik statisticheskikh materialov, 1989* (Moscow: Finansy i statistika, 1990), p. 142; USSR Goskompriroda, *Sostoyanie . . . v 1988 g.*, p. 145. Another source notes that three-quarters of irrigation channels lack cement linings, leading to a water loss rate of 40 percent. L. Vashchukov, "Uluchshit' sokhrannost' i ispol'zovanie zemel'nykh i vodnykh resursov strany," *Vestnik statistiki*, No. 7, 1988, p. 42.

15. *Zarya Vostoka*, May 4, 1989, p. 2. USSR Goskomstat reported that losses in Georgia averaged a third of supplies. USSR Goskomstat, *Okhrana okruzhayushchei sredy*, p. 108.

16. Grigorii Reznichenko, "I stakana chistoi vody ne pribavilos'," *Novyi mir*, No. 1, 1990, p. 204.

17. Rozengurt, *Water Policy Mismanagement*, pp. 48–49; K. S. Losev, "Sotsial'no-ekonomicheskie i ekologicheskie posledstviya ispol'zovaniya vody: Vozmozhnye puti razvitiya," *Izvestiya Akademii Nauk SSSR: Seriya geograficheskaya*, No. 6, 1988, p. 49.

18. *Izvestiya*, February 7, 1990, p. 3.

19. *Zarya Vostoka*, May 4, 1989, p. 2. A survey reported by USSR Goskomstat revealed that the demand for water-metering devices exceeded supply by 350 percent. USSR Goskomstat, *Okhrana okruzhayushchei sredy*, p. 109.

20. USSR Goskomstat, *Okhrana okruzhayushchei sredy*, p. 109.

21. Vashchukov, "Uluchshit'," p. 43.

22. USSR Goskomstat, *Okhrana okruzhayushchei sredy*, p. 109. The breakdown by republics for saturation irrigation using furrows is as follows: Turkmenistan 100 percent, Uzbekistan 99 percent, Azerbaijan 96 percent, Armenia 91 percent, and Georgia 88 percent. Another USSR Goskomstat source puts the use of furrows for irrigation as follows: Tajikistan 91 percent, Georgia 89 percent, Armenia 83 percent, and Uzbekistan 81 percent. Vashchukov, "Uluchshit'," pp. 43–44.

23. *Izvestiya*, February 7, 1990, p. 3. Rozengurt, writing about Central Asia and Kazakhstan in *Water Policy Mismanagement*, pegs efficiency there at 30–40 percent (p. 48).

24. Rozengurt, *Water Policy Mismanagement*, p. 47. Where the soil is very saline, particularly in regions affected by salt borne in wind off the Aral Sea's bed, farmers attempt to flush the salt out with applications of more water, thereby exacerbating the problem of overwatering. For more on this topic, see Chapter 4.

25. Kukhar', "Nekotorye," p. 109.

26. USSR Goskomstat, *Okhrana okruzhayushchei sredy,* p. 109. Of 656 agricultural enterprises surveyed, 82 percent had established guidelines for irrigation required, and over one-third of enterprises were found to be irrigating in excess of these guidelines.

27. A. N. Kashtanov, "Ekologizatsiya sel'skogo khozyaistva," *Vestnik Akademii Nauk SSSR,* No. 11, 1988, p. 58.

28. USSR Goskompriroda, *Sostoyanie prirodnoi sredy i prirodookhrannaya deyatel'nost' v SSSR v 1989 godu* (Moscow: Institut Molodezhi, 1990), p. 6.

29. Vladimir I. Luk'yanenko, "Vliyanie gidrostroitel'stva na vosproizvodstvo promyslovykh ryb," *Vestnik Akademii Nauk SSSR,* No. 12, 1989, p. 52.

30. Rozengurt, *Water Policy Mismanagement,* p. 10.

31. N. A. Lopatin, "The Development, Effectiveness, and Prospects of Hydroelectric Power," *Energetik,* No. 6, 1990, in JPRS-UEA-90-038, p. 115.

32. Aleksei Yablokov, presentation at conference on Democratic Federalism and Environmental Crisis in the Republics of the Former Soviet Union, Moscow, August 1991.

33. *Kul'tura,* No. 12, 1991, p. 3, translated in JPRS-TEN-92-003, p. 54.

34. USSR Goskompriroda, *Sostoyanie ... v 1988 g.,* p. 58.

35. USSR Goskomstat, *Narodnoe khozyaistvo SSSR v 1988 g.* (Moscow Finansy i statistika, 1989), p. 379.

36. D. Ya. Ratkovich, "O probleme vodoobespecheniya strany s uchetom trebovanii po okruzhayushchei sredy," *Vodnye resursy,* No. 5, 1989, p. 7.

37. Luk'yanenko, "Vliyanie gidrostroitel'stva," p. 52.

38. Ibid., pp. 52–53.

39. TASS, April 5, 1990; *Izvestiya,* January 7, 1990, p. 1.

40. Ratkovich, "O probleme," p. 6.

41. *Izvestiya,* February 7, 1990, p. 3.

42. Robert G. Darst, Jr., "Environmentalism in the USSR: The Opposition to the River Diversion Projects," *Soviet Economy,* Vol. 4, No. 3, 1988, pp. 223–252.

43. Kukhar', "Nekotorye," p. 109.

44. USSR Goskomstat, *Narodnoe khozyaistvo SSSR v 1988 g.,* p. 445.

45. Lopatin, "Development, Effectiveness and Prospects," p. 115.

46. *Izvestiya,* March 26, 1990, p. 2.

47. USSR Goskomstat, *Narodnoe khozyaistvo SSSR v 1988 g.,* p. 252; see also Kukhar', "Nekotorye," p. 107.

48. USSR Goskomstat, *Okhrana okruzhayushchei sredy,* pp. 14, 35.

49. *Pravda,* August 11, 1989, p. 2.

50. L. I. Globa et al., "Kachestvo pit'yevoi vody: proekt, kotoryi predstoit realizovat'," *Vestnik Akademii Nauk SSSR,* No. 4, 1991.

51. *Vestnik statistiki,* No. 6, 1990, p. 43.

52. Toomas Frei, minister of environment, in *Sovetskaya Estoniya,* December 2, 1990, p. 3.

53. Fedor Morgun, "Ekologiya v sisteme planirovaniya," *Planovoe khozyaistvo,* No. 2, 1989, p. 62.

54. USSR Goskompriroda, *Sostoyanie ... v 1989 godu,* p. 222.

55. *Moskovskaya pravda,* July 5, 1989, p. 2.

56. *Ekologiya i my*, No. 1, 1990, p. 2.

57. *Vestnik statistiki*, No. 11, 1991, p. 64.

58. Radio Riga, cited in Radio Free Europe/Radio Liberty Daily Report, August 9, 1991.

59. USSR Goskomstat, *Okhrana okruzhayushchei sredy*, p. 34.

60. *Vestnik statistiki*, No. 6, 1990, p. 43.

61. *Ekologiya i my*, No. 1, 1990, p. 2.

62. USSR Goskomstat, *Okhrana okruzhayushchei sredy*, p. 30; USSR Goskompriroda, *Sostoyanie . . . v 1989 godu*, p. 99.

63. USSR Goskompriroda, *Sostoyanie . . . v 1989 godu*, p. 99.

64. A. K. Kuchushev and N. M. Matveev, "Sokhranit' zdorov'e zemli," *Vestnik Akademii Nauk SSSR*, No. 3, 1990, p. 34.

65. USSR Goskomstat, *Okhrana okruzhayushchei sredy*, p. 139.

66. B. Babich et al., "Okhrana," p. 99. See also Vladimir Luk'yanenko, "O general'noi kontseptsii okhrany vodoemov ot zagryaznenii," *Vestnik Akademii Nauk SSSR*, No. 12, 1989. For comparison, the process efficiency of a conventional activated-sludge process system in the United States rates at between 85 and 95 percent efficiency in treating organic matter. Metcalf and Eddy, Inc., *Wastewater Engineering: Treatment, Disposal, Reuse* (New York: McGraw-Hill, 1979), p. 484.

67. USSR Goskomstat, *Press-vypusk*, No. 79, February 23, 1990.

68. USSR Goskomstat, *Okhrana okruzhayushchei sredy*, p. 9.

69. *Izvestiya*, July 15, 1989, p. 6, and February 9, 1990, p. 2; *Ekho planety*, No. 31, 1989, p. 18; and *Trud*, March 1, 1990, p. 1.

70. *Pravda Ukrainy*, January 18, 1990, p. 2.

71. Boris N. Laskorin and Vladimir I. Luk'yanenko, "O kachestve vody Volgo-Kaspiiskogo basseina," *Vestnik Akademii Nauk SSSR*, No. 10, 1990, pp. 17–18.

72. Sergei Pomogaev, personal communication, St. Petersburg, June 1991.

73. *Vestnik statistiki*, No. 11, 1991, p. 64.

74. V. Tregobchuk, "Economics and the Environment," *Pod znamenem Leninizma*, No. 4, 1990, translated in JPRS-UPA-90-019, p. 79.

75. M. G. Sofer, "O vode zhivoi i mertvoi," *Energiya: Ekonomika, tekhnika, ekologiya*, No. 7, 1988, pp. 35–36; *Trud*, July 30, 1989, p. 3.

76. USSR Goskomstat, *Okhrana okruzhayushchei sredy*, p. 75.

77. Losev, "Sotsial'no-ekonomicheskie," p. 46; Kashtanov, "Ekologizatsiya," p. 57. According to research by USSR Goskompriroda, 200,000 tons of pesticides leach into waterways annually in Russia. Sergei Bobylev, professor of economics, Moscow State University, "APK: Ekologizatsiya ili krizis?" unpublished manuscript, 1991, p. 10.

78. N. N. Prikhod'ko, "Osnovnye napravleniya okhrany malykh rek Ukrainskoi SSR ot zaileniya i zagrazneniya agrokhimikatami," *Vodnye resursy*, No. 2, 1989, p. 147.

79. *Vestnik statistiki*, No. 11, 1990, p. 64.

80. Rozengurt, *Water Policy Mismanagement*, p. 43.

81. *Sovetskaya Rossiya*, July 14, 1989, p. 4.

82. Kaunas Economics Institute, "Urgent Ecological Problems in Lithuania," briefing submitted to the Lithuanian Council of Ministers, November 1988.

83. Losev, "Sotsial'no-ekonomicheskie," p. 48. The number of compounds for which norms have been established grew rapidly: from 13 in 1940 to 70 in 1960 and to 500 in 1980.

84. Although existing pollution standards are generally adequate for guaranteeing human health, they may not be strict enough to protect other wildlife. USSR Goskompriroda, *Sostoyanie . . . v 1988 g.*, p. 163.

85. Losev, "Sotsial'no-ekonomicheskie," p. 48.

86. M. I. Biritskii et al., "O pervichnom uchete ispol'zovaniya vod," *Vodnye resursy*, No. 4, 1989, p. 173. Responsibility for monitoring was split between three agencies at the all-Union level: the USSR State Committee for Hydrometeorology (surface waters such as lakes, reservoirs, and rivers), the USSR Ministry of Geology (underground water reserves), and the USSR Ministry of Water Resources Construction (water use and effluent discharge).

87. USSR Goskompriroda, *Sostoyanie . . . v 1988 g.*, p. 48; Bobylev, "APK," p. 9.

88. Bobylev, "APK," p. 9; USSR Goskompriroda, *Sostoyanie . . . v 1989 godu*, p. 39.

89. K. K. Rebane, "Severo-vostok Estonii: Bolevaya tochka sostoyaniya okruzhayushchei sredy," *Izvestiya Akademii Nauk SSSR*, No. 11, 1988, p. 155.

90. Novosti Press Agency, April 2, 1990.

91. USSR Goskomstat, *Press-vypusk*, No. 226, June 7, 1990. When agricultural runoff (particularly from the rice fields of the southern Volga region) is added, the total rises to 20 cubic kilometers, or almost half of all wastewater produced in the former Soviet Union. B. N. Profir'yev, "Ekonomicheskie i organizatsonnogo-upravlencheskie problemmy ekologicheskoi politiki v SSSR," *Izvestiya Akademii Nauk SSSR, Seriya ekonomicheskaya*, No. 3, 1990, p. 22.

92. "Ekologicheskaya obstanovka v respublike," *Kommunist Tatarii*, no author, No. 3, 1990, p. 54.

93. USSR Goskompriroda, *Sostoyanie . . . v 1988 g.*, p. 48. See also Vladimir M. Kotlyakov et al., "O degradatsii vodnykh i zemel'nykh resursov na Russkoi ravnine," *Vestnik Akademii Nauk SSSR*, No. 12, 1989.

94. Rozengurt, *Water Policy Mismanagement*, p. 42.

95. USSR Goskompriroda, *Sostoyanie . . . v 1988 g.*, pp. 39–40, 51–52, 121.

96. Ibid., pp. 120–121.

97. Ibid., p. 121; *Izvestiya*, November 27, 1990, p. 3.

98. *Trud*, October 6, 1989, p. 4.

99. Luk'yanenko, "O general'noi kontseptsii," pp. 77–78.

100. Luk'yanenko, "Vliyanie gidrostroitel'stva," pp. 52, 57.

101. Kuchushev and Matveev, "Sokhranit' zdorov'e zemli," p. 35.

102. Vladimir I. Luk'yanenko, "A Toxicological Crisis in the Bodies of Water," *Rybnoe khozyaistvo*, No. 6, 1990, translated in JPRS-TEN-90-011, p. 55. See also Laskorin and Luk'yanenko, "O kachestve vody."

103. *Izvestiya*, November 13, 1990, p. 7.

104. Gennadii G. Matishov, "More na grani opustosheniya," *Priroda*, No. 3, 1990, p. 30.

105. Mikhail Dubrovskii, "Zashchita Vorontsova," *Poisk*, No. 28, 1989, p. 4.

106. Kuchushev and Matveev, "Sokhranit' zdorov'e zemli," p. 35.

107. *Sotsialisticheskaya industriya,* July 11, 1989, p. 4.

108. Helsinki Radio, January 9, 1990, translated in FBIS–SOV–90–007, p. 89.

109. *Glasnost',* cited by Novosti Press Agency, October 22, 1990.

110. L. I. Globa et al., *Vestnik Akademii Nauk SSSR,* No. 4, 1991, pp. 35, 37.

111. *Vestnik statistiki,* No. 11, 1991, p. 61.

112. USSR Goskomstat, *Okhrana okruzhayushchei sredy,* p. 36.

113. Yu. A. Rakhmanin, Academy of Medical Sciences Institute of General and Municipal Hygiene, cited in Globa et al., *Vestnik Akademii Nauk SSSR,* p. 36. The difference in reporting may be because water supplies in the major cities, which tend to have better treatment facilities, are likely to be tested more often.

114. USSR Goskomstat, *Okhrana okruzhayushchei sredy,* p. 36.

115. "Ekologicheskaya obstanovka v respublike," pp. 54–55.

116. See, for example, *Sovetskaya Rossiya,* May 24, 1989, p. 2; *Trud,* November 30, 1989, p. 2; and *Rabochaya tribuna,* July 27, 1990, p. 3.

117. Boris P. Namestnikov, prosecutor, Moscow oblast, cited in *Moskovskaya pravda,* August 8, 1991, p. 2.

118. *Nedelya,* No. 42, 1989, p. 5.

119. *Pravda,* May 13, 1990, p. 2.

120. *Izvestiya,* April 30, 1990, p. 2.

121. TASS, March 30, 1990.

122. Radio Moscow, August 23, 1990; TASS, August 24, 1990. Both reports are translated in FBIS-SOV-90-165, p. 88.

123. *Komsomol'skaya pravda,* February 21, 1991, p. 2.

124. On this point, the weekly *Glasnost'* issued a pessimistic assessment in December 1990 alleging that as much as two-thirds of the water supply in Russia did not meet health standards. *Glasnost',* cited by Novosti Press Agency, October 22, 1990.

125. USSR Goskomstat, *Okhrana okruzhayushchei sredy,* p. 14.

126. Radio Moscow, July 30, 1990.

127. *Turkmenskaya iskra,* April 27, 1990, p. 2.

128. *Izvestiya,* November 19, 1990, p. 1; *Meditsinskaya gazeta,* May 23, 1990. According to the latter newspaper, over 70 percent of the tests of the water in the city of Khiva near Urgench on the lower Amu Darya failed health standards for chemical content alone.

129. *Ekonomika i zhizn',* No. 6, 1992, p. 13.

130. US Centers for Disease Control, "Public Health Assessment—Russian Federation, 1992," *Morbidity and Mortality Weekly Report,* February 14, 1992, pp. 1–2.

131. USSR Goskomstat, *Okhrana okruzhayushchei sredy,* p. 133.

132. *Vestnik statistiki,* No. 8, 1989, p. 57.

133. USSR Goskomstat, *Narodnoe khozyaistvo SSSR v 1987 g.* (Moscow: Finansy i statistika, 1988), pp. 574–575.

134. USSR Goskompriroda, *Sostoyanie ... 1988 g.,* p. 126.

135. *Izvestiya,* May 4, 1989, p. 2.

136. Ibid.

137. USSR Goskomstat, *Okhrana okruzhayushchei sredy,* pp. 22–23.

138. The four resolutions were dated January 21, 1969; June 16, 1971; July 21, 1977; and April 13, 1987.

139. USSR Goskomstat, *Narodnoe khozyaiastvo SSSR v 1987 g.*, p. 574. It should be pointed out that although the new system, on paper, greatly reduced the volume of effluent labeled "wastewater" being dumped into Baikal, the discharges were relatively clean to begin with, and therefore this change did not contribute to a significant lowering of the level of pollutants entering the Baikal basin.

140. *Vestnik statistiki*, No. 8, 1989, p. 57.

141. Ibid., p. 56.

142. *Nash Baikal*, No. 3, 1990.

143. *Izvestiya*, May 4, 1989, p. 2. An environmental impact study indicated that the development of another large industrial complex in Ust-Ilimsk would further aggravate already serious environmental problems there.

144. *Literaturnaya gazeta*, No. 1, 1988.

145. *Los Angeles Times*, October 27, 1991, p. A5.

4

The Land

The land has been exhausted . . . our cropland urgently needs treatment everywhere.
—R. A. Giniyatullin, chair, Uzbek Ministry of Land Reclamation
and Water Resources

For those who want to admire the beauties of Aral, the best thing now is to take
an airplane.
—*Kommunist* (February 1990)

One of the most telling indictments of the Soviet economic system was the persistent queues for food at state stores even as the government spent billions of dollars to import massive quantities of grain. This condition stood in stark contrast to the role of the Russian Empire as a major grain exporter before the Bolshevik revolution. The region's food supply problems rested, to a large extent, on the unproductive nature of collective agriculture, unrealistic prices, and an inefficient and wasteful food processing and distribution system. In addition to its tax on the economy, Soviet agricultural development policy emphasized massive investments in mechanization, chemicals, and irrigation that proved catastrophic for the state of land resources and compounded the region's food supply problems. In a special report on agriculture to the Russian parliament, agricultural economist Sergei Bobylev criticized the technocratic approach to farming: "One of the principal reasons for present conditions is the underestimation, and even the complete lack of understanding, of the role of ecological factors in agricultural development."[1]

Moreover, studies indicate that the food available to consumers often is unsafe for human consumption because of inappropriate or negligent practices. In September 1989, 100 students fell ill while helping with the onion harvest outside Yekaterinburg (formerly Sverdlovsk). Many of the students had to be flown to a nearby hospital for treatment, and some were incapacitated for months. Tests revealed that the students were suffering from "toxic polyneurosis" as a result of coming into contact with soil laced with "a number of pesticides." The farm's director maintained that the students simply suffered from exhaustion, but a government investigation revealed that pesticides were improperly stored and handled on the farm and that soil samples contained concentrations of chemicals exceeding safe limits by as much as 120 times. Use of some preparations present had been banned. The onions were impounded, but the harvest apparently continued later.[2] Responding to a report of the incident, a woman from Murmansk queried: "Who will answer for the poisoning not only of the students from Sverdlovsk but also of all the Russian land?"[3]

Soviet agricultural policies have had a negative impact not only on farmland but on the environment at large. One Kyrgyz parliamentarian related the following story about how local farmers avoided fulfilling the state's plan for fertilizer use:

> When asked to fulfill [the plan], farmers begin looking for ways to avoid doing so. One method is to take the fertilizer outside of city and regional boundaries and bury it there. Recently, several places where fertilizers had been buried were found near our unique lake Issyk-Kul. There are 100 tons of fertilizer there. The neighboring People's Republic of China has been asking for fertilizer, so it would have been very easy to simply sell it. Instead farmers transported it to this region and buried it, thereby polluting [the lake].[4]

Despite the benefits to be reaped from radical economic reforms like privatization and marketization of agriculture, producers, consumers, and nature alike will be burdened for the foreseeable future by the environmental legacy of Soviet agriculture.

A POOR INHERITANCE SQUANDERED

The territory that comprises the former Soviet Union, though vast, is composed to a large extent of tundra, taiga, mountains, semidesert, and desert—terrain that is relatively unsuitable for intense economic activity and is very susceptible to degradation. Similarly, agricultural land (which covers 6 million square kilometers, or about one-quarter of former Soviet territory) tends to be rocky, low in humus and essential nutrients, hilly, exposed to wind erosion, and subject to flood and drought. To make matters worse, productive lands, such as the rich black earth zone (*chernozem*), were badly abused by Soviet agriculture. Degradation of the *chernozem* is particularly troubling because this region accounted for 60 percent of the cultivated land and produced 80 percent of the USSR's marketable grain.

In the words of Goskompriroda's 1988 report on the state of the environment: "The condition of land resources is a cause of great concern."[5] When the condition of land resources is analyzed by region, Moldova has suffered the worst; the Caucasus, Central Asia, and the central *chernozem* zone are not much better off.[6] The most serious problem has been erosion that has affected half of agricultural land, a fifth of it critically (see Map 4.1). The Soviet environment agency estimated that wind, rain, and melting snow eroded 1.5 billion tons of topsoil from farmland annually.[7] The agroindustrial agency, USSR Gosagroprom, was more pessimistic, putting losses of fine soils (*melkozem*) from Soviet farmland at 2–3 billion tons annually. In addition, the agency pegged the loss of humus and fertilizer at 100 and 43 million tons, respectively.[8] According to a 1988 report to the USSR Academy of Sciences, the region's farmland has been scarred by almost 1 million kilometers of gullies and washouts.[9]

In consequence, the humus content of the soil has been maintained in only a few regions: the Baltic states, Belarus, and several oblasts in Ukraine and Russia. In parts of the *chernozem*, up to one-third of the humus has been lost.[10] In Ukraine, erosion has affected almost a third of all arable land, resulting in the production loss of "millions of tons" in wheat in 1990.[11] Researcher M. N. Zaslavskii estimated that the effect of erosion in grain-growing regions of the Soviet Union reduced potential production by 90 million tons per year.[12] As an indication of the scale of the problem, this equaled about half of total Soviet annual production in the late 1980s, and the Soviet Union imported 35 million tons of grain in 1988.[13] Agricultural analyst A. N. Kashtanov reported in 1988 that agricultural output averaged 15 to 60 percent below its potential because of erosion, resulting in annual losses costing the USSR 7–8 billion rubles. Fertilizers lost to erosion added another 2.5 billion rubles to the toll. The total impact of erosion on land and water resources added up to 11–15 billion rubles per year.[14] Zaslavskii was more pessimistic, putting the loss at 15–20 billion rubles annually;[15] when other costs to the economy were added, the bill rose to 30 billion rubles, over 10 percent of total agricultural production.[16]

In addition, large-scale irrigation of arid and semidesert regions and overirrigation, as outlined in the previous chapter, had caused the soil in many areas to become waterlogged and saturated with salt. Of arable land in the former USSR, 13 percent was reported to be excessively saline.[17]

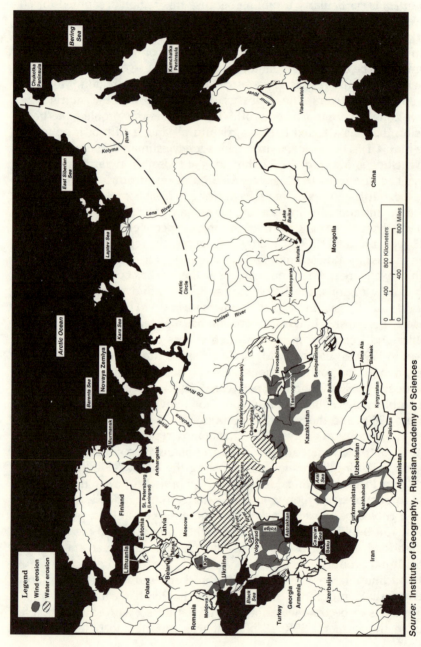

Source: Institute of Geography. Russian Academy of Sciences

MAP 4.1 Agricultural regions subject to a high rate of erosion, late 1980s

Like other natural resources in the Soviet Union, agricultural land suffered heavily from the extensive nature of its exploitation. Many problems can be traced to the Virgin Lands Program instituted in the 1950s by Nikita Khrushchev. Dissatisfied with the low yields on existing farmland, Khrushchev initiated a drive to open up vast new tracts of land to farming as a means of solving the Soviet Union's food supply problems. Most of the virgin lands were grassland of marginal quality, however, and very prone to erosion when planted with row crops and not allowed to lie fallow for long periods. Though the program was abandoned, these marginal lands continued to be cropped continuously as farmers were under constant pressure to boost output. As a result, an average of 30–50 percent of the humus was lost, turning parts of southern Siberia and northern Kazakhstan into a virtual dust bowl.

With erosion, pressure on pastureland by overgrazing and the cutting of too much hay has given rise to desertification, particularly in Central Asia. In Tajikistan, the "long term, unsystematic cutting and overgrazing" of grasslands have led to "a catastrophic worsening" in the state of grasslands there, and the productivity of the land has decreased 10–50 percent.[18] In Kyrgyzstan, 85 percent of the republic's territory consists of grassland: "Unfortunately, we are losing this wealth," noted Apas Dzhumagulov, the republic's prime minister, in a 1989 address devoted to ecological issues.[19] Over the 1950s–1980s, the yield from the republic's grasslands decreased by a third: "If we do not take essential measures, what will we leave to our descendants?" he asked.

To combat the decreases in harvest that resulted from soil degradation, the Soviet government funded major land reclamation projects, but it proved to be a losing battle. In spite of the fact that over a half million hectares of agricultural land were reclaimed in 1989, according to official reports, water erosion continued to grow, claiming 100,000–150,000 hectares.[20] Between 1975 and 1985, the area of saline land nearly doubled. Most of the reclamation work funded by the government did not entail restoration of degraded lands per se but the extension of irrigation and drainage systems. Moreover, many of the land improvements documented existed only in the reports to economic planners; as in other sectors of the Soviet economy, the quality of work was poor. According to a report that appeared in the agricultural newspaper *Sel'skaya zhizn'* (Rural Life), land reported to have been improved and brought into economic use in the Russian Federation between 1981 and 1986 needed "major" repairs by 1990.[21] In 1975, 4.8 million hectares of irrigated land were in need of capital work; by 1985, the area increased to 5.6 million hectares; and by 1988, it reached 7 million hectares—almost one-third of all irrigated land.[22] In the paradoxical words of a USSR Gosplan official:

"The improved state of a significant portion of these lands is constantly worsening."[23]

In sum, between 1968 and 1988, poor land use rendered 6 million hectares of the most productive agricultural land barren—an area the size of West Virginia.[24] According to N. Z. Milashchenko, first vice-president of the Academy of Agricultural Sciences, "These figures underscore the problems in investment policies and also the environmentally dangerous trends in farming."[25] In a review of the environmental impact of Soviet agriculture, Kashtanov, writing in the *Bulletin of the USSR Academy of Sciences*, noted the following as the fundamental causes of the poor state of Soviet land resources:

> a lack of an individual responsibility for the land; the ecological illiteracy of many agricultural specialists and managers; unsatisfactory government control of the regulation and conservation of soil productivity and of [those who cause] erosion; the lack of a specialized government erosion control service . . . the lack of the technical means to conduct soil conservation; and the low level of scientific expertise in the conservation of the soil and the environment.[26]

As mentioned in Chapter 2, land resources have been damaged not only by destructive agricultural development but also by exogenous factors such as airborne pollution. Aleksei Yablokov labels industrial pollution and its threat to the food supply as Russia's number two environmental threat.[27] On this point, USSR Goskompriroda chair Nikolai Vorontsov made the following comment:

> When industrial plants discharge a ton of sulfur onto a square kilometer of farmland, the properties of the soil are substantially degraded, to put it mildly. Let us see where our chief producers of noxious waste are concentrated—on the mightiest *chernozem* soils: Zaporozhye, Dnepropetrovsk, Dneprodzerzhinsk, the entire Donbass. . . . We will try to introduce new and more progressive soil protection measures—contour plowing, using the very gentlest implements, limiting the amounts of chemicals that go into the soil, and so on, but the poison will continue to be showered from above.[28]

The accumulation of industrial pollutants has been greatest near metallurgical centers—such as Ukraine's Donets Basin and Russia's Kola Peninsula and southern Urals region—where zinc, copper, cobalt, cadmium, vanadium, and numerous other elements have been found in the soil in concentrations far above permitted levels.[29] An official at the Georgian State Planning Committee reported contamination of the soil by these and other metals around the cities of Tbilisi, Rustavi, and Batumi.[30]

In a vain attempt to compensate for the myriad of ills besetting Soviet agriculture—low productivity of the soil, an undeveloped infrastructure, squalid rural living conditions, a lack of effective financial incentives, and poor farm management, to name a few—planners often turned to technological quick fixes. Beginning with the Khrushchev regime, the Soviet government poured hundreds of billions of rubles into agriculture in an attempt to put more food on the table. Along with state ownership of the land and collective agriculture, heavy mechanization and the extensive use of agrochemicals were portrayed as an unquestionable good.

Contrary to officials' intentions, many investment programs were ill-conceived and misdirected and served only to promote further the deterioration of regions they were supposed to help. USSR Goskompriroda estimated that between 1965 and 1988, capital investment in agriculture increased 5-fold, fertilizer and pesticide use went up comparably, and the total area of irrigated and drained agricultural land doubled. Yet gross agricultural output over the same period increased by a mere 20 percent—not enough to keep pace with the growth of the population.[31]

TROUBLE WITH TRACTORS

In 1988, Soviet factories turned out 559,000 tractors, six times the volume produced in the United States.[32] In addition to being ubiquitous, Soviet-designed tractors were uniformly big and heavy—so big and heavy that they were described by USSR Goskompriroda as being one of the principal factors contributing to soil degradation and causing "a massive loss in agricultural production."[33] Juhan Aare, a member of the committee on the environment in the Estonian parliament, complained that "our small fields and plains are being destroyed by gigantic machines designed for the needs of the enormous Russian and Ukrainian steppes. . . . Heavy tractors mean death for our land."[34] *Sel'skaya zhizn'* carried the following commentary on Soviet tractors:

> Modern technology—powerful and heavy—is damaging the land and excessively compacting it. After numerous passes by a Kirovets, Don, or KamAZ [tractor], a tight ear of wheat will not develop, no matter how much the soil is fertilized. According to specialists' calculations, the excessive compaction of the soil prevents the country from producing 15 million tons of wheat yearly.[35]

The problems, according to *Sel'skaya zhizn'*, began in 1959, when Nikita Khrushchev visited the farm of Roswell Garst in the United States and saw that U.S. tractors were equipped with tires. Back in the USSR, Khrushchev demanded that Soviet tractors also be outfitted with tires instead of the customary Caterpillar tracks. Khrushchev, did not, however, pay attention to all the details, such as the weight of the tractor or the air pressure needed in the tires. In comparison studies, the K-700 model tractor equipped with tires exerted up to twice as much pressure on the soil as lighter models with wheels or vehicles of comparable weight with Caterpillar tracks. The result was a drop in crop yields estimated to be as much as 25 percent.

Once the soil has been excessively compacted it takes years to recover. Agronomists began in the mid-1970s trying to undo the harm wrought by Khrushchev's scheme, but to little avail. Extensive research indicated that using different tires or reverting to Caterpillars would improve the situation, and new standards were adopted by the government accordingly. The tractor manufacturers, however, balked at the new regulations and managed to get them shelved—an easier task than building lighter tractors or fitting Caterpillar tracks to existing models.[36]

"STUFFED WITH FERTILIZER"

With Khrushchev's crash campaign to "chemicalize" agriculture, begun in the early 1960s, fertilizer became one of the most important weapons in the Soviet struggle to produce more food. Planners measured success in terms of gross output of fertilizer, not food: In 1960, Soviet fertilizer production amounted to less than half that of the United States; by the late 1960s, the Soviet Union had drawn even in fertilizer output. In 1988, the USSR produced more than 37 million tons, nearly twice as much as its rival.[37] In contrast with many of Khrushchev's other challenges to the West, the USSR won the fertilizer battle, but it lost the food production war.

Despite the increase in fertilizer output, agriculture officials often pointed out that overall fertilizer use was relatively low in comparison to that in Western countries. On average, one hectare of arable land in the Soviet Union received about 120 kilograms of fertilizer per year in the 1980s; the rate in Western Europe, according to Soviet comparisons, often was 5 to 6 times as high during the same period. Such comparisons, however, were faulty: Fertilizer use under Soviet central planning, like many other indicators, was very uneven, and the discrepancies were not accurately reflected in government statistics. Belarus, Lithuania, and Latvia, for example, averaged over 300 kilograms per hectare, whereas one-quarter of all Soviet land under cultivation normally received no fertilizer at all. Kazakhstan registered the lowest average fertilizer use under the Soviet system, only 34 kilograms applied per hectare.[38] Yet great discrepancies existed in the republic also: In 1989, *Sel'skaya zhizn'* reported that in the southern section of Kazakhstan, "the land literally has been stuffed with fertilizers."[39]

While state planners focused on boosting output, other aspects of the fertilizer drive—distribution, storage, and, most important, application—were overlooked. An audit conducted by the state planning agency USSR Gosplan revealed that 11 percent of all fertilizers never reached the field because of transport and storage problems. *Pravda* provocatively recommended that farmers sow their crops along railroad tracks because so much fertilizer was lost from loaded trains on the way from factory to farm.[40] When supplies did reach the farm, they often were left out in the open: Turkmenistan's agricultural agency reported that in one region, only one-quarter of farms had necessary storage facilities.[41] The problem is likely to continue for the new republics because the construction of special facilities for the storage of agrochemicals dropped 30 percent across the USSR in the late 1980s.[42]

While agronomists worked out in detail how to apply fertilizers properly, farmers and rural specialists were often oblivious to these guidelines. An academician interviewed by *Pravda* complained that the government poorly trained farmers in the use of agrochemicals. Boris A. Yagodin, a member of the Academy of Agricultural Sciences, complained that agricultural chemistry was not being taught at technical schools and that several agricultural institutes had been closed down. Moreover, ignorance was compounded by negligence: "Technological discipline is . . . low. It is easier for a manager to report the quantity of fertilizer applied than to bother with a troublesome, scientifically based system of chemical use for each individual field."[43] As a result, farmers often dumped agricultural chemicals on the soil without regard for the specific needs of the crop, the weather, the season, soil conditions, or the type of product being applied.

Gosplan estimated that across the Soviet Union, rain and irrigation washed a third of all fertilizer out of the soil and into groundwater.[44] Accordingly, N. Z. Milashchenko wrote in 1989: "An increase in nitrate contamination of ground and surface waters has been noted in all areas in recent years." Toxicologists estimated that over 16.6 million tons of lead, 3.2 million tons of cadmium, and a half ton of mercury had been added to the soil with phosphorous fertilizers alone—then there was fluorine, strontium, and uranium. "Unfortunately," wrote Milashchenko, "the biological aspects of this problem . . . still have not been worked out."[45]

PROBLEMS WITH PESTICIDES

About 25 percent of all agricultural land was treated with chemical-based pesticides during the Soviet era; improper application of these preparations, however, caused considerable harm to the environment, crops, and farm workers.[46] As with fertilizers, little training was given in the use of pesticides, and technical support was poor. In addition, farmers often lacked the necessary equipment to apply properly the pesticides supplied to them. As a consequence, more than just plants were treated: According to one source, half of all pesticides were used in an "unsatisfactory" manner, and aerial crop dusting proving particularly problematic.[47]

Farmland has been "significantly contaminated" by pesticides (i.e., insecticides, herbicides, and fungicides) in Azerbaijan, Armenia, Kyrgyzstan, Moldova, Tajikistan, Uzbekistan, and elsewhere.[48] Pesticide use was particularly heavy in rice- and cotton-growing regions during the Soviet era. According to a report in the business weekly *Ekonomika i zhizn'*, pesticide use averaged 15–25 kilograms per hectare of rice in the 1980s. "This is only in theory," added the authors, "[and] in practice, far more pesticides are used." Damage was compounded when farmers flooded the paddies immediately after treating them, sending the pesticides directly into the water table.

In 1987, almost a third of all fish in the Volga Basin reportedly died from pesticide poisoning.[49] In many regions, such as the cotton belt of Central Asia, reports indicated that pesticides were turning up in the drinking water supply. In the Krasnoarmeiskii region of southern Russia's Krasnodar region, the use of pesticides on rice crops has taken a heavy toll on the health of the population. According to a statement in 1989 by a health official in the region, the incidence of cancer among the general population increased by 50 percent over the previous five years, and children's immune systems weakened. Yevgenii Rybailov complained: "The fields are being attacked with over one hundred preparations. They arrive at the state farms without any accompanying documentation, without instructions—the workers just do not know how to use them. We are wasting money and paying for it with our health."[50] Uzbekistan Goskompriroda reported that more than 250,000 containers holding 6,000 tons of "banned toxic chemicals," including DDT and the highly toxic defoliant butifos, had piled up on the republic's farm.[51]

DDT was banned in the Soviet Union in 1970, but the environment has continued to suffer the effects of this long-lived pesticide. Of soil samples tested in late 1988, one-half showed residual levels and about 15 percent (accounting for 8,300 hectares of land) contained concentrations of DDT that exceeded the maximum level specified in health regulations. The republics most affected—with average concentrations from 2 to 8 times the established norm—are Azerbaijan, Armenia, Uzbekistan, and Moldova. Traces of the pesticide have been found not only in cotton-growing areas, where it was used most heavily, but also in regions where other crops are raised; in Kyrgyzstan, soil under wheat and vegetable crops reached 33–46 and 9–20 times the norm, respectively. Soil samples from Novosibirsk oblast contained concentrations of DDT as high as 56–192 times the permissible norm, suggesting that use of the preparation continued after the ban.[52] The government also ran down its stocks of DDT by exporting the pesticide. Between 1986 and 1989 (the only years for which data are available), Soviet entrepreneurs sold approximately 14,000 tons of the pesticide abroad.[53]

A review of the state of the environment in Ukraine summed up the effect of the Soviet government's chemicalization drive in these words:

> The unshakable belief that intensive chemicalization of agriculture would substantially increase yields turned out to be premature. Unscientific and intensive chemicalization brings with it serious negative social and ecological consequences. It has already been established that it is the fundamental cause of the increase in illness among the population living in regions of intensive application of pesticides. The increase in infant mortality and illness in rural regions causes alarm. The monitoring for the contamination of foods with various chemicals has prompted serious concern.[54]

FROM FIELD TO TABLE

Soviet consumers added a new word to their daily vocabulary and daily concerns in the 1980s—*nitraty*, or nitrates—prompted by a spate of media reports on Soviet agriculture and its impact on the food supply.[55] Yet the region's food supply is threatened not only by nitrate contamination, a function of the improper use of fertilizers, but also by pesticides, heavy metals, and even radioactive elements. In his 1991 report to the Russian parliament, Bobylev wrote: "The quantity of produce which contains radionucleides presently consumed by the public is great."[56] Sadly, chronic food shortages and high prices mean that the public has no choice but to continue eating such tainted produce.

According to official data, over 1.8 million tests were carried out on food products in the Soviet Union in 1988. One-tenth of the produce examined failed to meet various government health standards. Uzbekistan had the worst record; nearly one-fifth of the food tested there did not pass inspection. Other republics with rates of contaminated food above the Soviet average were Kyrgyzstan, Tajikistan, Kazakhstan, and

Russia.[57] In terms of nitrates, one-quarter of all crops tested in Estonia and Moldova were reportedly contaminated in 1989; in Russia, Belarus, Kazakhstan, and Lithuania, the share was one-sixth.[58] In Russia, over 28 percent of potatoes tested registered above-norm levels of nitrates.[59] In Lithuania, over half of the potatoes, a third of the cabbages, and over a quarter of onions tested failed government standards for nitrates in 1987; results of these inspections and others for Lithuania are outlined in Table 4.1.

Of food supplies tested specifically for pesticide residues in 1989, 3.9 percent on average contained levels higher than the permissible norm (see Table 4.2). Georgia had the most serious problem that year, with 11.7 percent of the food tested exceeding the limit.[60] Reports of these government studies did not mention at which point the tests were conducted—whether in the field, processing plant, or point of sale—or what was done with produce that failed. In April 1989, Goskompriroda's Fedor Morgun admitted that health codes occasionally were ignored, and "products contaminated above established norms are being sold."[61] Other sources reported worse figures. Bobylev claimed that 17 percent of Russian produce was contaminated with "residual quantities" of pesticides.[62] Russian environmentalist Aleksei Yablokov has been one of the most outspoken about the threat to the food supply and, citing 1987 data, alleged that in some areas of the USSR, up to half of foodstuffs tested were contaminated with pesticides and unfit for human consumption.[63] A third of produce tested in St. Petersburg that year contained quantities of pesticides at levels hazardous to health.[64]

Food quality standards, like other public health norms, were established by the USSR Ministry of Health. Like water and air quality stan-

TABLE 4.1   Nitrate concentration of produce in Lithuania, 1987

	Number of Samples Tested	Percent Within Norm	Percent 1–2 Times Permissible Limit	Percent Exceeding Twice Permissible Limit
Potatoes	2,124	42.1	48.8	9.1
Cabbage	449	61.3	24.7	14.1
Onions	143	73.0	25.3	1.7
Green onions	116	81.4	16.3	2.3
Beets	391	87.2	12.5	0.3
Cucumbers	52	88.5	9.6	1.9
Tomatoes	62	91.9	4.9	3.2
Carrots	505	92.7	6.1	1.2

Source: Kaunas Economics Institute, "Urgent Ecological Problems in Lithuania," briefing submitted to the Lithuanian Council of Ministers, November 1988, p. 36.

TABLE 4.2   Pesticide contamination of soil and produce by republic, 1989 (percentages)

	Samples with Residual Levels		Samples with Above-Norm Levels	
	Soil	Produce	Soil	Produce
USSR average	33.4	25.0	4.6	3.9
Azerbaijan	58.4	42.4	29.2	na
Belarus	37.2	10.0	24.8	3.4
Georgia	63.8	55.1	24.4	11.7
Kazakhstan	17.8	9.8	1.4	3.5
Kyrgyzstan	2.8	1.0	4.9	0.6
Lithuania	1.6	16.0	5.6	4.1
Moldova	30.2	8.8	11.7	6.9
Russia	25.8	17.1	1.4	5.1
Tajikistan	66.6	34.8	3.9	0.0
Turkmenistan	33.6	60.9	na	0.0
Ukraine	54.2	29.6	0.7	0.5
Uzbekistan	65.3	53.4	4.7	2.9

Source: USSR Goskompriroda, *Sostoyanie prirodnoi sredy i prirodookhrannaya deyatel'nost' v SSSR v 1989 godu* (Moscow: Institut Molodezhi, 1990), p. 107.

dards, those for food were strict. "Regarding our standards matching international norms," Morgun assured the public, "they are, in general, fully comparable." But, he added: "There are also examples of [levels of] maximum permissible concentrations being revised upwards unjustifiably."[65] In 1988, the health ministry increased the concentrations of nitrates permitted in many vegetables and fruits; standards for potatoes and cabbage, for instance, more than tripled.[66]

In December 1989, *Komsomol'skaya pravda* looked into the issue of contaminated foods in Ukraine. Over a period of four months in 1989, public health specialists conducted 542 tests on food in the republic's capital; a quarter revealed excessive levels of nitrates. The chair of the department of biophysics and radiobiology at the Ukrainian Academy of Science Botany Institute, Dr. D. M. Grodzinskii, related the following story to the newspaper: "In our laboratory, we have 14 colleagues living in 13 districts of Kiev. And so we decided that each of us would bring to the laboratory milk, vegetables, and fruit from our districts. We ran tests. The results were stupefying . . . a very high level of contamination."[67]

With the active participation of scientific institutions, two journalists from *Moskovskaya pravda* investigated produce from three state farms serving the capital. After running tests for the presence of heavy metals, they concluded: "The results of the analysis, unfortunately, exceeded the most pessimistic fears. . . . It turns out that of the three state farms, only one was 'clean.'" Carrot samples exceeded permissible concentrations for cadmium by a factor of between 3 and 8, and in beets by 10–14. The presence of zinc in beets was 2–3 times above the maximum permissible concentration.

The newspaper revealed that the main wastewater treatment facility serving Moscow had been disposing sludge at dozens of farms on the outskirts of the city. As many industrial enterprises in the capital released their wastes into the city sewage system indiscriminately, the precipitate produced by the city's two wastewater treatment plants contained high levels of heavy metals. Fields fertilized with the precipitate contained concentrations of mercury 10 times higher than those found in untainted soil; concentrations of silver and chromium were 3–10 times higher; and zinc, copper, arsenic, strontium, vanadium, nickel, and cobalt levels were elevated as much as 3 times.[68] The chief engineer of the Kuryanovo plant dismissed the threat as unwarranted. On the grounds of the sewage plant, juicy tomatoes and cucumbers thrived in greenhouses built to supply plant personnel. Tellingly, he conceded that the facility's produce was not grown with sludge.[69]

THE TECHNOCRATIC APPROACH TO AGRICULTURE RECONSIDERED

The reliance on agrochemicals permitted the stagnation of efforts to improve farmland in more constructive ways—for example, by introducing lighter farm equipment, shallow tilling, contour plowing, and crop rotation, not to mention reforming collective agriculture. *Sel'skaya zhizn'* characterized the state of affairs in Kazakhstan thus: "The pursuit of instant success and victorious reports through the introduction of monocropping led to such an impoverishment of the soil that one might as well remove them from production and let them lie fallow for a long time."[70]

As Soviet society began to question the efficacy of collective farming and public ownership of land, policymakers also started to reconsider the traditional technocratic approach to agriculture. For example, USSR Goskompriroda's Valentin Sokolovskii blamed the state of Soviet agriculture on a modernist "fetishization of scientific and technical progress," adding, "The belief that technology, fertilizers, [and] pesticides can boost productivity infinitely has led to stagnation in the development of agricultural science and the unrestrained spending of the soil's reserves."[71] Petr I. Poletaev, another official at USSR Goskompriroda, related the following telling anecdote: The chairman of a collective farm was asked once why he was using so much fertilizer. "Our land is like a drug addict," the farmer replied. "It cannot survive without it." Poletaev's wry retort was "Alas, a drug addict does not last long either."[72]

Fertilizer use began to taper off in 1988. Deliveries of fertilizer decreased by one-fifth by 1990, but gross agricultural output remained relatively steady.[73] The drop in fertilizer use may be attributed to two causes: bottlenecks in the supply system as a result of economic dislocation (particularly transport slowdowns and a drop in petroleum production), and attempts by farms to economize on inputs in the wake of economic reforms—namely, the shift to financial independence and sharply rising input prices. The application of chemical-based pesticides peaked in 1985, and by 1990 had dropped over 50 percent, while the use of herbicides alone fell by over 60 percent.[74] As in the case of fertilizers, this reduction likely reflected farm managers' attempts to cut costs. Another probable cause was a decrease in the availability of pesticides and a tightening of regulations. Production of a number of ineffective preparations was curtailed, and the use of other pesticides, such as butifos, was banned.[75] Finally, many farm managers appear to have been adversely affected by heavy media attention on the misuse of agrochemicals, particularly of herbicides in Central Asia, moving them to avoid their use.

As a result of the decrease in the use of pesticides and a greater awareness of their proper application, the share of food and soil samples registering above-norm levels of pesticides tapered off (see Figure 4.1). Similarly, the share of many common vegetables registering above-norm levels of nitrates decreased from 12.3 percent in 1988 to 6.8 percent in 1989.[76]

Meanwhile, the use of organic methods to protect crops was increasing—organic farming was up by 10 percent between 1986 and 1988 alone. Despite the increase, however, the share of agricultural land being thus treated remained small, only 4 percent.[77] It is interesting to note that the original impetus to pursue organic farming came from high Soviet officials who sought to obtain a safe supply of food for their families. Enterprises like the Ala-Tal state farm outside of Alma-Ata, which raised apples, strawberries, tomatoes, and even trout, were directed to do so with minimal chemical inputs.[78] The motivation to grow organic foods became strong as media reports indicated that produce certified "organic" in urban peasant markets sold briskly, despite higher prices.[79] In response to the deteriorating quality of the republic's food supply, the Kazakh government passed a resolution mandating punitive fines for those found selling tainted produce.[80] In May 1990, the Soviet government announced it would pay a premium for grain grown with-

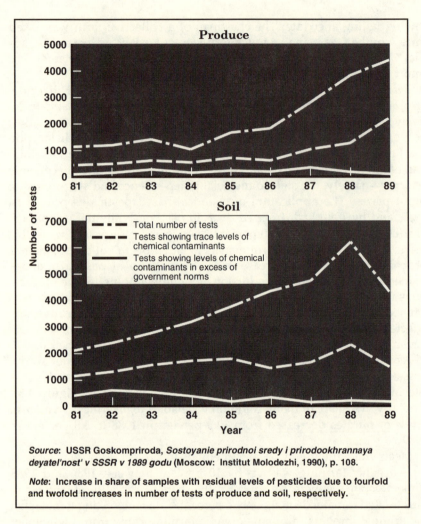

FIGURE 4.1 Trends in pesticide contamination of soil and produce, 1981–1989

out chemical pesticides as part of its larger program to promote grain sales to the state.[81] Parliamentarians from Central Asia met in Tashkent in October 1991 to coordinate the republics' environmental policies. The representatives announced an ambitious plan to halt the use of pesticides and herbicides in the region by 1995.[82]

INTERSECTION OF LAND AND WATER USE: THE CASE OF THE ARAL SEA AND CENTRAL ASIAN AGRICULTURE

The Aral Sea was once the world's fourth-largest inland lake, with a surface area greater than the state of West Virginia. A fleet operating out of the port town of Muinak on the Amu Darya delta to the south regularly hauled in over 40,000 tons of fresh-water fish a year from this verdant, self-sustaining ecosystem. Around its shores in Kazakhstan, Uzbekistan, and Turkmenistan, nomadic tribes raised livestock.[83]

In Central Asia, agricultural development under the Soviet regime was epitomized by the dominance of cotton, as the Kremlin aggressively sought self-sufficiency in what planners dubbed "white gold." In the late 1950s, the Central Asian republics, most notably Uzbekistan, began to fulfill their "internationalist duty" by rapidly expanding irrigation in arid zones and plowing up their market gardens and orchards to obtain extra acreage for cotton. Between 1960 and 1988, the production of raw

Abandoned fishing trawlers on the dry Aral Sea bed near the former port city of Aralsk, Kazakhstan. Photo: Y. Kudin, Novosti from Sovfoto.

cotton was boosted 80 percent in Uzbekistan and over 350 percent in neighboring Turkmenistan.[84]

In the early 1990s, Soviet Central Asia was the world's third-largest cotton-growing region and accounted for 12 percent of world exports, a share second only to that of the United States. Uzbekistan accounted for over 60 percent of total Soviet cotton production, with cotton plantations occupying up to three-quarters of the republic's agricultural lands. Despite the monetary reward, the price paid by the people of Central Asia for the cotton monoculture has been high.

To help fulfill this duty, engineers built the 1,100-kilometer V. I. Lenin Karakum Canal to bring water from the Amu Darya to new cotton acreage in the Turkmen desert. Water also was drawn off at numerous other points along the Amu Darya and Syr Darya in Turkmenistan, Uzbekistan, and Kazakhstan on their way to the Aral. Whereas these rivers once fed the sea 50–70 cubic kilometers of water annually, the inflow to the Aral had been reduced to a trickle by the 1980s. In the most favorable years, the sea has received no more than 20 cubic kilometers. Meanwhile, water has evaporated from it at a rate of 33–36 cubic kilometers annually. By the 1990s, the water level of Aral had dropped by more than 15 meters, and the sea had shrunk to almost half its former size, causing the sea to split into two: "Little Aral" to the north fed by the Syr Darya, and "Big Aral" in the south fed by the Amu Darya (see Map 4.2). Thus, the Aral Sea is fast becoming the Aral Desert.

The demise of Aral can be ranked as a major land-use disaster. As the water has fallen, its salinity has increased sharply (from 10 percent in 1960 to 27 percent at the end of the 1980s), wiping out 20 of 24 species of fish. With nothing to catch, abandoned trawlers now lay beached on the sand 70 kilometers from water. In a futile attempt to preserve the 1,100 jobs at the Muinak and Aralsk fish-processing plants (now located far from the coast), the Soviet government resorted to shipping in frozen fish by rail from the Pacific and Atlantic. Windstorms rake the exposed lake, whipping up tens of millions of tons of sand, salt, and accumulated agricultural chemicals into the air. In 1988, USSR Goskomstat reported that an average hectare of agricultural land in the region had received over one-half ton of airborne salt, leading to the destruction of crops and forests.[85] The salt also travels for thousands of kilometers, reaching the Pamir Mountains of Tajikistan along the Afghan and Chinese border and accelerating spring snowmelts there. Meanwhile, the reduced surface area of the lake has modified the weather in the Aral region. The climate is more continental—summer heat has become hotter and drier, winters are more severe, and the growing season has been reduced by up to a fortnight.

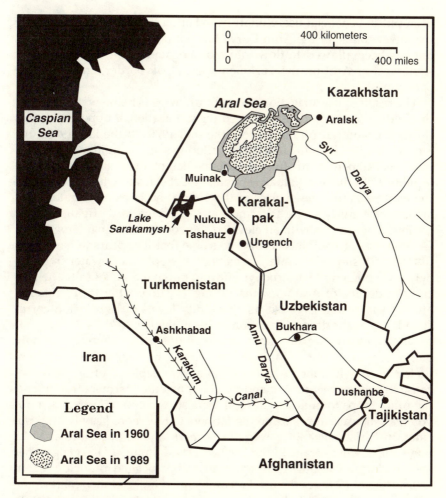

MAP 4.2 Aral Sea region

All this has ensued while irrigation canals upstream leak profusely—
on the order of one-half the volume of water diverted away from the Aral
Sea.[86] Since the early 1970s, engineers in Ashkhabad, the capital of
Turkmenistan, have been struggling to prevent the city from being inundated by seepage from the Karakum Canal by drilling 150 relief wells to
pump the water out of the city.[87] The use of leaky and rudimentary water
delivery systems in the fields has resulted in uneven and often excessive
irrigation, and a lack of adequate drainage systems prevents the return of
groundwater to the rivers or its reuse. When runoff is collected, it has not

been put to beneficial use. Runoff from cotton and rice irrigation along the lower course of the Amu Darya has not been returned to the river, but has been allowed to flow into a desert depression, 200 kilometers southwest of Aral on the Turkmen-Karakalpak border, creating Lake Sarakamysh.

The result of overirrigation and poor drainage is rising water levels in the fields, a factor that has promoted the salinization of upper soil layers through evapotranspiration. From the mid-1970s to the late 1980s, the area of irrigated land in Uzbekistan suffering saline conditions increased by almost 40 percent to affect almost one-half of all irrigated land in the republic.[88] In the Karakalpak republic of Uzbekistan, which borders on the Aral Sea, only one-quarter of the 485,000 hectares of irrigated land are not excessively saline as farmers are forced to draw irrigation water coming downstream with an elevated salt content.[89] In many regions of Central Asia, the soil has become so saline that it appears to have been dusted with snow. In winter, farmers often apply more water in a desperate yet often more destructive effort to purge the soil of salt. The precipitous decline of Aral notwithstanding, existing patterns of irrigation are not sustainable because rising salinity levels in Uzbekistan corresponded with the dropoff in cotton yields in the 1980s.[90]

Unfortunately, the ambitious diversion of water resources tells only half of the story. The region's cotton plantations came to be dependent on fertilizers when the poor desert soils were depleted of nutrients because the government's demanding plan prevented farmers from planting other crops to build up the soil. Persistent cotton cropping also favored an increase in pests, forcing farmers to rely more heavily on pesticides. In Turkmenistan, for example, farmers applied pesticides at 20–25 times the Soviet average in the 1980s.[91] David Smith, a U.S. geographer specializing in Central Asian agriculture, has pegged pesticide use in Uzbekistan at 10 times the level recommended in the United States.[92] Finally, farmers turned to heavy doses of potent defoliants in autumn to facilitate harvesting the cotton crop.

The inordinate use of fertilizers, pesticides, and defoliants on cotton crops has contaminated groundwater supplies as excessive irrigation has flushed much of the agrochemicals off the field and into the water table. Downstream cities like Chardzhou, Urgench, Tashauz, and Nukus, the capital of Karakalpakistan, not to mention the small towns and villages that line the two rivers and their tributaries, have minimal sewerage treatment capability; municipal and industrial wastes therefore are released directly into the rivers. The toxic brew of agrochemicals, minerals, and waste that continues down the river has made it unfit for consumption by humans and even livestock, yet settlements along the lower reaches of the Amu Darya in Karakalpakistan must draw up to two-thirds of their drinking water from the river; this water is untreated for lack of any alternative.[93]

Assaulted by agrochemicals from above and tainted water from below, the land in the vicinity of Aral is being threatened by what one scholar described as this "slow Chernobyl"—a strain the region's health-care system is woefully ill-equipped to handle. Kakimbek Salykov, chair of the USSR Supreme Soviet Committee on Ecology, noted in 1990 that three-quarters of the population of his native Karakalpakistan suffer from various diseases.[94] *Argumenty i fakty* reported that official infant mortality statistics for the region had risen from 44.7 deaths per 1,000 live births in 1965 to as high as 90 by 1986. Four-fifths of the women and children in the region suffer from anemia. In Kazakhstan's Kzyl-Orda oblast to the northeast of Aral, the incidence of typhoid fever increased 30 times between 1974 and 1989, with viral hepatitis up 7 times. Incidences of tuberculosis and cancer also have been on the rise.[95] Recent outbreaks of bubonic plague epitomize the region's regression to pre-modern conditions.[96] In sum, Goskompriroda's Vorontsov labeled the Aral crisis "the greatest ecological catastrophe of our planet."[97]

These consequences were foreseen several decades ago, but planners failed to implement plans to conserve irrigation water or to allow the farms to switch to less water-intensive crops. Consequently, many scientists now believe that Aral is beyond recovery and the best that can be hoped for in the immediate future is that conditions will not deteriorate as fast as they have been. In a September 1988 joint resolution, the Soviet government and CPSU Central Committee called for "a complex of radical measures" to rescue the sea from "the serious deficiencies" of the past. The first section of the tripartite plan contained measures to address environmental degradation, such as reducing the amount of water diverted to agriculture, renovating and upgrading existing irrigation systems, and restricting work on new large-scale projects after 1991. The plan also called for the planting of vegetation in coastal areas and on the exposed lake bed to prevent further wind erosion. The second aspect of the program addressed public health concerns, mandating the rapid construction of municipal water supply systems, strict observation of water quality standards, and improved healthcare services. Finally, the third section called for a multifaceted plan of economic development to combat accumulated social ills in the region.[98]

By the summer of 1990, 50 different projects were reported to be under way to address the region's problems, but evidence suggested any improvement would be a long way off, if not totally elusive.[99] In late 1991, *Pravda* reported that drinking water quality in the region had not improved: Only half of the money allocated for construction and capital repairs of irrigation and municipal water systems had been spent.[100] A principal fault with the government/Communist Party plan was that its conservation measures were not enough to halt the catastrophic decline in the level of Aral. The plan called for a minimum of 8.7 cubic kilometers of water for the sea in 1990 to increase gradually to 20–21 cubic kilometers by 2005. Obviously, even these levels fall far short of the volume of water required just to keep pace with natural evaporation from the lake (33–36 cubic kilometers). Second, efforts to improve drinking water quality for downstream populations along the Amu Darya and Syr Darya focused on diverting agricultural runoff directly into Aral via thousands of kilometers of special drainage canals paralleling the rivers. The approach does not address the fact that vast quantities of agrochemicals will continue to leach into return water that eventually will reach Aral. The benefit to the sea from the plan, therefore, is dubious.[101]

The key to saving Aral and obtaining sustainable economic growth lies with reforming agriculture in Central Asia. One option would be to cut the demand for water by substantially reducing the size of cotton plantations and converting farms to growing less water-consumptive crops. Some suggest growing high-value produce; Uzbekistan, for instance, once had a great reputation for its bounty of fruits, vegetables, and nuts.[102] Local political leaders have expressed an interest in reducing their cotton acreage, but the cost in the short term would be great because cotton exports are the region's principal source of hard currency, netting the region $700 million annually in the early 1990s.[103]

A second option would be to improve the efficiency of water use through the repair and maintenance of existing networks—much of which are in very poor condition—and employment of new water-saving technologies and techniques, such as laser leveling of fields. The largest water savings (up to 30–40 cubic kilometers) could be achieved through the reduction of evaporation and seepage from irrigation projects by lining canals and replacing furrowed irrigation with drip systems.[104] This task would be monumental and expensive because there are over 180,000 kilometers of irrigation canals in Central Asia, less than 10 percent of which have antifiltration linings.[105]

Other costly aspects of dealing with the Aral Sea disaster remain, and all of them—such as controlling water pollution, providing clean drinking water, and addressing the health crisis—entail competing for scarce funds. As Lester Brown of the WorldWatch Institute has pointed out, the region's population has been growing about 3 percent annually, a rate matched only in Africa. This puts a double burden on the environment while exerting downward pressure on living standards: A rapidly growing population increases demand on the local water supply even more, yet scarce government money must be stretched to meet social needs as well as to restore the environment.[106] More people will require more jobs in the future, increasing pressures to maintain the status quo in agriculture.

Although the Soviet government intended to scrap the Sibaral project in its planning stage in 1986, many in Central Asia continue to see the diversion of Siberian water to the south as the only way out of the Aral Sea crisis and the greater water shortage plaguing Central Asia. Alleging that Aral represented a "second Chernobyl," Ulmas Umarbekov, deputy prime minister of Uzbekistan, argued in the republican daily *Pravda vostoka* that the Aral region needed help from wealthier neighbors: medicines, health personnel, clean food, construction materials, and water. Invoking classical communist slogans of the past, he concluded that the river diversion represented "the greatest gesture in history of brotherly cooperation [and] friendship of the peoples of the our country."[107] "The Central Asian region must live and develop. Clearly its own water resources are obviously inadequate for this," wrote two officials of the Sredazgidrovodkhlopok water resource development agency in the same newspaper. Taking a conventional prodevelopment position held by many in the West, they argued that Aral was essentially a hopeless case. Rather than spend scarce resources to revive the sea, planners should focus on saving the inhabitants, and the best way was to improve their standard of living. The expensive water conservation projects and plans to reduce allocations for agriculture, therefore, should be scrapped for projects that would provide safe drinking water, improve health care and housing, and boost agricultural output while causing less environmental degradation.[108]

The likelihood of diverting Siberian waters to the south vanished with the rise of Russian national consciousness and independence. With the collapse of Soviet power, the likelihood of significant inflows of investment funds to restructure the Central Asian economy on the scale described here also disappeared. Despite the disintegration of the Soviet Union, Central Asian parliamentarians again raised the issue of water diversions at a regional environmental meeting as late as October 1991.[109]

In their efforts to find a solution to the problem, analysts routinely ignore one of the most glaring causes for poor land and water use in the region: the fact that irrigation water has been supplied to farmers virtually free of charge over the decades. Raising the price of water to agricultural users would prompt more efficient use of inputs and investment in water-saving measures, not to mention create a source of revenue to fund a revival of Aral. Officials have not attempted such a move, however, because of political pressure by the region's powerful farm managers and fears that rising costs would render farms uncompetitive and hurt exports. Taking advantage of its warm climate, Central Asia may replace thirsty cotton with exports of fresh produce to the north—a traditional emphasis of the region's farmers before Moscow's cotton drive. Central Asian farmers may opt for another high-profit crop: opium.[110] Ultimately, nature may preclude any option. According to the Academy of Sciences Institute of Geography, the portion of irrigated land already salinized from excessive irrigation ranges from 35 percent in Tajikistan to 80 percent in Turkmenistan.[111] The land soon could be rendered barren, obviating any alternative to the dismal legacy of the Soviet cotton culture. Said Sabyr Komalov, a local scientist: "We have no more than ten years left to prevent total disaster."[112]

Notes

1. Sergei N. Bobylev, professor of economics, Moscow State University, "APK: Ekologizatsia ili krizis?" briefing prepared for the Russian Federation Supreme Soviet, 1991,unpublished manuscript, 1991, p. 1.

2. *Sovetskaya Rossiya*, September 5, 1989, p. 4, and October 24, 1989, p. 4.

3. *Sovetskaya Rossiya*, October 24, 1990, p. 4.

4. Anatolii Grebenyuk, deputy chair, Committee on Ecology, Supreme Soviet of Kyrgyzstan, presentation at conference on Democratic Federalism and Environmental Crisis in the Republics of the Former Soviet Union, Moscow, August 1991.

5. USSR Goskompriroda, *Sostoyanie prirodnoi sredy v SSSR v 1988 g.* (Moscow: VINITI, 1989), p. 68.

6. USSR Goskomstat, *Okhrana okruzhayushchei sredy i ratsional'noe ispol'zovanie prirodnykh resursov v SSSR* (Moscow: Finansy i statistika, 1989), p. 8. For more on the state of the *chernozem* region, see I. V. Priputina, "Lowering of the Humus Content of the Chernozem Soils of the Russian Plain as a Result of Human Action," *Vestnik Moskovskogo gosudarstvennogo universiteta, geografiya*, No. 5, 1989, translated in *Soviet Geography*, No. 12, 1989, pp. 759–762.

7. USSR Goskompriroda, *Sostoyanie . . . v 1988 g.*, p. 70. Agricultural specialist Sergei Bobylev also pegs soil loss at about 1.5 billion tons annually, including 75 million tons of humus and more than 30 million tons of nitrogen, phosphorus, and potassium. Sergei N. Bobylev, "Puti povysheniya effektivnosti ispol'zovaniya zemel'nykh resursov," in T. S. Khachaturov and K. V. Papenov, eds., *Effektivnost' prirodookhrannykh meropriyatii* (Moscow: Izdatel'stvo Moskovskogo Universiteta, 1990), p. 65.

8. USSR Gosagroprom cited in A. N. Kashtanov, "Ekologizatsiya sel'skogo khozyaistva," *Vestnik Akademii Nauk SSSR*, No. 11, 1988, p. 57. Valentin G. Sokolovskii, the first deputy chairman of USSR Goskompriroda, also cited a figure of 3 billion tons for annual soil loss. A. K. Kuchushev and N. M. Matveev, "Sokhvanit' zdorov'e zemli," *Vestnik Akademii Nauk SSSR*, No. 3, 1990, p. 37.

9. Kashtanov, "Ekologizatsiya," p. 57.

10. USSR Goskompriroda, *Sostoyanie . . . v 1988 g.*, p. 69; Aleksei Yablokov, "The Current State of the Soviet Environment," *Environmental Policy Review,* January 1990, p. 5; V. Ivashchenko, "Intensifikatsiya zemledeliya–osnovnoi put' realizatsii prodovol'stvennoi programmy," *Planovoe khozyaistvo,* No. 8, 1988, p. 106; V. P. Kukhar', "Nekotorye aktual'nye ekologicheskie problemy Ukrainskoi SSR," *Vestnik Akademii Nauk SSSR,* No. 11, 1988, p. 109.

11. Kukhar', "Nekotorye," p. 109; V. Tregobchuk, "Economics and the Environment," *Pod znamenem Leninizma,* No. 4, 1990, translated in JPRS-UPA-90-019, p. 79.

12. M. N. Zaslavskii cited in Bobylev, "Puti povysheniya effektivnosti," p. 66.

13. USSR Ministry of Foreign Economic Relations, *Vneshnie ekonomicheskie svyazi SSSR v 1988 g.* (Moscow: Finansy i statistika, 1989), p. 42. In 1988, the grain harvest totaled 195 million tons. In 1990, the harvest exceeded 240 million tons, a record crop.

14. Kashtanov, "Ekologizatsiya," pp. 57–58.

15. Nikolai Vorontsov pegged losses resulting from erosion at 15–16 billion rubles. USSR Goskompriroda, *Sostoyanie prirodnoi sredy i prirodookhrannaya deyatel'nost' v SSSR v 1989 godu* (Moscow: Institut Molodezhi, 1990), p. 8.

16. In 1989, agricultural output was valued at 225 billion rubles (in 1983 prices). USSR Goskomstat, *Narodnoe khozyaistvo SSSR v 1989 g.* (Moscow: Finansy i statistika), p. 7. Ruble measures of degradation are provided as an illustration of Soviet analysis of the situation. Such analysis is highly problematic given that prices under the Soviet regime were severely distorted.

17. USSR Goskompriroda, *Sostoyanie . . . v 1988 g.*, p. 115.

18. A. N. Maksumov, "Ob ekologicheskoi obstanovke v Tadzhikistane," *Vestnik Akademii Nauk SSSR,* No. 11, 1988, p. 142.

19. *Sovetskaya Kirgiziya,* July 30, 1989, p. 2.

20. Kashtanov, "Ekologizatsiya," p. 57.

21. *Izvestiya,* February 7, 1990, p. 3.

22. USSR Goskompriroda, *Sostoyanie . . . v 1988 g.*, p. 102.

23. Ivashchenko, "Intensifikatsiya," p. 107.

24. USSR Goskompriroda, *Sostoyanie . . . v 1988 g.*, p. 115.

25. N. Z. Milashchenko, "Solving Ecological Problems in Farming," *Zemledelie,* No. 5, 1989, translated in JPRS-UES-89-025, p. 59.

26. Kashtanov, "Ekologizatsiya," p. 58.

27. *Kul'tura,* No. 12, 1991, p. 3, translated in JPRS-TEN-92-003, p. 54.

28. Nikolai Vorontsov, "The Sofia Ecoforum: Much Work Ahead," *International Affairs,* No. 2, 1990, p. 34.

29. USSR Goskompriroda, *Sostoyanie . . . v 1988 g.*, pp. 73–74.

30. *Zarya vostoka,* January 9, 1990, p. 2.

31. USSR Goskompriroda, *Sostoyanie . . . v 1988 g.*, p. 69; USSR Goskomstat, *Narodnoe khozyaistvo SSSR v 1988 g.* (Moscow: Finansy i statistika, 1989), p. 444; USSR Central Statistical Agency, *Narodnoe khozyaistvo SSSR v 1970 g.* (Moscow: Statistika, 1971), p. 339.

32. USSR Goskomstat, *Narodnoe khozyaistvo SSSR v 1988 g.*, pp. 676–677.

33. USSR Goskompriroda, *Sostoyanie . . . v 1988 g.*, p. 74.

34. *Svenska Dagbladet*, July 29, 1990, translated in FBIS-SOV-89-161, p. 53.

35. *Sel'skaya zhizn'*, November 10, 1988, p. 2.

36. Ibid.; also *Sel'skaya zhizn'*, February 17, 1989, p. 2.

37. Central Intelligence Agency, *Handbook of Economic Statistics, 1985* (Washington, DC: Government Printing Office, 1985), p. 165; USSR Goskomstat, *Narodnoe khozyaistvo SSSR v 1988 g.*, pp. 674–675.

38. USSR Goskomstat, *Okhrana okruzhayushchei sredy*, p. 99; USSR Goskomstat, *Sel'skoe khozyaistvo SSSR* (Moscow: Finansy i statistika, 1988), p. 114.

39. *Sel'skaya zhizn'*, March 28, 1989, p. 2.

40. *Pravda*, January 29, 1990, p. 3.

41. *Turkmenskaya iskra*, April 27, 1990, p. 2.

42. Storage space for 2,284,400 tons of agrochemicals built with government and kolkhoz funding was inaugurated in 1986. The figure fell to 1,988,600 and 1,589,300 in 1987 and 1988, respectively. USSR Goskomstat, *Press-vypusk*, No. 168, April 22, 1989.

43. *Pravda*, May 25, 1989, p. 2.

44. *Pravda*, January 29, 1990, p. 3.

45. Milashchenko, "Solving Ecological Problems," p. 59.

46. USSR Goskomstat, *Okhrana okruzhayushchei sredy*, p. 99.

47. A. F. Kosenko, "Integrated Protection: Conditions and Prospects," *Zashchita rastenii*, No. 10, 1989, translated in JPRS-UEA-90-004, p. 52.

48. USSR Goskomstat, *Okhrana okruzhayushchei sredy*, p. 99.

49. *Ekonomika i zhizn'*, No. 13, 1990, p. 6.

50. *Literaturnaya gazeta*, No. 34, 1989, p. 12.

51. *Pravda vostoka*, November 21, 1989, p. 3.

52. USSR Goskompriroda, *Sostoyanie . . . v 1989 godu*, pp. 59, 69–70, 107.

53. USSR Ministry of Foreign Economic Relations, *Vneshnie ekonomicheskie svyazy SSSR v 1989 g.* (Moscow: Finansy i statistika, 1990), p. 30; USSR Ministry of Foreign Economic Relations, *Vneshnie ekonomicheskie svyazy SSSR v 1988 g.* (Moscow: Finansy i statistika, 1989), p. 27; USSR Ministry of Foreign Economic Relations, *Vneshnyaya torgovlya SSSR v 1987 g.* (Moscow: Finansy i statistika, 1988), p. 27.

54. Kukhar', "Nekotorye," p. 109.

55. Zeev Wolfson, "'Nitrates'—A New Problem for the Soviet Consumer," *Report on the USSR*, No. 20, 1989.

56. Bobylev, "APK," p. 17.

57. USSR Goskomstat, *Okhrana okruzhayushchei sredy*, p. 101.

58. USSR Goskompriroda, *Sostoyanie . . . v 1989 godu*, p. 109.

59. Bobylev, "APK," p. 20.

60. USSR Goskompriroda, *Sostoyanie . . . v 1989 godu*, p. 107.

61. *Argumenty i fakty*, No. 13, 1989, p. 2.

62. Bobylev, "APK," p. 16.

63. Yablokov, "The Current State," p. 5.

64. *Literaturnaya gazeta*, No. 21, 1989, p. 12.

65. *Argumenty i fakty*, No. 13, 1989, p. 2.

66. In accordance with USSR State Sanitary Code No. 42-123-4616-88, permissible nitrate (NO_3) concentrations for potatoes were increased from 80 to 250 milligrams per kilogram; for cabbage from 150 to 500 milligrams per kilogram; and for tomatoes from 60 to 150 milligrams per kilogram. The permitted concentration in onions was increased from 60 to 80 milligrams per kilogram; that for beets was unchanged. Kaunas Economics Institute, "Urgent Ecological Problems in Lithuania," briefing submitted to the Lithuanian Council of Ministers, unpublished manuscript, November 1988, pp. 36–39; Bobylev, "APK," p. 17.

67. *Komsomol'skaya pravda*, December 22, 1989, p. 2.

68. *Moskovskaya pravda*, January 16, 1990, p. 2. The findings in the article were then corroborated by USSR Goskompriroda chair Nikolai Vorontsov. *Moskovskaya pravda*, January 18, 1990, p. 1.

69. Fedor Dainenko, chief engineer, Kuryanovo Wastewater Treatment Plant, personal communication, Moscow, June 1991.

70. *Sel'skaya zhizn'*, March 28, 1989, p. 2.

71. Kuchushev and Matveev, "Sokhranit' zdorov'e zemli," p. 36.

72. Petr I. Poletaev, "Vosstanovit' garmoniyu prirody i cheloveka," *Zdorov'e*, No. 6, 1989, p. 1.

73. USSR Goskomstat, *Narodnoe khozyaistvo SSSR v 1990 g.* (Moscow: Finaury i statistika, 1991), p. 447.

74. USSR Goskomstat, *Narodnoe khozyaistvo SSSR v 1990 g.*, p. 448.

75. Kosenko, "Integrated Protection," p. 49.

76. USSR Goskompriroda, *Sostoyanie . . . v 1989 godu*, p. 110.

77. USSR Goskomstat, *Okhrana okruzhayushchei sredy*, p. 99.

78. Hamida and Rafael Yernazarov, staff members, Kazakh Ecological Fund, personal communication, Los Angeles, April 1992.

79. For more reporting on the market for organic food, see, for example, *Pravda*, August 8, 1989, p. 2; and *Izvestiya*, September 11, 1988, p. 2.

80. TASS, December 21, 1989.

81. *Sel'skaya zhizn'*, November 10, 1988, p. 2.

82. *Pravda vostoka*, October 21, 1991, p. 2.

83. The Aral region (in Russian, Priaralye) is generally considered by commentators to include Kazakhstan's Kzyl-Orda oblast, the Karakalpak republic (Karakalpakistan) and Khorezm oblast in Uzbekistan, and Turkmenistan's Tashauz oblast.

84. Known padding of production figures aside, the output of raw cotton in Uzbekistan grew from 2.9 million tons in 1960 to 5.4 million tons in 1988. The corresponding figures for Turkmenistan are 363,000 tons and 1.3 million tons. USSR Central Statistical Agency, p. 319; USSR Goskomstat, *Narodnoe khozyaistvo SSSR v 1988 g.*, p. 455. Overall agricultural production grew four times (in value terms) between 1950 and 1988. *Sobranie postanovlenii pravitel'stva Soyuza Sovetskikh Sotsialisticheskikh Respublik*, No. 33, 1988, p. 563.

85. USSR Goskompriroda, *Sostoyanie . . . v 1988 g.*, p. 117.

86. USSR Goskompriroda, *Sostoyanie . . . v 1989 godu*, p. 95.

87. K. S. Losev, "Sotsial'no-ekonomicheskie i ekologicheskie posledstvia ispol'zovaniya vody: vozmozhnye puti razvitiya," *Izvestiya Akademii Nauk SSSR, seriya geograficheskaya,* No. 6, 1988, p. 49; Michael A. Rozengurt, "Water Policy Mismanagement in the Southern USSR: The Ecological and Economical Impact," National Council for Soviet and East European Studies, November 1989, pp. 48–49.

88. *Pravda vostoka,* November 21, 1989, p. 3.

89. *Komsomolets Uzbekistana,* July 26, 1989; David R. Smith, "Salinization in Uzbekistan," *Post-Soviet Geography,* January 1992, p. 30.

90. Smith, "Salinization in Uzbekistan," p. 22.

91. USSR Goskompriroda, *Sostoyanie . . . v 1988 g.,* p. 131.

92. David R. Smith, "Growing Pollution and Health Concerns in the Lower Amu Darya Basin, Uzbekistan," *Soviet Geography,* October 1991, p. 560.

93. Ibid., p. 556.

94. TASS, June 14, 1990; Grigorii Reznichenko, "I stakana chistoi vody ne pribavilols'," *Novy mir,* No. 1, 1990, p. 202.

95. *Argumenty i fakty,* No. 51, 1989, p. 4; Radio Moscow, November 23, 1990. For more on the region's health problems, see Annette Bohr, "Health Catastrophe in Karakalpakistan," *Report on the USSR,* No. 29, 1989; *Meditsinskaya gazeta,* May 23, 1990; and *Sem'ya,* No. 19, 1990.

96. Philip Micklin, "Touring the Aral: Visit to an Ecologic Disaster Zone," *Soviet Geography,* February 1991, p. 94; TASS, July 18, 1991.

97. USSR Goskompriroda, *Sostoyanie . . . v 1989 godu,* p. 6.

98. For the text of the resolution, consult "O merakh po korennomu uluchsheniyu ekologicheskoi i sanitarnoi obstanovki . . . ." Incidentally, the committee that drafted the plan was headed by the chair of the USSR State Committee for Hydrometeorology, Yurii Izreal'.

99. TASS, June 14, 1990.

100. *Pravda,* October 15, 1991.

101. In 1989, the Uzbek government began construction of a 400-kilometer diversion canal to run parallel to the Amu Darya. TASS, December 16, 1989. Plans have been in the works for a 1,500-kilometer canal extending all the way up to Termez on the Afghan border. N. T. Kuznetsov, "Otkrytoe pis'mo uchenym, pisatelyam, vodokhozyaistvennikam, vsem, kogo volnuet ekologicheskaya situatsiya v Priaral'ye," *Izvestiya Akademii Nauk SSSR, seriya geograficheskaya,* No. 6, 1988, p. 130.

102. By the 1980s, however, Uzbekistan ranked lowest in the Soviet Union in consumption of vegetables, fruit, meat, and milk. Gregory Gleason, "'Birlik' and the Cotton Question," *Report on the USSR,* No. 24, 1990, p. 22.

103. John Stead, Dunavant Enterprises, Inc., presentation at conference on Central Asian Development in the Future, Scottsdale, Arizona, June 1992.

104. *Pravda,* April 20, 1990, p. 1.

105. Reznichenko, "I stakana," p. 204.

106. Lester R. Brown, "The Aral Sea: Going, Going . . . ," *WorldWatch,* January–February 1991, p. 27.

107. *Pravda vostoka,* June 6, 1990, p. 4.

108. *Pravda vostoka,* January 4, 1990, p. 3. For a rebuttal by the leaders of the Committee to Save the Aral, see *Pravda vostoka,* January 19, 1990, p. 3.

109. *Pravda vostoka,* October 21, 1991, p. 2.

110. *Economist,* September 21, 1991, p. 59.

111. Brown, "The Aral Sea," p. 23.

112. *Guardian,* November 9, 1990.

5

Solid and Hazardous Waste

The basic policy used to be to collect basically everything in sight and send it away—
the farther away the better.
—Moscow city offical responsible for hazardous waste, 1991

Rain is expected. Background [radiation] is normal.
—Voronezh Weather Forecast

In January 1990, *Trud* reported that an ampule emitting dangerous levels of gamma radiation had been found in a heap of scrap metal located on the grounds of the Vtorchermet Production Cooperative in the Tajik capital of Dushanbe. The ampule was discovered by specialists conducting a routine survey of radiation levels across the republic. The report did not say whether anyone was affected by the radiation, but noted that contact with the ampule for just two or three hours would have caused radiation sickness and eventual death. How and when the ampule got there was unclear. Such ampules had been produced decades before for use in devices to monitor the water level in reservoirs, but they had not been registered anywhere, there had been no monitoring of their radioactivity, and no provision had been made for their proper disposal.[1]

Two months later, the Soviet government made an unusual concession to farmers in Kazakhstan: It promised to clear away space debris that had accumulated on their fields.[2] According to *Pravda*, 5,000 tons of metal debris—the remains of rockets launched from the USSR's Baikonur cosmodrome—had fallen on the republic over the past thirty years, creating "a considerable obstacle to agriculture."[3] Two months later, a similar program was launched to clean up rocket debris that had fallen on the tundra from launches at the Plesetsk military cosmodrome near

Arkhangelsk. The military promised that from then on, "painstaking efforts" would be made to clean up after every rocket launch.[4]

These two events epitomize the paradoxical situation of solid waste management in the Soviet era: The USSR made great strides in producing many of the sophisticated and high-technology goods of an advanced industrialized society, but planners failed to develop a suitable and environmentally sound means to dispose of the associated high-tech by-products. Once created, waste was allowed to fall where it would.

Essentially, the issue of solid waste was treated as an afterthought for which little provision was made and for which few people were prepared to take responsibility. Of all the threats to the environment in the region, solid wastes, and particularly hazardous wastes, were the least documented. As a consequence of this ignorance, they may prove to be the most dangerous threat—to humans as well as to the environment. "Today, the most acute problem is neutralizing, utilizing, and disposing of hazardous industrial wastes," Fedor Morgun, former chairman of USSR Goskompriroda, told the weekly *Argumenty i fakty* in 1989. "The main trouble is that instead of reprocessing and utilization, it is being carted off to dumps in increasing quantities. As a result, not only the soil but also the groundwater are being polluted. This is having a direct effect on people's health."[5] One year later, the Collegium of the USSR Prosecutor's Office convened to look into the problem, and its conclusions were similarly pessimistic. The group noted that established regulations governing the disposal and decontamination of industrial and hazardous wastes were "not being adhered to strictly" and that "environmental laws were often grossly violated." Such a state of affairs moved the Collegium, like Morgun, to assert that hazardous waste was "the sharpest problem" threatening the land and groundwater and, therefore, people's health.[6]

REPORTING ON WASTE ISSUES

Despite the magnitude of the problem, the issue of solid waste disposal has not commanded the level of public attention that other environmental issues, such as water and air pollution, have received. Reporting on waste disposal in the media, as illustrated in the anecdotes in this chapter, largely has been limited to stories about the discovery of illegally dumped hazardous wastes. One reason may be that the issue of solid waste management does not have the dramatic appeal of, say, the desiccation of the Aral Sea or the threat to Lake Baikal. Another factor is that unlike the United States or western Europe, most of the territory of the former Soviet Union has huge expanses of open space that provide great opportunities to conceal discarded wastes, making the problem less visible to the public than other forms of environmental pollution. Government officials themselves often reveal their lack of knowledge of the generation and fate of solid wastes, as appropriate data have not been collected. Commenting on his first months as chief of the new environment agency, Morgun observed in 1988:

> Recently, I asked leading specialists at Goskompriroda what would seem like an elementary question: "What is the volume, even the approximate amount, of urban household and industrial solid waste in our country?" No one could give an approximate figure, let alone an exact one. No one in the country ever had made such an estimate.[7]

The Soviet government took a belated step to remedy the situation in May 1990 when the USSR Council of Ministers Commission on Emergency Situations ordered state ministries to conduct a one-time inventory of the hazardous wastes they produced.[8] Oblast governments in Ukraine had begun to register and classify commercial wastes the previous year, but officials found that "some managers, risking liability, continue to conceal the quantity and type of wastes" their firms produced, reported *Stroitel'naya gazeta*.[9] In 1989, the Moscow city government formed Ekotekhprom, a public concern to build and operate hazardous waste treatment facilities for the city. Lacking sufficient information, managers of the firm decided first to inventory the types of wastes being generated in the city so that they could then determine how best to handle them.[10]

Finally, data on wastes produced by the military-industrial complex— wastes that in the West have proved to be some of the most dangerous and most problematic to treat and dispose of—were hidden by the veil of secrecy that obscured all defense activities under the Soviet regime. Environmentalists frequently charged that military officials classified information on hazardous waste to prevent public access to damaging reports. The desire for secrecy on this issue is understandable because the military feared a public backlash if its actions were disclosed.

In the summer of 1989, citizens rapidly organized and blocked the opening of the military's new chemical weapons–destruction facility in the central Russian city of Chapaevsk (see Chapter 7). Ongoing protests likewise have threatened the completion of a nuclear waste treatment and storage facility near Krasnoyarsk. Reports of the alleged dumping of chemical weapons and radioactive waste in the Kara and Barents seas have stirred public controversy in Murmansk and Arkhangelsk. On the Pacific coast, citizens have challenged the navy's plans to dismantle nuclear-powered submarines.

Often it is only after calamity strikes that a problem is unveiled and citizens are forced to confront the waste hazards accumulating in their own backyards. In May 1990, *Rabochaya tribuna* (Labor Tribune) reported that three coal mines in the eastern Ukrainian town of Gorlovka were closed after fifty miners were poisoned by a bluish substance seeping into a mine shaft at the Uglegorskaya mine.[11] This was not the first such incident in the region; the preceding December, three miners had died and hundreds of others had fallen ill after toxic chlorobenzene had seeped into a shaft at the nearby Aleksandr-Zapad mine. Preliminary tests indicated that chlorobenzene, benzene, styrene, phenol, acetone, and other compounds were present in the Uglegorskaya mine, and suspicion immediately was directed at a defense ministry explosives plant located 600 meters directly above.

A crew from the evening news program "Vremya" was allowed to visit the grounds of the secret defense plant and managed to take pictures of several evaporation ponds filled with toxic wastes. Standing before the foul-looking lagoons, Deputy Minister of the Defense Industry N. G. Puzyrev flatly denied that his plant was the cause of the miners' troubles, asserting that no toxic chemicals were being produced at the site. He did not, however, say they were not being used there.[12] Within several weeks, a special investigative commission revealed that waste from the plant had been "indiscriminately discarded for decades." Formaldehyde leaking from the plant combined with toxic wastes percolating through the soil to create the potent poison that struck down the miners.[13] According to Nikolai Surgai, chairman of an investigative commission sent to the region by the Ukrainian government, the mixture resulted in a concoction of 1,500 various compounds, "some of which were previously unknown."[14] None of the plant's managers was prosecuted for the incident, but the formaldehyde operation was scheduled to be shut down.[15] According to *Trud*, the situation, if not rectified, threatened the drinking water supplies of nine cities in Donetsk and Lugansk oblasts.[16]

Incidents such as these have produced fear in the bureaucracy of continued upheavals. Thus, government and military officials alike have been slow to release data on the generation and fate of hazardous wastes in the post-Soviet era.

EXAMINING THE WASTE STREAM

Given the lack of available data, it remains impossible to say conclusively how much waste the region's economies produce, how it is treated, or where it is disposed. According to a 1988 estimate by economist Nikolai Pirogov, a USSR Gosplan official responsible for recycling programs, the generation of solid wastes from all sources was approximately 9 billion tons annually.[17] This estimate probably included all forms of waste—from domestic and commercial refuse to wastes from industry, agriculture, and mining.

The most comprehensive official information published on solid wastes concerns common household refuse, or *bytovye otkhody*.[18] Because of the slow pace of innovation and the otherwise much-criticized neglect of the consumer goods and service sectors of the Soviet economy, the USSR did not experience an explosion of waste from surplus goods, elaborate packaging, and disposable products. Indeed, persistent shortages of such basics as paper, glass, plastic, and even food promoted a tradition of conservation at the individual level. Basically stated, consumers did not have much to waste. As a result, the Soviet economy produced an average of only 56–57 million tons of domestic and commercial waste a year in the late 1980s,[19] or about 195 kilograms of waste per capita.[20] Output ranged widely within the USSR—according to one report, from 160 to 240 kilograms per capita.[21]

In comparison, the United States (the world's greatest trash producer) created about 163 million tons annually, equaling about 655 kilograms per capita.[22] Table 5.1 illustrates the differences in the waste stream between the United States and the Soviet Union in the late 1980s. Of note is the large share of Soviet waste classified as food products, despite perennial food shortages. This phenomenon can be attributed to two factors: a smaller volume of plastic, paper, and metal discarded (a function, in part, of modest packaging practices) and a large share of food wasted in the processing and transport phase of the food chain.

In contrast, problems with industrial wastes are much more acute. The Soviet economy was notorious for its inefficiency, and inefficiency bred waste. Correspondingly, discussion of industrial wastes in the Soviet Union generally was framed in terms of resource conservation. In 1989, for example, mining and refining activities in the coal, fertilizer, building materials, and metal industries used just 39 percent of materials extracted, producing about 2 billion tons of detritus and costing the economy 6 billion rubles in lost resources.[23] Soviet metal refiners produced another 100 million tons of slag yearly.[24] The metal-working industry annually scrapped over 100 million tons of steel and iron—one-fifth of its input. Half of the scrap was composed of swarf because metal castings produced by Soviet enterprises tended to be very rough in form and this required extensive milling and grinding to bring a piece down to specification.[25]

TABLE 5.1 Comparison of U.S. and USSR municipal solid waste generation, disposal, and recovery, 1988

	United States	Russian Federation
Annual waste generation		
Total (million metric tons)	162.9	56.0[a]
Per capita (kilograms)	655	195[a]
Generation of waste by category (percent)		
Paper and cardboard	40.0	20–36
Glass	7.0	5–7
Metals	8.5	2–3
Plastics	8.0	3–5
Textiles	2.1	3–6
Rubber and leather	2.5	1.5–2.5
Wood	3.6	1–4
Food	7.4	20–38
Other	20.9	10–35.5
Disposal methods (percent)		
Recovery	13.1	1.3[a]
Incineration	14.2	2.2[a]
Landfilling	72.7	96.5[a]

[a] 1989 data for the Soviet Union.

Sources: Adapted from U.S. Bureau of the Census, *Statistical Abstract of the United States: 1991* (Washington, DC: Government Printing Office, 1991), p. 212. USSR Goskompriroda, *Sostoyanie prirodnoi sredy v SSSR v 1988 g.* (Moscow: VINITI, 1989), p. 64; USSR Goskompriroda, *Sostoyanie prirodnoi sredy i prirodookhrannaya deyatel'nost' v SSSR v 1989 godu* (Moscow: Institut Molodozhi, 1990), p. 32; TASS, May 21, 1990.

In Ukraine's coal-producing regions, industrial waste assumed particularly large proportions during the Soviet era. Mining operations occupied a total of 270 square kilometers of land in the republic—one-fifth of which has been marred by excavation and by more than 1.2 billion cubic meters of tailings and overburden, piled up in 1,600 heaps.[26] Loggers across the USSR discarded a reported 60 million tons of wood as waste at felling sites, and the timber industry scrapped 100 million cubic meters of wood yearly in the 1980s, bringing total losses in processing to 40 percent.[27] Similar problems faced agriculture: High rates of spoilage and waste during harvesting, storage, transport, and processing translated into at least one-third of the fruit and vegetable crops never making it to the Soviet dinner table. Similarly, 20–25 percent of the Soviet wheat crop and 10–15 percent of meat and dairy production traditionally was lost in processing.[28] The problem with industrial waste grew to such proportions that the Soviet government attempted to use nuclear devices to create artificial craters in which to dump wastes from the Bashkir metallurgical centers of Sterlitamak and Salavat.[29]

Comprehensive data on the generation of hazardous waste were a closely guarded secret under the Soviet regime because many firms that created the waste were part of the defense industry. In 1990, the Soviet government conducted its first comprehensive accounting of toxic waste inventories and producers and pegged total output of toxic waste *(toksicheskie otkhody)* at 302 million tons that year—roughly equal to the volume created in the U.S., according to Soviet calculations. According to this survey, 80 percent of the toxic waste was generated by metallurgical enterprises (see Table 5.2).[30] Table 5.3 illustrates the volume of waste generated by type, according to the 1990 study.

METHODS OF WASTE DISPOSAL

To paraphrase Gosplan's Pirogov, the attitude of most managers under Soviet central planning was that wastes were not the problem of those who created them. This mentality was reinforced by the uneven

TABLE 5.2 Generation and disposal of toxic waste by sector, 1990[a]

Sector	Volume Generated (thousands of metric tons)	Percent Recovered and Safely Disposed
Total	302,083	11.85
Ferrous and non-ferrous metals	241,500	9.8[b]
Construction materials	11,100	4.5
Fertilizer	7,200	9.5
Chemicals and petrochemicals	5,900	32.3
Energy	5,300	33.5
Automobiles and farm equipment	3,800	17.2
Lathes and instruments	1,600	7.3
Electronics	400	3.8
Pharmaceuticals	400	25.0
Coal	300	30.0
Heavy machinery	200	20.0
Other	22,583	26.5[b]

[a]Based on a survey of 10,300 enterprises. Data do not include air emissions or wastewater discharge to surface water.

[b]Approximate.

Source: USSR Goskomstat, *Okhrana okruzhayushchei sredy i ratsional'noe ispol'zovanie prirodnykh resursov* (Moscow: Informtsentr Goskomstata SSSR, 1991), p. 130.

TABLE 5.3   Generation and disposal of toxic waste by type, 1990[a]

Waste Type	Volume Generated (thousands of metric tons)	Percent Recovered or Safely Disposed
Total	302,083	11.85
Lead and lead compounds	44,292	4.0
Nickel and nickel compounds	25,298	6.0
Arsenic and arsenic compounds	4,785	0.3
Inorganic fluorine compounds	1,816	0.8
Hexavalent chromium compounds	1,002	30.0
Waste from galvanic processing	958	26.0
Used solvents	205	22.0
Phenols and phenol compounds	197	53.0
Expired chemicals and pesticides	17	53.0
Mercury and mercury compounds	8	4.0
Other	222,752	14.1

[a] Based on a survey of 10,300 enterprises. Data do not include air emissions or waste-water discharge to surface water.

Source: USSR Goskomstat, *Okhrana okruzhayushchei sredy i ratsional'noe ispol'zovanie prirodnykh resursov* (Moscow: Informtsentr Goskomstata SSSR, 1991), p. 131.

manner in which the Soviet economy developed. Central planners ensured that the economy produced goods expected of an advanced industrialized economy, and little attention was paid to the environmental consequences of such production—in particular, to the proper handling and disposal of waste. Lacking strict regulation, Soviet enterprises did not have to pay appreciable costs to dispose of their waste material output. Thus, the Soviet Union acted as a major industrial power that managed its waste disposal as do less-developed nations.

According to Soviet practice, almost all solid wastes were landfilled, yielding an estimated total of over 50 billion tons of waste piled up on land occupying 1,400 square kilometers.[31] According to the government's 1990 survey mentioned above, the volume of toxic wastes accumulated totaled 6.7 billion tons.[32] Yet over half of the almost 6,000 official municipal and industrial landfills monitored by the Soviet government did not meet public health norms at the end of the 1980s. More than three-quarters of the landfills in noncompliance were located in Uzbekistan, Georgia, Moldova, Latvia, and Turkmenistan.[33] Commenting on urban landfills in Russia, USSR Goskompriroda concluded that "The majority . . . are in an unsatisfactory condition; substances from wastes get into the soil and contaminate ground and surface water." In Latvia, for instance, leaching chemicals contaminated groundwater in a radius of up to 1.5 kilometers from landfills serving Riga, Jurmala, Daugavpils, and other cities. In addition to the poor preparation of landfills, contamination problems have been exacerbated by a lack of heavy machinery (such as crawlers and scrapers) to grade, compact, and cover the waste properly.[34]

In March 1990, *Sovetskaya kul'tura* (Soviet Culture) featured a story about the dismal fate of Ilinka, a small town encircled by the ash heap of a power plant and by a landfill serving the Far Eastern city of Khabarovsk. An investigation after a fatal accident at the site revealed that the landfill had been operating unmonitored for almost twenty years. Both domestic and industrial wastes—often containing dangerous and toxic substances—were being dumped indiscriminately. The city of Khabarovsk spent no money to ensure that the landfill was operated in a safe manner, and though a cooperative enterprise had been put in charge of the landfill in 1989, the incoming refuse continued simply to be raked about, without any attempt to classify or process it. Residents living as close as three hundred meters from the landfill were threatened by swarms of insects, noxious fumes, and contaminants percolating through the soil. In the words of *Sovetskaya kul'tura:* "It seems that everything was done against common sense." The newspaper labeled the dump "a model ecological catastrophe," but it was quick to point out that the situation was not uncommon but rather "a gloomy symbol of what is happening all over the country."[35]

In February 1990, *Turkmenskaya iskra* (Turkmen Spark) filed the following report on a dump located ten kilometers outside of Ashkhabad, the republic's capital:

> The dump for common refuse begins far from its official boundaries. All around in a radius of about one kilometer, trash, scrap metal, and rags are scattered about. [Truck] drivers from industrial enterprises and even local residents do not drive up to the dump proper, but discard [rubbish] all about. One and one half kilometers from the site, homes stand in the village of Choganly. But the dump has no borders and, therefore, no sanitary zone. Trash is everywhere. But not simply common trash. People often illegally dump industrial wastes containing toxic substances . . . even though they should be disposed in specially arranged facilities.[36]

As alluded to in the preceding passage, the press has carried news stories about the frequent discovery of improperly disposed hazardous wastes. The picture pieced together from such reports is, in essence, one of enterprises dumping their wastes wherever and however it is conve-

In August 1992, officials in the Siberian oblast of Tomsk began testing a proto-
type incinerator for liquid hazardous wastes. In the background, construction of
the oblast's first hazardous waste treatment facility begins. Photo: DJ Peterson.

nient for them, with little monitoring by officials and no threat of prose-
cution for violation of environmental codes.

As in the case of the defense plant in Gorlovka, the general practice
among plant managers has been to let materials accumulate on-site indefinitely because the plants often lack access to officially permitted
treatment and storage facilities for wastes. A casual survey of the Soviet
industrial landscape reveals factory grounds littered with discarded
waste and disused equipment. In Kyrgyzstan, managers have no choice
in this matter: "The fact that we have no waste sites and store everything
in our factories is a serious problem," asserted one local parliamentarian
in 1991.[37] Industries with the greatest accumulation of toxic wastes on-
site include metal refining, asbestos, chemicals, electric power, and oil
refining.[38] An option for unscrupulous managers is illegal dumping off-
site; *Stroitel'naya gazeta* carried the following commentary on the subject:

> It is possible to cite numerous examples of enterprises surreptitiously
> carting away to dumps and ravines or releasing into the sewers or directly
> into the water table highly concentrated inorganic toxics and heavy metal

compounds, which migrate through the soil or water into our homes and into the food on the table. Indeed, how can it be any other way, when the public health service and committee for environmental protection still do not have lists of enterprises' wastes and their permissible concentrations? Spot checks reveal only the most grave violations.[39]

The Soviet government monitored about 6,000 landfills nationwide, but this clearly raises a question: How many dumps went unregistered or unmonitored? For obvious reasons, comprehensive data on illegal waste sites are unavailable, but the number probably runs into the thousands. The number of large abandoned dumps around Moscow alone has been estimated at about 100.[40] In the 1980s, the Russian capital averaged 6 million tons of industrial refuse generated yearly; of this, one-sixth was discarded untreated in unlicensed dumps because the waste did not meet the sanitary norms required for it to be deposited in landfills having proper permits.[41] The prime minister of Kyrgyzstan acknowledged in 1989 that in the republic's capital of Bishkek (formerly Frunze), "five hundred tons of highly toxic waste are stored without observing essential sanitary norms."[42] In its review of waste disposal practices, the Collegium of the USSR Prosecutor cited the chemical, petrochemical, electronics, and metallurgical industries as having the worst record for disposing of hazardous wastes. According to USSR Goskompriroda, metallurgical enterprises, the largest producers of hazardous waste, managed to "recycle or detoxify" (read incinerate or properly landfill) just 10 percent of the waste they produced.[43] As a result of such performance, the Soviet government estimated that every year enterprises illegally dump 170,000 tons of waste sludge derived from galvanic processing, 74,000 tons of petroleum-based waste, 39,000 tons of phenol compounds, and 11,000 tons of used solvents. In addition, illegally dumped hazardous wastes contained an estimated 688,000 tons of arsenic, 251,000 tons of chromium, 129,000 tons of nickel, and 41 tons of lead. Finally, the improper disposal of mercury vapor lamps alone added more than 11 tons of mercury to the environment.[44]

In 1972, the government began experimenting with waste incineration to a limited extent. Seven incinerators were built in Russia with imported technology and are located in Moscow (two plants), St. Petersburg, Vladimir, Nizhnii Novgorod (formerly Gorkii), Murmansk, Vladivostok, Sochi, and Pyatigorsk. Three have been built in Ukraine, in Kiev, Sevastopol, and Kharkov. About 2.3 percent of all solid wastes in the late 1980s was incinerated, compared with 14 percent in the United States.[45] More incinerators are under construction. Burning waste is a controversial issue, however: Although it helps alleviate the storage problem and can be used to generate steam, the by-products of incineration (fumes

Final preparation of an interim landfill for solid hazardous waste in Tomsk oblast. The facility was built to mitigate the large volume of waste improperly stored at local enterprises while construction proceeds on the oblast's treatment facility. Photo: DJ Peterson.

and ash), if not strictly controlled, can prove to be more of a pollution menace. Indeed, efforts to burn trash have resulted in serious problems: *Trud* reported that an incinerator located in the resort town of Sochi dumped wastes containing pollutants as high as 3,000 times the legal norm into the Black Sea.[46] Associated pollution control technologies were not purchased when the city of Moscow imported its two incinerators from France and Denmark; as a result, public health officials have required the incinerators to operate at low capacity in order to minimize their emissions.[47]

WASTE RECOVERY AND RECYCLING

Resource reclamation and recycling under the Soviet regime did not reach the scale found elsewhere in the world (see Table 5.1). The reasons for this lag are closely linked with the causes of the Soviet economy's resource intensiveness and inefficiency. In short, the extensive input orientation of Soviet development focused on the acquisition of virgin raw materials rather than on conservation and resource recovery—a policy reinforced by subsidized prices for such inputs that discouraged enterprises from seeking alternative, recyclable resources. This practice was sustained by the image of plenty in the minds of planners and managers: of limitless forests and huge, untapped reserves of coal, oil, and other natural resources. Finally, the cost of waste disposal was insignificant. Laws against illegal dumping were haphazardly enforced, and the maximum fine for violating environmental regulations averaged only 500–600 rubles.[48] Some enterprise managers found it expedient to pay repeated fines for violation of environmental laws rather than handle their wastes properly.[49]

As the waste accumulated, however, the inefficiencies dragged down the economy. The Soviet government attempted to correct the situation by using administrative means. In 1980, it enunciated the first of a series of resource conservation initiatives, a comprehensive and detailed resolution entitled "On Measures for the Long-Term Improvement of the Use of Recycled Materials in the National Economy." An excerpt illustrating the intent of the measure follows:

> With the goal of the long-term improvement in the use of recycled resources in the national economy, the USSR Council of Ministers resolves that:
>
> 1. USSR Gossnab [the USSR State Committee for Material and Technical Supply], USSR Gosplan, USSR ministries and organizations, the Councils of Ministers of the union and autonomous republics, the [executive committees] of the oblast, city, district, and rural soviets of People's Deputies, [and] managers of associations, enterprises, and organizations consider as [their] most important task the fundamental improvement of [their] work to organize the collection and most complete use of all forms of wastes from production and consumption, and also by-products, [and] that they consider the use of recycled resources to be an important reserve in increasing the effectiveness of social production.
>
> 2. By 1981, 1985, and 1990, USSR Gossnab [state supply agency], Tsentrosoyuz [rural trade organization], and the Councils of Ministers of the union republics implement the purchase of used paper, used textiles, used polymers, worn-out tires, and cullet in volumes as stipulated in Enclosure No. 1....[50]

The effort achieved some success: Between 1981 and 1987, the volume of recycled slag, wood, and paper increased by 30 percent, recycled petroleum products grew by 60 percent, and the volume of coal ash put to use increased by 80 percent. According to the state statistical agency, resource recovery efforts saved the economy from consuming an additional 55 billion rubles worth of raw materials during the 1986–1989 period.

Nevertheless, the disincentives to recycling prevailed, and the increase in resource recovery barely managed to outpace growth in consumption. During the 1980s, for example, the volume of wasted lumber left in forests increased by 40 percent, despite intensive conservation efforts in the logging industry.[51] Consequently, the overall "waste content" (*otkhodoemkost'*) of the Soviet economy declined by a mere 1.8 percent.[52] In its 1989 survey, USSR Goskompriroda estimated that coal- and oil-fired power plants produced 110 million tons of ash annually. Only 13 percent of this ash—largely that from plants burning oil shale in the Baltic region—was put to constructive use. The rest reportedly was land-filled.[53] For comparison, about 27 percent of the paper and cardboard in the Soviet Union was produced using recycled materials in the late 1980s, about the same rate as in the United States; in Hungary, Britain, and Japan the rate was over 50 percent.[54]

The modest achievements of the Soviet government's program can be attributed to its "command-administrative" nature that allowed detailed directives to be subverted easily by uncooperative ministries and enter-prises. Planning and plan fulfillment frequently were uncoordinated, prompting the ubiquitous Soviet-style production bottleneck. One such bottleneck created a "used-paper crisis" in the mid-1980s. In the 1980 law previously mentioned, the government mandated that all enterprises and government agencies collect their waste paper for recycling. But by mid-decade, it became apparent that not enough processing capacity could be brought on line in time to handle the mounting quantities of paper col-lected. "Every day a bonfire burns in the courtyard of our building," re-ported the editor of *Mayak kommunizma* (Beacon of Communism), a local newspaper in Perm oblast. "The recycling center is not accepting paper for recycling and we have nowhere to store it."[55]

In its attempts to teach good citizenship, the Communist Party drafted its army of youthful aspirants to help the government with its recycling efforts. Again, the command-administrative system took its toll; although marginally effective, the mandatory recycling drives, with their heavy political content, imbued weary participants with faint identity with their Soviet state or Communist Party and scant sympathy for nature. An engineer emigrating from St. Petersburg related the following anecdote to Radio Liberty in 1989:

> When our little granddaughter joined the Pioneers, she was instructed to gather 10 kilos of old paper, to sell 3–4 rubles worth of handicrafts (to be made by her), to take a bouquet of flowers to the Piskarev Cemetery, and to gather 80–100 kilograms of scrap metal. Since a small child could not do

this on her own, the task inevitably fell to us. We took the flowers to the cemetery, and the entire family went out collecting old books and newspapers which we took in two trips to the collection center. Rather than producing and selling the handicrafts, we simply gave our granddaughter three rubles. The toughest part was finding 80 kilos of scrap metal. We were fortunate enough to find an old iron bed in the street, but we had to pay a handyman to take it to the collection point.

Children were more zealous about recycling in Moscow, a mechanical engineer from the capital told Radio Liberty:

Although the idea is for the children to help clean up the city by gathering bits and pieces of discarded metal, they have realized that it is far less trouble to get hold of some large metal object. Since large metal objects generally are not left on the streets, the children simply steal them. I worked at a hardware accessories factory, and old presses and other metal parts always were left lying about under the awning in our yard. Pioneers would get into the yard through holes in the fences and steal everything they could. When I caught them, they said: "But these are being thrown out anyway." During these scrap metal drives, production dropped since factory workers had to be stationed as guards in the yard. The Pioneers also uncoupled the sidecar from my uncle's motorcycle and loaded part of the metal fence from his house on to it before pushing it to the collection point. . . . The [police] do not interfere in these incidents and simply tell us not to leave things without supervision.[56]

Other reports indicate that some resource recovery efforts may have been detrimental to the environment. An environmental group from the Ural Mountains city of Kirovgrad wrote *Trud* about an enterprise that recovered copper from old wiring:

The insulation is burned and the copper remains. During this procedure, phenol and hydrogen chloride are released into the air. The resulting levels by which this exceeds the maximum permissible concentration is simply fantastic—from 20- to 750-fold.[57]

The challenge of disposing of municipal waste will only increase in the future as economic reform gathers momentum in the post-Soviet era and the region's economies become commercialized. The end of government subsidies for raw materials will help provide effective stimulation to reduce unnecessary consumption of material inputs and to increase recycling and resource reclamation. After their legalization in 1987, the cooperative movement dramatically expanded the opportunity for recycling and resource recovery. In many instances, entrepreneurial workers at a state enterprise formed cooperatives to make use of valuable goods wasted at their place of work. In 1990, over 3,200 cooperative firms engaged in the production of everything from troughs for livestock farms to plastic packaging materials and toys, grossing over 1.2 billion rubles in the process.[58]

Despite these improvements, significant bureaucratic obstacles remained. Over years of operation, the Motorstroitel (Motorbuilder) enterprise, a Zaporozhye-based aircraft engine manufacturer, accumulated hundreds of tons of high-quality scrap metal. Motorstroitel had tried to sell the metal to local companies, including the state-owned Vtorchermet recycling enterprise, but the pieces were too big to comply with state standards and Motorstroitel had no means to cut up the scrap. In 1989, Motorstroitel negotiated a barter deal with an international-trading cooperative, Inzhener. In exchange for 200 tons of scrap metal, Motorstroitel received three Volvos, a Nissan microbus, 300,000 disposable syringes, and 1.2 million rubles. Amid claims that the firm had engaged in the "export of strategic minerals," it was charged with "destruction of socialist property" for illegally moving the scrap off its territory. After a two-year investigation involving the KGB, it was determined that Motorstroitel had not violated the law, and, indeed, the state netted a half million rubles on the deal.[59]

RADIOACTIVE WASTE

Although official data on solid wastes are scarce, official information on the generation and fate of radioactive waste is for the most part unavailable—first because of poor monitoring, but more important, because of military secrecy. Secrecy and "national security interests" spell bad news for the environment, as has become starkly evident to U.S. citizens who have recently learned of decades of mishaps at U.S. nuclear weapons facilities. It is reasonable to assume that the Soviet military establishment experienced similar problems with its nuclear weapons programs.

As part of the response to the Chernobyl accident, the government began monitoring background radiation levels at 2,200 stationary meteorological stations across Soviet territory. USSR Goskompriroda reported in 1989 that with the notable exception of the oblasts in the Russian Federation, Belarus, and Ukraine affected by Chernobyl, "the radiation situation does not differ substantially with background levels."[60] Published scientific studies also indicated that in the vicinity of nuclear power plants, radiation levels were within norm.[61] Despite this reassuring evidence, the Soviet media began to report isolated mishaps involving low- and medium-level wastes in 1989. Subsequent efforts by public health agencies to monitor radiation levels, often using detectors mounted on helicopters, uncovered even more problems. The anecdotal evidence brought forth to date suggests that the situation is alarmingly severe.

For example, in the town of Sillamae in northeastern Estonia, nearly 300 children attending two kindergartens suffered a loss of hair in 1989. When the story first broke in March of that year, the Soviet press agency, TASS, reported that specialists initially had suspected the cause to be natural radioactivity emanating from local shale deposits. Subsequent tests, however, revealed that background radiation in the town was normal. After months of speculation and controversy, the former director of the Baltiets enterprise, a local defense industry, revealed that his company had dumped radioactive wastes in the town. The two kindergartens were built over the dump, separated from it by only a thin layer of sand.[62]

In Kirovgrad, gravel from uranium mining was used for road construction, causing radiation levels to exceed health norms in twelve locations around the city.[63] In Brest, situated on the Polish-Belarusian border, a source of radiation was discovered only a few hundred meters from the ancient fortress located in the city center. Radiation levels in the area were reported in the media to be up to 900 microroentgens per hour—60 times greater than normal background levels. (The Soviet health standard is 18 microroentgens per hour.) Since the early 1960s, the location had been the site of a secret facility for transferring uranium ore coming into the Soviet Union from mines in Eastern Europe. According to Novosti Press Agency, the uranium arrived in open train cars and was transferred by hand "in a primitive fashion." In the autumn of 1989, the transfer facility was relocated outside of Brest, and some soil from the site was removed and discarded outside of town.[64]

Twenty-six "radiation-related accidents" were registered in the Turkmen capital of Ashkhabad in 1989, according to the republican newspaper *Turkmenskaya iskra*. Fourteen of these incidents involved the misplacing of instruments containing radioactive components. A worker at a local medical research institute discarded 238 vials containing radioactive residues. This was only one of seven such violations at the institute caused by a "casual attitude" toward handling radioactive materials and lax supervision by public health officials.[65] In the scientific research center of Novosibirsk, a helicopter survey of the city revealed 84 "radiation anomalies." Again many sources were determined to be components from instruments "mindlessly and recklessly thrown away." But other sources were "homemade"—enterprising locals had pilfered construction materials to build houses and the like. Why "hot" bricks, beams, and such items were radioactive was not explained. The city's chief health officer added:

From the helicopter water mains that at one time had carried radioactive pulp to a factory were discovered in the Zarya 1 truck farm cooperative near the settlement of Pashino. Many years ago a kilometer of pipe was stolen from an enterprise and sold to the cooperative. The gardeners watered their plots with radium-226 remaining in the pipes.[66]

In June 1990, "No Trespassing" signs appeared in Moscow's Izmailovskii Park warning passersby that decontamination work was under way in the area. As part of a routine survey, "acute sources of radiation" were detected. The reason: The popular park had served as a landfill for household and industrial wastes during the 1950s.[67] The park was not the only radioactive site found in the capital. Between 1982 and 1991, the Geo-ekotsentr concern, traversing the entire capital by car and by foot, discovered and eliminated approximately 600 radioactive sources. By 1991, only 15 remained to be decontaminated.[68] "As a result of someone's carelessness [or] negligence, many radioactive sources, which are used in many branches of industry, turn up now and then in the most unexpected places," commented a city council member studying the problem.[69] Included among those "unexpected places" were almost three-quarters of city schools: "Even experienced specialists were disturbed," noted *Rabochaya tribuna*.[70] The newspaper published a previously classified map of Geo-ekotsentr's work on its front page, creating a stir in the city (see Figure 5.1).

In most cases, the radioactivity was confined to an extremely small point and did not present a serious health hazard. But a half-hour exposure to a source at the upper end of the spectrum (2,570–2,570,000 millirems per year) could have produced a dosage in excess of the U.S. safety standard for one year.[71] Work with radioactive materials in Moscow dates back to the late 1940s, a period when there were no regulations governing the management of radioactive wastes. "People handled the problem simply," commented *Moskovsk Pravda*: "Into the dump truck and go a ways."[72] In many instances, radiation patches were found along city thoroughfares as well as highways leading out of Moscow,[73] but several sources also were discovered in residential districts. As the city rapidly grew outward in the postwar years, construction workers turned up long-forgotten dumps containing the hazardous materials.

Despite the number of radiation accidents in Moscow, the city does have radioactive waste disposal services. In 1990, the Radon Scientific

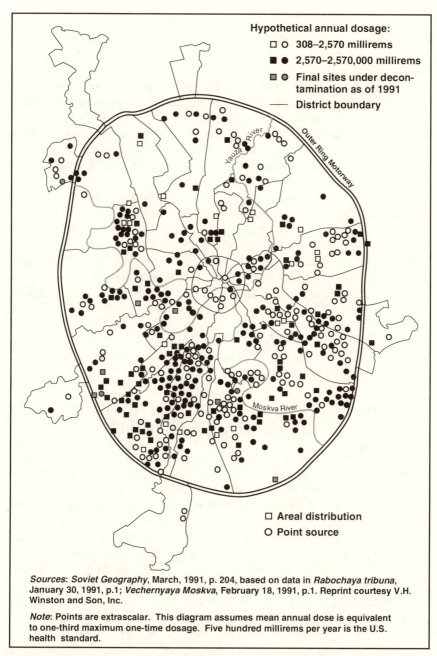

FIGURE 5.1 Mean annual biological gamma radiation dosage for Moscow at sites of above-mean background radiation.

Production Enterprise collected waste from over 1,300 businesses, research institutes, and hospitals in Moscow and neighboring oblasts. According to reports, the materials are trucked (with police escort) to a disposal facility near the city of Zagorsk where they are buried in lead and cement receptacles. Sixteen such facilities *(spetskombinat)* operated throughout Russia in 1990, and more were under development in Kazan, Ufa, and Chelyabinsk. The respected weekly *Pravitel'stvennyi vestnik* pointed out ominously, however, that many of Russia's storage facilities are "not sufficiently equipped with special technical equipment. They lack transport vehicles and measurement and dosimetric apparatuses."[74]

Notwithstanding Moscow's cleanup work—and there has without doubt been progress—uneasiness remains there and elsewhere about contaminated cities, and the media have been strong voices in the concern expressed. For example, in St. Petersburg, 1,500 radioactive "patches" were found, only a fraction of which have been decontaminated. "The situation is close to critical," reported Yu. N. Shchukin, chairman of the city's commission on radiation monitoring, in 1990. A radiation map of the city was drafted, but it was placed "under lock and key."[75] Reporting on the discovery of radioactive wastes in Tashkent oblast and Samarkand, a television newscaster mused, "Why are radioactive dumps multiplying?"[76] When it reported about a radiation incident at Dushanbe, *Trud* led with the query: "Is there a guarantee against 'micro-Chernobyls'?"

RADIOACTIVE WASTE: THE CASE OF THE SOVIET NUCLEAR WEAPONS COMPLEX

One partial answer to these questions is the fact that despite improvements in access to environmental information, glasnost in the Soviet era largely failed to penetrate the military-industrial complex. The prevailing shroud of secrecy was most opaque when it involved the core of the Soviet defense structure: nuclear weapons. Referred to only by their numerical postal abbreviations, entire cities involved in nuclear weapons production were closed to all but those who worked there. Three major facilities located east of the Ural Mountains in Russia produced material for Soviet nuclear weapons: Chelyabinsk-40, Krasnoyarsk-26, and Tomsk-7. In the haste to build up its nuclear weapons arsenal, the Soviet leadership was willing to take great risks and to sacrifice the environment as well as the public's health for the sake of national security. In the post-Soviet era, these nuclear cities have begun to emerge from behind the curtain and, in the process, have started to reveal their environmental woes. As one *Izvestiya* reporter concluded: "Nothing good came of the excessive secrecy."[77]

Five nuclear reactors at the Siberian Atomic Energy Station at Tomsk-7 produced nuclear material to be processed at the nearby Siberian Chemical Combine. The Tomsk-7 complex, located 15 kilometers northwest of the Siberian provincial center of Tomsk, first started operations in 1958 and served as the USSR's main processing facility in its waning years.[78] Over three decades, "127,000 tons of solid and 33 million cubic meters of liquid radioactive waste" produced at Tomsk-7 reportedly were stored underground in a sandy bed located 10–12 kilometers from the River Tom, a tributary of the Ob. According to the manager of the Siberian Chemical Combine (abbreviated Sibkhimkombinat), data on the radioactivity of buried wastes were classified, and total radioactivity in the region was unknown.[79]

Accusations of waste management problems at the complex date back at least to 1968, when a plant worker reported to the CPSU's Central Committee that managers had dumped "several tons of enriched atomic material into the reservoir."[80] At one point, a senior engineer responsible for monitoring the storage of "special produce" *(spetsproduktsiya)* reported radiation problems to General Secretary Leonid Brezhnev. Though A. Grigor'yev was rebuked for his bold action, officials apparently attempted to remediate the situation.[81] In 1991, workers at the Sibkhimkombinat alleged to *Izvestiya* that plant management had "discharged liquid radioactive wastes directly into the Tom for many years."[82]

In May 1990, *Izvestiya* reported that 38 people in Tomsk-7 were contaminated after consuming wild game tainted with radioactivity. Describing the situation as "very threatening," the newspaper noted that there were "contaminated reservoirs, open to all," including the wild game. A facility for storing radioactive wastes from the plant was not properly fenced off and allowed wild animals to enter the area. Whereas *Izvestiya* described the situation as a danger, local officials held to the traditional line: *Vse tam prekrasno* (everything there is fine).[83]

The Krasnoyarsk-26 complex, located on the Yenisei River 50 kilometers north of the central Siberian city of Krasnoyarsk, began to produce plutonium for Soviet warheads in the early 1950s.[84] Three reactors at the facility, known officially as the Order of Lenin Mining-Chemical Combine, were encapsulated in a massive cement structure 250 meters underground—secure from "a nuclear strike."[85] Despite these safety precautions, studies made thousands of kilometers to the north at the mouth of the Yenisei reportedly revealed high levels of radiation.[86]

Standing above Reactor No. 3 of the Order of Lenin Mining-Chemical Combine located at Krasnoyarsk-26. In December 1991, officials opened the top-secret site to a handful of local journalists and environmentalists in an effort to assure them of the facility's safety. Photo: Aleksandr Preobrazhenskii.

Another story, appearing in the environmental journal *Priroda i chelovek* (Man and Nature), alleged that gamma radiation levels in the Yenisei River at points below discharge from the Krasnoyarsk-26 facility were 120–150 times above normal.[87] Speaking with *Izvestiya* in November 1991, the director of Krasnoyarsk-26 denied any release of radiation resulting from an accident—a statement that did not rule out the possibility of radioactive by-products released as a part of regular operations.[88]

The tragic history of the Mayak enterprise near the city of Kyshtym in the Ural Mountains epitomizes the problem of handling nuclear waste and the potential for disaster. Mayak, located in the top-secret town of Chelyabinsk-40, formed the core of the early Soviet nuclear weapons program. Its reactors, code named "Object A" and "Object B," started operations in 1948. They were the first industrial reactors in the USSR and provided the material for its first atomic bomb, detonated the following August.[89] Between 1949 and 1952, "several million curies" of untreated high-, medium- and low-level radioactive wastes from processing work at Mayak were released directly into the Techa River, a tributary of the Ob. Intense radiation levels immediately caused widespread fish kills along the course of the Techa. Eventually, traces of radioactivity showed up in the Arctic Ocean—nearly 1,000 miles downstream. Sensing that "something was not right," in the measured words of Soviet Deputy Prime Minister Lev Ryabev, authorities fenced off the river with barbed wire and evacuated some 7,500 people from villages along its course.[90]

Next, the plant's directors decided to divert wastes from the plant into nearby Lake Karachai. Because the small lake lacked an outlet, it shortly accumulated radioactivity totaling 120 million curies. (By comparison, an estimated 50 million curies of radiation were released by the accident at Chernobyl.) Standing on the lake shores for an hour without protection would result in a lethal dose of radiation.[91]

Engineers turned to a third disposal method—a series of 16 underground storage tanks made of cement. But on September 29, 1957, the cooling system broke down in one tank holding 70,000–80,000 tons of radioactive sludge. An uncontrolled fission reaction ensued, resulting in a massive explosion that blew off the tank's cement lid and spewed 2.1

Yurii Pirogov, a local opponent of Krasnoyarsk-26, measures the radioactivity of silt taken from the Yenisei River near the outfall of cooling water from the reactor site. Photo: Vladimir Mikheev.

million curies of radioactive isotopes of cesium, ruthenium, and strontium as high as 1 kilometer into the atmosphere. The spray of radioactive
materials precipitated over a swath of land over 100 kilometers long in
Tyumen, Chelyabinsk, and Yekaterinburg (Sverdlovsk) oblasts—an area
marked by 217 settlements and inhabited by 270,000 people. Ten thousand people were permanently evacuated from some of the most
dangerous locations; entire villages were razed and their names removed
from the map.[92] Although the accident was the subject of a 1979 book by
dissident biologist Zhores Medvedev published in the West, the event
officially was confirmed by *Izvestiya* only in 1989—thirty-two years after
the incident.[93]

   In 1967, a severe drought plaguing the Ural Mountains region caused
the level of Karachai to drop and to expose radioactive materials on the
dry shores of the lake. Gusting winds subsequently picked up this material, dispersing 600 curies of cesium and strontium over about 2,000
square kilometers and affecting more than 40,000 people.[94] According to
Petr Somin, chair of the Chelyabinsk regional parliament, a total of
437,000 residents of the area were exposed to radioactivity as a result of
these mishaps, with chronic radiation sickness diagnosed in 935 cases.[95]

Radiation meter near village of Muslyumovo along the Techa River (Chelyabinsk
oblast, Russia) reads 0.4 millirem per hour in 1992, forty years after high-level
radioactive wastes were dumped in river. Photo: James Lerager.

Local environmental activists contend that in reality more people probably were afflicted over forty years of negligence, but doctors, while carefully studying victims' development, were forbidden to tell their patients that they had been exposed to radiation.[96]

In the 1970s, a new waste storage facility was constructed at Mayak, but even this facility reportedly has been prone to breakdowns of its cooling system and to regional power outages. Meanwhile, a half million tons of solid wastes have been buried in 200 "trench-type" storage facilities "lacking monitoring equipment."[97] The total radioactivity of liquid wastes confined in a parcel 30–40 square kilometers around Mayak has been pegged at 1 billion curies—20 times the radioactivity released by the Chernobyl accident.[98] Soil and groundwater down to a depth of 100 meters have been contaminated around Karachai, and the area of contamination has been spreading out at the rate of about 80 meters per year, threatening a reservoir supplying the city of Chelyabinsk.[99] In the late 1960s, workers started filling in Lake Karachai with rock and soil, and plant engineers expect to seal it over with concrete eventually by the mid-1990s, but a 1991 government commission concluded such an approach was "a crime" that threatened to exacerbate the leaching of radioactive isotopes into the groundwater.[100]

Before the USSR disintegrated, Soviet Deputy Prime Minister Ryabev claimed that 80 percent of the land contaminated by the explosion had been decontaminated and restored to "economic activity" by the end of the 1980s and that the remainder would be recovered by the middle of the 1990s. Forty years after the contamination of the Techa, *Moscow News* noted: "People continue to use the river and grow contaminated food which they eat themselves and ship to the city. Not a single large village has been evacuated, because it is too expensive to resettle large numbers of people. Only small villages were evacuated and people were offered flimsy prefab constructions to live in."[101]

To prevent the further spread of radioactivity down the Techa River, engineers built a series of dams in the region of Chelyabinsk-40 that created a cascade of several reservoirs. Today these reservoirs hold a total of 500 million cubic meters of radioactive water containing almost 200,000 curies of radioactivity. While the Mayak reactors were in operation, the contaminated water from these reservoirs was used as a coolant and through evaporation helped regulate their level. Now the reservoirs have become unstable, and many fear that without intervention, they may overflow their banks. To help resolve the situation, the nuclear power ministry started construction of the South Urals Atomic Energy Station in 1983.[102] Rising protests from around Chelyabinsk oblast, however, effectively stopped work on the project in 1989.

The official attitude toward nuclear waste characterized the general approach of the Soviet regime toward the environment: The vast reserve of nature was capable of accommodating and mitigating any form of pollution created by society. "Who knew it would turn out this way?" commented Mayak's chief engineer on the original decision to dump radioactive waste into the Techa:

> We reckoned that the river water would dilute the radionuclides to safe levels. We failed to take into account—we simply did not know—that the radioactivity would be absorbed by the silt on the bottom; it bound and concentrated two million curies of radioactivity in the upper course of the river. Knowledge about the atom among academics then was at the level of today's tenth graders.[103]

PUBLIC OPINION AND THE IMPLICATIONS FOR WASTE MANAGEMENT

The revelations under glasnost of such radiation catastrophes have led to a state of mind among the public dubbed "nuclear syndrome" and "radiophobia"—a state of mind characterized by the assumption that every health problem is related to radiation. "It seems that Novosibirsk is far away from Chernobyl," noted *Izvestiya*, "but two or three months cannot pass without a rumor circulating the city about some form of radiation [problem] here." When the meat ration in the Siberian city suddenly was raised from one to three kilograms per coupon, people were not happy but suspicious. Shoppers assumed the meat was radioactive because media reports had told of meat shipments originating from regions contaminated by Chernobyl. Tests by specialists reportedly revealed, however, that the food was not tainted.[104]

In May 1990, millions of dead starfish and other sea animals washed up on the beaches of the White Sea. Owing to the presence of several important navy bases in the region, speculation immediately focused there. Was the phenomenon the result of an accident aboard a nuclear submarine? Apparently not, concluded a team of investigators sent to the region, although the exact cause was not ascertained.[105] That summer, local residents concluded that suspicious tremors in the city of Dimitrovgrad were caused by the injection of liquid radioactive wastes into underground deposits on a reserve of the nearby Atomic Reactors Scientific Research Institute. A commission of international experts was called in to investigate; they concluded that the tremors were from explosions set off by prospectors searching for oil in the region.[106]

In Voronezh, the site of one of the oldest Soviet-built nuclear power stations, the local radio station broadcasts radiation levels during its morning weather forecast. Electronic signs installed on the city hall and train stations in Arkhangelsk indicate radiation levels in that city. Nevertheless, citizens remain skeptical and distrustful of such information. "Over the past two years, our newspaper has regularly informed its readers about background radiation in Moscow," noted the evening paper *Vechernyaya Moskva*. "If we do not mention a particular district for three or four days, distressed phone calls come pouring in from there asking: 'Did something happen here?'"[107] In the same way people in the United States engaged in a purchasing run on radon test kits in the 1980s, people in the former Soviet Union have been grabbing up as many radiation dosimeters as can be produced. After a profile of the Izotop enterprise and its "Bella" hand-held dosimeter appeared in a Ukrainian newspaper, the firm was inundated with orders—so many that it had to suspend accepting new orders for two years.[108] Despite these developments, only 5 percent of the population polled in 1990 expressed satisfaction with the amount of information available on radiation conditions.[109]

In a new effort to come to terms with the country's hazardous waste management problems, USSR Goskompriroda in 1990 called for the construction of special facilities "to store and to reprocess industrial toxic wastes," proposing that "no less than ten" be opened in Ukraine's Donets-Dnieper region alone by 2005.[110] Although these recommendations never were adopted by the Soviet government, they would have come under fire. Given past problems with the handling and disposal of hazardous wastes, citizens have organized to oppose the siting and operation of hazardous waste facilities in their communities. Similar to that in the West, oppposition in the former Soviet Union has been based on the "not in my backyard" argument, under which local residents see little benefit and great hazard from having such a facility located nearby. The demise of Soviet authority and the rise of citizen activism and regionalism have reinforced this trend.

For example, residents of the towns of Izhora and Tosno outside St. Petersburg have demanded the closure of the twenty-year-old Krasnyi Bor hazardous waste incinerator and storage facility, which serves 860 enterprises in the St. Petersburg region. The government had elaborated plans to increase the facility's processing capacity from 80,000 tons to 120,000 tons of toxic waste annually, but the local Izhora Green movement used the occasion to mount a vigorous opposition to Krasnyi Bor, citing the plant's numerous violations of existing environmental protection regulations.[111] In the provincial town of Zagorsk (renamed Sergiev Posad), the city council voted in 1989 to cancel a huge new facility proposed to process and store 100,000 tons of hazardous wastes per year. "The cleaning of Moscow at the cost of Zagorsk does not look very noble, especially since Zagorsk itself is in need of an ecological cleansing," wrote a group of residents.[112] The Kremlin had been considering siting a large nuclear waste storage facility on the Kola Peninsula. In the summer of 1990, the Murmansk oblast soviet asked Boris Yeltsin to move the project, scheduled to be completed in the mid-1990s, to the uninhabited island of Novaya Zemlya, site of a nuclear weapons test range.[113] In October 1990, the city soviet of nearby Arkhangelsk banned the production or import of any radioactive materials without the express consent of the local government; Arkhangelsk, they declared, was a "nuclear-free zone."[114]

At the First USSR Congress of People's Deputies, convened in May–June 1989, it was revealed that a decade-old secret project being built across the Yenisei from Krasnoyarsk-26 was to process and store wastes from commercial nuclear power plants. Initiated in the 1970s without public comment and consent, the project was planned to be the largest such facility in the world. As part of its operations, the reprocessing plant was to convert high- and low-level radioactive waste to liquid form to be pumped through a 2-kilometer pipeline (dubbed the "Krasnoyarsk subway") under the majestic Yenisei River and injected into a clay formation 700 meters underground on the other side. The reaction to the news of such a scheme being built near Siberia's largest city, with a population of over 1 million people, was "like an exploding bomb," wrote *Sotsialisticheskaya industriya*. Local authorities ordered an immediate halt to construction pending the outcome of an environmental impact study. Citizens' anger that such a project (estimated to cost 2 billion rubles) could be conceived and built under their backyards without prior consent virtually has ensured that it will not be completed as planned.[115]

The problem of nuclear waste disposal is exacerbated by the fact that the USSR was a waste importer. As part of its arrangements to build nuclear power plants in Eastern Europe, Finland, and Cuba, the Soviet government contracted to provide its clients with nuclear fuel and then to receive the spent material for reprocessing. Responding to citizens' accusations that Russia was being used as a nuclear waste dumping ground, the quasi–democratically elected Russian Congress of People's Deputies under the leadership of Boris Yeltsin passed a resolution calling for laws to be drafted prohibiting the burial of nuclear waste from abroad as well as from other Soviet republics.[116]

Public opposition to waste treatment and disposal schemes will force policymakers to reconsider the activities that contribute to the situation. The lack of ready disposal sites in Russia for radioactive waste, for in-

In 1989, opponents forced Krasnoyarsk officials to halt the construction of a top-secret facility, known as RT-2, ostensibly intended to reprocess spent nuclear fuel from civilian reactors. Photo: Vladimir Mikheev.

stance, may force Lithuania and Ukraine to reconsider their reliance on nuclear power in the long term. But this will not solve the problem of handling existing waste. In an attempt to overcome public resistance to the construction of a large-scale decontamination facility to handle the Chernobyl cleanup, Viktor Bar'yakhtar, chair of the Ukrainian Academy of Sciences, pointed out: "It's not worth questioning the necessity of such a beneficial complex; we can't do without it."[117] Writing on the Krasnyi Bor scandal, a commentator noted the alternative to having no treatment facility at all: "The one million tons [of waste treated] would have ended up in forests, rivers, lakes, and on the bottom of the Gulf of Finland."[118]

Notes

1. *Trud,* January 17, 1990, p. 3.
2. Radio Moscow, March 18, 1990.
3. *Pravda,* January 11, 1991, p. 3.
4. Radio Moscow, May 5, 1990.
5. *Argumenty i fakty,* No. 13, 1989, p. 1.
6. TASS, May 21, 1990.
7. "Vrachevat' rany zemli" (no author), *Politicheskoe obrazovanie,* No. 6, 1989, p. 34.
8. TASS, May 30, 1990.

9. *Stroitel'naya gazeta,* October 26, 1989, p. 2.

10. *Izvestiya,* July 26, 1989, p. 6. For more on Moscow's waste management program, see Semyon Feldman, "Digging for Gold," *Business in the USSR,* November 1990.

11. *Rabochaya tribuna,* May 8, 1990.

12. Central Television, "Vremya," May 10, 1990.

13. TASS, May 22, 1990; *Trud,* May 26, 1990.

14. *Izvestiya,* May 10, 1990, p. 6.

15. Central Television, "Vremya," May 22, 1990.

16. *Trud,* May 26, 1990. For more on the incident, see *Ogonek,* No. 26, 1990.

17. N. L. Pirogov, "Chto zhe delat' s otkhodami?" *Energiya: Ekonomika, tekhnika, ekologiya,* No. 12, 1988, p. 23.

18. The term *bytovye otkhody* (literally, everyday or domestic waste) is misleading. Although not defined, data on *bytovye otkhody* are probably based on the volume of waste collected by municipal services from residences and offices and from some commercial or industrial enterprises.

19. TASS, May 21, 1990. A figure of 56 million tons was cited at a meeting of the Collegium of the USSR Prosecutor's Office convened to examine problems with waste disposal. In its long-range environmental protection plan, USSR Goskompriroda pegged the volume at 57 million tons. *Ekonomika i zhizn',* No. 41, 1990, insert page 1.

20. The Russian economy produced 27 million tons of trash (about 48 percent of the Soviet total), or 186 kilograms per inhabitant. USSR Goskompriroda, *Sostoyanie prirodnoi sredy v SSSR v 1988 g.* (Moscow: VINITI, 1989), p. 66; USSR Goskompriroda, *Sostoyanie prirodnoi sredy i prirodookhrannaya deyatel'nost' v SSSR v 1989 godu* (Moscow: Institut Molodezhi, 1990), p. 32.

21. D. N. Ben'yamovskii and E. M. Bukreev, "Zavod dvoinogo naznacheniya," *Energiya: Ekonomika, tekhnika, ekologia,* No. 9, 1987, p. 29.

22. U.S. Bureau of the Census, *Statistical Abstract of the United States: 1991* (Washington, DC: Government Printing Office, 1991), p. 212.

23. USSR Goskompriroda, *Sostoyanie . . . v 1988 g.,* p. 82; USSR Goskomstat, *Press-vypusk,* No. 494, November 1, 1989.

24. Pirogov, "Chto zhe delat'," p. 23.

25. Ibid.; USSR Goskomstat, *Okhrana okruzhayushchei sredy i ratsional'noe ispol'zovanie prirodnykh resursov v SSSR* (Moscow: Finansy i statistika, 1989), p. 154; *Ekonomika i zhizn',* No. 6, 1990, p. 17.

26. *Ekonomika i zhizn',* No. 12, 1990, p. 14.

27. Pirogov, "Chto zhe delat'," p. 23; V. I. Naidenov et al., "Chem dal'she v les," *Energiya: Ekonomika, tekhnika, ekologiya,* No. 4, 1988, p. 17; *Ekologicheskaya gazeta,* Nos. 11–12, 1991, p. 6, cited in JPRS-TEN-92-008, p. 75. According to research conducted by USSR Gosplan, the Soviet forest products industry used just over one-quarter of all wood harvested. *Ekonomicheskaya gazeta,* No. 19, 1986, p. 2.

28. S. N. Bobylev and A. Sh. Khodzhaev, *Bor'ba s poteryami sel'skokhozyaist-vennoi produktsii,* cited in T. S. Khachaturov and K. V. Papenov, eds., *Effektivnost'*

prirodookhrannykh meropriyatii (Moscow: Izdatel'stvo Moskovskogo Universiteta, 1990), p. 80.

29. Radio Moscow, citing Interfax, February 21, 1990.

30. *Vestnik statistiki*, No. 11, 1990, p. 64. The study was conducted by USSR Goskomstat, USSR Goskompriroda, and the USSR Ministry of Health and covered 10,300 enterprises.

31. USSR Goskompriroda, *Sostoyanie* . . . *v 1988 g.*, p. 82; O. V. Gorbatyuk et al., "Fermentery geologicheskogo masshtaba," *Priroda*, No. 9, 1989, p. 72.

32. *Vestnik statistiki*, No. 11, 1990, p. 64.

33. USSR Goskomstat, *Okhrana okruzhayushchei sredy* . . . *v USSR*, p. 37.

34. USSR Goskompriroda, *Sostoyanie* . . . *v 1988 g.*, pp. 32, 34, 65.

35. *Sovetskaya kul'tura*, March 24, 1990, p. 4.

36. *Turkmenskaya iskra*, February 21, 1990, p. 4.

37. Anatolii Grebenyuk, deputy chair, Committee on Ecology, Supreme Soviet of Kyrgyzstan, presentation at conference on Democratic Federalism and Environmental Crisis in the Republics of the Former Soviet Union, Moscow, August 1991.

38. *Vestnik statistiki*, No. 11, 1990, p. 64.

39. *Stroitel'naya gazeta*, October 26, 1989, p. 2.

40. Feldman, "Digging for Gold," p. 96.

41. *Izvestiya*, July 26, 1989, p. 6.

42. *Sovetskaya Kirgiziya*, July 30, 1989, p. 2.

43. USSR Goskomstat, *Okhrana okruzhayushchei sredy i ratsional'noe ispol'zovanie prirodnykh resursov* (Moscow: Informtsentr Goskomstata SSSR, 1991), p. 130.

44. *Vestnik statistiki*, No. 11, 1991, p. 64.

45. USSR Goskompriroda, *Sostoyanie* . . . *v 1989 godu*, p. 32. U.S. Bureau of the Census, *Statistical Abstracts, 1991*, p. 212. Between 10 and 12 percent of refuse from Moscow is reportedly incinerated, Gorbatyuk et al., "Fermentery geologicheskogo," p. 72.

46. *Trud*, October 6, 1989, p. 4.

47. *European*, January 11, 1991.

48. Mikhail Galyatin, staff assistant, RSFSR Council of Ministers, presentation at conference on Democratic Federalism and Environmental Crisis in the Republics of the Former Soviet Union, Moscow, August 1991.

49. See, for example, *Stroitel'naya gazeta*, October 26, 1990, p. 2.

50. "O merakh po dal'neishemu uluchsheniyu ispol'zovaniya vtorichnogo syr'ya v narodnom khozyaistve," *Sobranie postanovlenii pravitel'stva Soyuza Sovetskikh Sotsialisticheskikh Respublik*, No. 7, 1980, pp. 163–172.

51. *Vestnik statistiki*, No. 11, 1991, p. 62. In 1990, 2.63 million cubic meters of lumber were discarded at the place of cutting.

52. Pirogov, "Chto zhe delat'," p. 24. Between 1981 and 1985, the volume of waste produced by the economy declined by more than 6 percent, but this improvement was largely negated in the following two years.

53. USSR Goskompriroda, *Sostoyanie* . . . *v 1988 g.*, p. 58. See also Khachaturov and Papenov, *Effektivnost'*, pp. 35–36.

54. USSR Goskomstat, *Okhrana okruzhayushchei sredy . . . v SSSR*, p. 156. It should be pointed out that until recently in the United States, the vast majority of recycled paper was made from scrap and defective goods that never made it out of the paper mills.

55. *Zhurnalist*, Nos. 2 and 11, 1986; No. 12, 1987; and No. 12, 1988.

56. Radio Liberty, Soviet Area Audience and Opinion Research, *Soviet Background Notes: Unevaluated Comments by Recent Emigrants*, SBN 4-89, May 1989, pp. 4–5.

57. *Trud*, January 18, 1990, p. 1.

58. *Vestnik statistiki*, No. 9, 1991, pp. 7–8. In 1990, cooperatives in the resource recovery sector accounted for 10–15 percent of all cooperatives and about 2 percent of total cooperatve income.

59. *Izvestiya*, June 28, 1991, p. 3.

60. USSR Goskompriroda, *Sostoyanie . . . v 1988 g.*, p. 35.

61. See, for example, A. E. Borokhovich and G. V. Shishkin, "Doza radiatsii po perimetru IAE im. I. V. Kurchatova," *Atomnaya energiya*, No. 5, 1990; and M. Ya. Chebotina et al., "Tritii v zone Beloyarskoi AES imeni I. V. Kurchatova," *Ekologiya*, No. 2, 1990.

62. United Press International (UPI), March 10, 1989; Reuter, March 11, 1989; *Vestnik narodnogo fronta* (Estonia), No. 8, 1989, p. 4; *Observer*, September 17, 1989.

63. Central Television, "Television News Service," September 18, 1990, translated in FBIS–SOV–90–182, p. 46.

64. Novosti Press Agency, September 11, 1990; see also Radio Moscow, September 6, 1990, cited in FBIS–SOV–90–174, p. 86.

65. *Turmenskaya iskra*, February 27, 1990, p. 2.

66. *Izvestiya*, January 8, 1990, p. 2.

67. Radio Moscow, June 10, 1990.

68. *Rabochaya tribuna*, January 30, 1991, p. 3; *Moskovskaya pravda*, May 16, 1991, p. 3.

69. L. Matveev, chair, Expert Commission on Radiation Safety of Moscow City Soviet Commission on Ecology, in *Vechernyaya Moskva*, February 18, 1991, p. 1.

70. *Rabochaya tribuna*, January 30, 1991, p. 3.

71. Andrew Bond, "News Notes," *Soviet Geography*, March 1991, p. 205. The radiation hazard was estimated by means of a rough translation of the Soviet measurement unit (microroentgens) into the U.S. measure.

72. *Moskovskaya pravda*, May 16, 1991, p. 3.

73. A total of 960 sources reportedly were found in Moscow oblast between 1982 and mid-1990. *Pravitel'stvennyi vestnik*, No. 34, 1990, p. 12. For reporting on radiation problems outside of Moscow, see *Rabochaya tribuna*, February 6, 1991, p. 2.

74. *Pravitel'stvennyi vestnik*, No. 34, 1990, p. 12.

75. "Safety Is Not Guaranteed," *Sovetskaya torgovlya*, March 1990, as translated in JPRS–UPA–90–030, p. 79.

76. Central Television, "Television News Service," April 25, 1990.

77. *Izvestiya*, August 1, 1991, p. 4.

78. Thomas B. Cochran and Robert Standish Norris, "Soviet Nuclear Warhead Production," *Nuclear Weapons Databook Working Paper*, NWD 90-3, October 19, 1990, pp. 22–23.

79. *Izvestiya*, August 1, 1991, p. 4.

80. Radio Rossii, May 27, 1991, as translated in JPRS–TEN–91–012, p. 63.

81. *Izvestiya*, May 3, 1990, p. 6.

82. *Izvestiya*, August 1, 1991, p. 4.

83. *Izvestiya*, May 3, 1990, p. 6.

84. Cochran and Norris, "Soviet Nuclear Warhead Production," p. 24.

85. *Izvestiya*, November 13, 1991, p. 6.

86. Aleksei Yablokov, presentation at conference on Democratic Federalism and Environmental Crisis in the Republics of the Former Soviet Union, Moscow, August 1991.

87. Mikhail Shutov, "'Metro' v preispodnyuyu," *Priroda i chelovek*, No. 3, 1991, p. 8.

88. *Izvestiya*, November 13, 1991, p. 6.

89. Cochran and Norris, "Soviet Nuclear Warhead Production," pp. 8–12. A total of five reactors operated at Mayak beween 1948 and 1990, when the last finally was shut down.

90. *Argumenty i fakty*, No. 34, 1989, p. 8; *Moscow News*, No. 19, 1991, p. 10.

91. Cochran and Norris, "Soviet Nuclear Warhead Production," p. 16.

92. *Izvestiya*, July 12, 1989, p. 6; A. I. Burnazyan, ed., "Itogi izucheniya i opyt likvidatsii posledstvii avariinogo zagryazneniya territorii produktami deleniya urana" (part 1), *Energiya: Ekonomika, tekhnika, ekologiya*, No. 1, 1990, pp. 51–52; Cochran and Norris, "Soviet Nuclear Warhead Production," pp. 16–21. The area of land contaminated totaled 15,000–23,000 square kilometers. For a comprehensive series of articles on the accident, see *Priroda*, No. 5, 1990.

93. *Izvestiya*, July 12, 1989, p. 6. See also *Izvestiya*, October 5, 1990, p. 7; *Pravda*, January 12, 1990, p. 3; and *Krasnaya zvezda*, October 19, 1990, p. 2. See Zhores A. Medvedev, *Nuclear Disaster in the Urals* (New York: Norton, 1979).

94. Radio Moscow, October 5, 1990, translated in FBIS–SOV–90–195, pp. 35–36.

95. Petr I. Somin, chair, Chelyabinsk oblast Soviet of People's Deputies, in testimony to RSFSR Congress of People's Deputies, Radio Moscow, December 10, 1990, translated in JPRS–TEN–91–001, p. 90. Also Central Television, "Vremya," September 12, 1991; *Moscow News*, No. 19, 1991, p. 10.

96. Natal'ya Mironova, Chelyabinsk Ecological Fund, personal communication, Moscow, June 1991; *Komsomol'skaya pravda*, October 29, 1991, p. 4. According to conclusions drawn by a USSR deputy minister of health, no major deviations from the norm in illnesses or mortality were observed among the population studied who lived in the contaminated zones at the time of the 1957 accident or in subsequent years after their evacuation. A. I. Burnazyan, ed., "Itogi izucheniya i opyt likvidatsii posledstvii avariinogo zagryazneniya territorii produktami deleniya urana" (part 3), *Energiya: Ekonomika, tekhnika, ekologiya*, No. 3, 1990, p. 24. See also *Izvestiya*, July 12, 1989, p. 6. According to the Natural Resources Defense Council (NRDC), workers at Mayak in the early years

received exceedingly "high exposures." Cochran and Norris, "Soviet Nuclear Warhead Production," p. 14, citing Boris V. Nikipelov et al., "Opyt pervogo predpriyatiya atomnoi promyshlennosti," *Priroda*, No. 2, 1990.

97. "USSR Ministry of Atomic Power and Industry commission to assess the ecological situation in the vicinity of the Mayak Production Enterprise," Moscow, 1990, cited by Natal'ya Mironova, presentation at USSR Nuclear Society conference on Radioactive Waste: Problems and Solutions, Moscow, June 1991; *Izvestiya*, March 3, 1991, p. 4.

98. Mironova, presentation citing USSR Ministry of Atomic Power and Industry commission. The figure of 1 billion curies was also reiterated by academician Anatolii F. Tsyb, head of the commission. Central Television, "Vremya," December 10, 1990.

99. Cochran and Norris, "Soviet Nuclear Warhead Production," p. 16.

100. TASS, November 14, 1991.

101. *Moscow News*, No. 19, 1991, p. 10.

102. The plant was designed to have three 800-megawatt fast-breeder reactors.

103. A. Suslov, cited in *Sovetskaya Rossiya*, April 20, 1991, p. 6.

104. *Izvestiya*, January 8, 1990, p. 2.

105. For more on the incident, refer to DJ Peterson, "An Environmental Disaster Unfolds," *Report on the USSR*, No. 27, 1990; *Pravda*, August 10, 1990, p. 6; and *Izvestiya*, August 29, 1990, p. 3.

106. *Izvestiya*, August 17, 1990, p. 6, and October 4, 1990, p. 6.

107. *Vechernyaya Moskva*, February 18, 1990, p. 1.

108. *Pravda Ukrainy*, July 7, 1990, p. 4.

109. *Vestnik statistiki*, No. 11, 1991, p. 65.

110. *Ekonomika i zhizn'*, No. 41, 1990, supp. pp. 2, 6.

111. See, for example, Yurii Porokhov, "Upravlenie spetstrans opytnyi poligon Krasnyi Bor," *Leningradskaya panorama*, No. 2, 1990.

112. *Ogonek*, No. 40, 1989, p. 3.

113. Helsinki Radio, July 2, 1990, translated in JPRS–TEN–90–007, p. 9.

114. TASS, October 22, 1990.

115. *Sotsialisticheskaya industriya*, July 23, 1989, p. 4. For more on the politics surrounding the Krasnoyarsk project, refer to *Komsomol'skaya pravda*, June 15, 1989, p. 1, and June 28, 1989, p. 1.

116. *Sovetskaya Rossiya*, June 28, 1990, p. 1.

117. TASS, December 18, 1989.

118. Porokhov, "Upravlenie."

6

Government Institutions and Environmental Policy

I agreed because I felt ashamed for our great country.
—Nikolai Vorontsov on why he decided to
accept the position as chief of the USSR
State Committee for the Protection of Nature

The Gorbachev administration went further than any of its predecessors in candidly acknowledging the extent of environmental damage in the Soviet Union and the need for new approaches to solving the problem. In addition to the official revelations of eco-glasnost outlined in the preceding chapters, two other significant developments in this reform process were the consolidation of environmental protection efforts within the State Committee for the Protection of Nature and the formation of the Committees on Ecology and Rational Use of Natural Resources in the parliament of the Union as well as those at the republican, regional, and local levels. The appearance of these two new institutions offered grounds for hope that the government would be better prepared to confront its enormous environmental problems.

Though both institutions at the Union level were disbanded with the breakup of the Soviet Union at the end of 1991, they served as the blueprint for their counterparts at the republic level. As a result, the experiences of environmental policymakers in the republics closely followed those in the Soviet government and parliament.

THE SOVIET GOVERNMENT AND THE USSR STATE COMMITTEE FOR THE PROTECTION OF NATURE

In recognition of the shortcomings of the regime's environmental protection efforts, the Soviet leadership in January 1988 created the first all-Union agency devoted exclusively to environmental protection: the USSR State Committee for the Protection of Nature, or Goskompriroda. The new agency, established by a joint resolution of the USSR Council of Ministers and the CPSU Central Committee, was intended to replace the hodgepodge of state committees and ministries that formerly shared responsibility for environmental policy in the Soviet Union.

The agency was charged with several tasks: to develop and administer environmental protection and remediation programs; to monitor environmental quality and the use of natural resources; to set norms for regulating pollution output and the use of natural resources; to conduct environmental impact studies of proposed development projects; to issue permits for disposal of toxic wastes, pollution emissions, geological prospecting, logging, and other uses of the land, water, and air; to manage plant and animal resources (including endangered species), nature reserves, and hunting; and to administer international agreements on nature protection.

In a significant change from the traditional Soviet view of environmental problems as discrete technological issues—such as devising measures to process the wastes of a particular enterprise or to minimize agricultural runoff—the structure of Goskompriroda reflected a progressive, systemic approach to environmental protection in recognition of the fact that environmental degradation had grown in size and complexity to become a regional, national, and international concern. The U.S. Environmental Protection Agency, in contrast, is separated into divisions responsible for particular problems (e.g., air, water, solid waste); consequently, there has been a tendency in the United States for, say, the air pollution section to encourage greater use of scrubbers, which results in the substitution of hazardous solid waste for air pollution. The systemic approach was considered better able to establish norms and procedures that reduce pollution comprehensively, because it tackled several problems simultaneously. Rather than focus on water pollution in Baikal alone, for example, researchers could study the state of the entire region, including its air pollution, logging activities, and agriculture. Such an approach also helps policymakers to focus better on causes of pollution rather than its symptoms.[1]

During its four-year existence, the all-Union environmental agency focused primarily on elaborating an entirely new environmental policy for the Soviet regime. The first step in this task involved gathering data and assessing the state of the environment. The results of this project were put together in a handbook, *The State of the Environment in the USSR,* published commercially in October 1989. The report was the first document to provide a comprehensive and authoritative (though not undisputed) review of environmental conditions in the USSR and represented a notable achievement on the part of its compilers, given a simple lack of information. "A shortage of timely and objective official ecological information still continues," the authors noted in the introduction. Obtaining accurate information was important, they added, not only for proper decisionmaking but also to counter rumors and erroneous reports circulating among the populace.[2]

A second principal task was preparing a comprehensive program of environmental cleanup and economic development for the Thirteenth Five-Year Plan (1991–1995) and up to 2005. The agency drafted this document, known as the Ecological Program (*Ekologicheskaya programma*) with the assistance of several outside agencies and scientists.[3] Although the Ecological Program was approved by the Presidium of the USSR Council of Ministers, it was never implemented because of the collapse of the Soviet regime.

The 1988 Council of Ministers' resolution that created USSR Goskompriroda also established affiliates at the republic, autonomous republic, and regional (krai and oblast) levels. As a Union-republic agency, Goskompriroda—like the Environmental Protection Agency in the United States—worked with its network of regional affiliates, which were closely modeled after the all-Union agency. For some republics, such as Belarus and Ukraine, the creation of the Goskompriroda system did not change the situation drastically; they had created their own agencies as far back as the 1960s. For the majority of republics and their regional subdivisions that did not have an environmental agency in 1988, the establishment of the unified Union-republic Goskompriroda system initiated the process of creating an environmental bureaucracy and assembling environmental expertise at the local level.

In the hierarchy of the Goskompriroda system, it was the republic-level agency that was central in implementing environmental policy. In the post-Soviet era, the republican authorities now have assumed sole responsibility for drafting programs to deal with problems of their region. In addition to executing and enforcing programs, local agencies are responsible for the basics of protecting the environment, such as ensuring a safe drinking water supply and disposing of municipal wastes.

THE CHALLENGE OF BUILDING A COMPETENT
ENVIRONMENTAL BUREAUCRACY

As a new entity, the Soviet environmental protection agency's first challenge consisted of building a capable bureaucracy. An effective state bureaucracy, especially one that is implementing reformist policies, requires a competent, motivated staff that is politically autonomous from the interests the members seek to regulate.[4] Unfortunately, the number of qualified experts available and willing to work for the environmental agency proved inadequate, a condition that has persisted in the post-Soviet era. Personnel problems began with the leadership of USSR Goskompriroda in Moscow.

The first chairman of USSR Goskompriroda, Fedor Morgun, was a Communist Party official specializing in agriculture who had worked his way up through the Ukrainian Communist Party apparatus. Despite his reportedly close ties with Mikhail Gorbachev, Morgun's performance proved disappointing. Morgun admitted that his lack of experience in environmental protection impaired his performance: "Every day I ran into dozens of unfamiliar terms and concepts. In places where an ecologist could take everything easily in stride, I had to become familiar with everything down to details, to get clarifications, and to ask questions repeatedly. At times, I simply felt awkward." Morgun also expressed frustration with his job: "I, accordingly, said what I thought [about environmental affairs] at meetings of the Council of Ministers, and I remained in the depressing minority, or more correctly, in criticized isolation."[5] After serving for fifteen months, Morgun resigned, evidently for a combination of reasons, including his inexperience, deteriorating health, and the desire of the USSR Council of Ministers to bring in fresh talent.

The government waited to choose a successor to Morgun until the popularly elected USSR Congress of People's Deputies, which was to assume the task of ratifying ministerial appointments, was first convened in June 1989. A further delay ensued when at least six top scientists refused offers to serve as head of USSR Goskompriroda. Those who were asked reportedly preferred to remain in academia, feeling that doing battle with government bureaucracies over the environment was a hopeless assignment. Soviet Prime Minister Nikolai Ryzhkov finally nominated Dr. Nikolai Vorontsov, a leading scholar at the USSR Academy of Sciences Institute of Biology. Vorontsov specialized in evolution, zoology, and genetics, and his credentials as an environmentalist also were impressive. According to his own account, in the 1960s Vorontsov helped kill a proposed "project of the century" to build a hydroelectric station on the lower Ob River, and he was an early and vocal opponent of the

Baikal Pulp and Paper Mill. Such activism was notable because at the time, being outspoken often threatened one's career. Vorontsov also distinguished himself by becoming the first non–Communist Party member to serve at a ministerial-level post in the Soviet government.

The shortage of capable specialists only increased as one moved down the hierarchy and was most acute in smaller offices and in republics with poorly funded agencies, such as those in Central Asia. In such circumstances, officials often served only as paper shufflers, compiling data from information that flowed into the office and reporting it to superiors at headquarters. In 1989, Nikolai Vorontsov admitted that very few people working at local environmental offices had a professional understanding of nature protection.[6]

One reason for the shortage of experts was that the Soviet higher educational system produced few people capable of fulfilling the tasks of a contemporary environmental professional. Although many universities had ecology departments, the curriculum traditionally focused almost exclusively on studying the science of ecosystems. Professional training paid inadequate attention to practical problems, such as how to evaluate the impact of development on the environment, how to prioritize environmental problems, and how to design economic policies to minimize environmental degradation.[7] On this point, one environmental activist commented: "You can count [the number of] ecologists on one hand without taking your mittens off."[8]

Personnel problems at the all-Union environmental agency were compounded by the fact that the bulk of its functions were assumed from other state committees and ministries, such as Goskomgidromet (the state meteorological service), the ministries of fisheries and water resources, and Gosagroprom (the agency overseeing the agricultural sector). Created in an era of fiscal austerity and a concerted campaign to cut government employment, Goskompriroda was instructed to absorb their staff, so as not to expand the overall size of the state apparatus. In many cases, the agencies losing departments and personnel used this game of bureaucratic musical chairs as an opportunity to rid themselves of incompetent or unproductive staff. Because of the shortage of experts, Goskompriroda had no choice but to accept these transferees. With the breakup of the Union, the Russian Federation under President Boris Yeltsin laid claim to the major share of Soviet institutions, inheriting the bulk of the Soviet technical and scientific establishment and, concomitantly, the bulk of Goskompriroda's paper shufflers.

In addition, many critics have charged that environmental protection organs, particularly at the local level, were staffed by Communist Party *apparatchiks* who obtained their positions through patronage connections rather than because of their environmental qualifications. As the centrally planned economy gave way to a nascent market economy, enterprising *apparatchiks* sought to transform their dwindling political capital into economic capital by using their connections to create lucrative business arrangements. Many environmental agencies, for example, attempted to use money earned from "polluter-pays" schemes (requiring polluters to pay the costs of environmental degradation and cleanup) to invest in pollution control projects at local enterprises or to create environmental technology and services businesses. The atmosphere of freewheeling, unregulated capitalism, however, contributed to the potential for fiscal malfeasance and conflicts of interest on the part of environmental officials in such government-sponsored ventures.

Despite being untested as an administrator, Nikolai Vorontsov's personal contacts and solid credentials as a scholar and environmentalist were seen as a plus in attracting talent to the environment agency. Nevertheless, Vorontsov's tenure at USSR Goskompriroda brought little improvement in personnel. The shortage of qualified and motivated environmental managers in the USSR's environmental bureaucracy distressed and demoralized environmentalists both in and out of the government, and environmental agencies at all levels were criticized heavily for their personnel policies. Aleksei Yablokov, for instance, complained that USSR Goskompriroda lacked environmental *entuziasty*, or zealots.[9] Asked whether he was concerned about the presence of so many *apparatchiks* in his organization, Vorontsov responded:

> Certainly I am. On the other hand, however, I am a scientist [who is] not conversant in the secrets of ministerial work, in the departmental tug-of-war. This is why I will need assistants and advisors from the ranks of the apparatus for as long as the current state structure exists. . . . I don't think *apparatchik* is a foul word. . . . Employees should bring real benefits to the cause they serve. If they think theirs are cushy jobs, if they are going to go easy on their former colleagues, if an enterprise director can get such officials to sign any statement favorable for him, then they must be kicked out mercilessly.[10]

Petr Poletaev, a deputy to Vorontsov, also defended his agency's position, tersely pointing out, "There are many scientists in the *apparat*."[11]

Finally, building bureaucratic capability was hampered by the atmosphere of uncertainty and chaos that has pervaded policymaking since the inception of perestroika in the mid-1980s. Reforms and reorganizations at all levels of government constantly shook up agencies and redefined their missions, budgets were volatile and unpredictable over the long term, and personnel changes came frequently. Given such conditions, many talented and motivated employees often left local environmental agencies after a short tenure to take jobs in the environmental movement or elsewhere because they felt they could accomplish more there. In Alma-Ata, for example, the local enterprise Eko-eksp (short for *ekologicheskaya ekspertiza*, or environmental study) was able to draw many environmental professionals away from the government to conduct environmental impact studies for local businesses. Moreover, the pay at Eko-eksp was better—2 to 5 times higher than a government job.[12] These uncertainties have only increased with the shakeup of governments, bureaucracies, and budgets in the post-Soviet era.

THE PROBLEM OF MEDIATING INTRAGOVERNMENTAL CONFLICT

Environmental agencies face pressure from all sides, most importantly other well-established interests, such as those of industry. Vorontsov once told an assembly of Soviet and foreign journalists, "I will not disturb my minister colleagues; I am convinced of this."[13] He was being exceedingly diplomatic. Instead, Goskompriroda officials discovered that their broad mandate impinged on the vested interests of virtually every ministry and state agency.

Conflict became most intense over enforcement of environmental regulations. In early 1988, USSR Deputy Prosecutor General Oleg V. Sorokoi stated that the Soviet Union's existing environmental regulations required strict control: "This still is absent," he said. But he pointed to the recent formation of Goskompriroda and added, "Now the situation must change."[14] Sorokoi was overly optimistic. Two and one-half years later, his successor, Vladimir Andreev, explained how the environment agency had to "beg on its knees" when it came to enforcing regulations because the ultimate decision to sanction an enterprise rested with the government:

> Let's take, for instance, a factory is polluting a river. The prosecutor sends the factory director a threatening letter: "You are violating the law in the grossest manner. I demand, etc." The letter gets zero attention. Stop production? Fire someone? No, the prosecutor only has the right to complain to higher-ups. No movement? Then . . . even higher. And so on, until one's head strikes the departmental ceiling. It's absurd, degrading.[15]

The following report in 1990 about a pharmaceutical enterprise in Kirovgrad, a city in the Ural mountains oblast of Sverdlovsk (now Yekaterinburg), illustrates the contradictory interests of government actors:

The regional public health department, the *gorispolkom* [city government], and other authorities on more than one occasion decided to close down the chemical production operation. But under the pressure of the ministry, these decisions never were carried out. The last time, the doors to the chlorosulfonic acid unit even were sealed. But on October 3, the director of the plant, V. Mazanik, broke the seal himself and restarted the department's work. And, once again, a ton of hydrogen chloride was released on October 25; workers were poisoned and had to be taken out of the polluted zone. On October 27, we all were astonished to hear the text of V. Mazanik's telegram sent to Sverdlovsk television and read on the air. It asserted that the chlorosulfonic acid unit presented no ecological danger, and hence the city committee for the protection of nature was sounding an alarm for no reason.[16]

The industrial ministries were not the only source of opposition. Although one of the objectives of creating the Goskompriroda system was to consolidate and to coordinate agencies working on environmental and resource affairs, this goal was accomplished to only a small extent during the Soviet era. One aspect of environmental policymaking particularly impeded by bureaucratic division was information gathering and analysis. Research on the environment in the former Soviet Union was conducted by over 1,000 institutions under the auspices of 70 different ministries and agencies.[17] The authors of USSR Goskompriroda's 1989 environmental handbook described serious bureaucratic challenges they encountered in gathering available information, not to mention assessing the information's reliability, because each agency had its own methodology for collecting and analyzing data. In the data-starved ex-Soviet system, access to information was as important as access to material resources, as each agency attempted to guard its prerogatives: "He who controls information," in the words of one Goskompriroda official, "has the power."[18] Commenting on the Soviet-era state of affairs in Ukraine, a writer in *The Economist* noted:

At least five different institutions, each with different kinds of equipment of varying quality, are conducting Chernobyl-related biological and environmental research, which they do not share with one another. All of these institutions are in conflict with their counterparts in Belarussia and with the top Soviet nuclear institute, the Moscow-controlled All-Union Centre for Radiation Research. . . . The central authorities in Moscow know that, if they keep tight control over the information they possess, they will also keep their contacts with foreigners and their access to foreign money. . . . [T]o get information about the effects of Chernobyl radiation on Ukrainians, the Ukrainian health ministry is reduced to begging Moscow for local medical statistics.[19]

A prolonged battle over management authority raged between Goskompriroda and Goskomgidromet, the meteorological service. The 1988 party/government resolution establishing Goskompriroda gave it power to monitor and to publish data on "the use of natural resources and on environmental protection efforts." Nevertheless, basic functions like air quality monitoring remained under the purview of the meteorology service. Vorontsov and his colleagues insisted, "All functions of state monitoring of the condition of the environment need to be transferred to Goskompriroda." Vorontsov went on to criticize bluntly the chairman of Goskomgidromet, Yurii Izrael', for refusing to give USSR Goskompriroda unimpeded access to the former agency's environmental data and for resisting Goskompriroda's efforts to play a larger role in environmental monitoring.[20]

Goskomgidromet's longevity and independence could be attributed directly to its chief—himself a political survivor. Appointed head of USSR Goskomgidromet in 1978, Izrael' was one of the last remaining bureaucrats from the Brezhnev era to survive in the era of perestroika.[21] Under his leadership, the meteorological service did nothing while it piled up data indicating that the nation's air was seriously polluted. It was also his agency that withheld information from the public in the crucial days, weeks, and even years after the Chernobyl accident.[22] The USSR deputy general prosecutor in late 1987 criticized Goskomgidromet—for its "weak control" of industry—and the existing environmental protection bureaucracy alike: "[While] possessing the most complete data on the ecological condition of the country," Oleg V. Sorokoi noted, "the Committee neither conducts thorough analyses of it, nor offers constructive recommendations. Workers in Goskomgidromet identify a problem, report it, and at that point consider their work finished."[23]

The feud between Goskomgidromet and Goskompriroda impaired the policymaking process, including the Soviet Union's initial response to the threat of global climate change. Goskomgidromet's stand on the issue was heavily influenced by the work of academician Mikhail Budyko, who constructed models showing that global warming would, on balance, prove beneficial to the Soviet Union by expanding the inventory of arable land, increasing rainfall, and lengthening the growing season. Goskompriroda, however, viewed climate change as a potentially disturbing phenomenon.[24]

Between debates about environmental policy, parliamentarians and environmental officials alike also have grappled with a related issue: the most effective institutional arrangements for environmental protection given the perceived weakness of the Goskompriroda system. One issue debated was the merit of elevating the political status of the environment agency by making it a full-fledged ministry on par, at least administratively, with the industrial ministries it sought to regulate. On the eve of the breakup of the Soviet Union, the Gorbachev administration elected to reorganize USSR Goskompriroda as the USSR Ministry of Environmental Protection and Rational Use of Natural Resources. Many republican authorities followed suit; in Russia, for example, the agency was reorganized as the RSFSR Ministry of Nature and Rational Use of Natural Resources (abbreviated Minpriroda). In a novel effort to give the Moldovan environmental agency the independence to monitor freely the activities of the government and its ministries, the agency was placed in direct subordination to the republican parliament.[25]

In the summer of 1991, the Russian government organized an environmental "bloc" consisting of several agencies, including environment, water resources, and forestry. Igor' Gavrilov was given a joint appointment as environment minister and deputy prime minister with oversight responsibility of all these agencies concerned with natural resources issues. The following November, the arrangement was reorganized yet again, with eleven different agencies being subsumed as committees in a bloc under Minpriroda. These committees included geodesy and cartography, water resources, geology and mineral resources, forestry, and hydrometeorology. The move by the Yeltsin administration to combine the functions of monitoring, resource management, and enforcement represented a significant advance for environmental protection, as the Gorbachev administration's failure to subordinate such powerful agencies as hydrometeorology and water resources undermined the status of USSR Goskompriroda. To the chagrin of the new environment minister, Viktor Danilov-Danil'yan, however, the committees for fisheries, hunting, and land reform quickly managed to reassert their bureaucratic independence from his superministry and "ruined this logical principle."[26]

GOVERNMENT SPENDING ON THE ENVIRONMENT

Of all the challenges facing the establishment of a capable and effective bureaucracy, the most important is obtaining adequate and stable sources of funding.

Throughout the years of the Gorbachev administration, state expenditures for environmental protection increased steadily.[27] Total spending by the Soviet government on nature protection and the "rational use of natural resources" in 1990 amounted to about 13 billion rubles, a 30 percent increase over levels in 1985.[28] Likewise, governmental allocations for capital investments in pollution abatement and control grew rapidly, surging 21 percent in 1989 and 18 percent in 1990; these increases are significant given the fact that in the latter year, the increase was the largest of any category, and overall government-funded investments had started to decline. A breakdown of spending in 1988 is given in Table 6.1.

The figures provided by the Soviet statistical agency in Table 6.1 do not tell the entire story, however. Most government spending was channeled directly through the branch ministries and their subordinate enterprises, not the environmental bureaucracy, an approach that raises the question of whether all money allocated was spent on environmental protection. Moreover, not all spending could be considered to be targeted directly at environmental protection; as illustrated in Chapter 4, moneys spent on land reclamation largely were allocated to irrigation and drainage projects, many of dubious benefit to the environment. Direct funding for the environmental bureaucracy occupied only a small fraction of government spending: for example, USSR Goskompriroda's budget for 1991, its last year of existence, was just 40 million rubles.[29] By

TABLE 6.1   Union-wide expenditures for environmental protection, 1988

	Rubles (millions)	Percent
Total[a]	11,592	100
Routine outlays		
Water pollution abatement, rational use of water resources	4,610	49.7
Air pollution abatement	1,510	13.0
Protection of land resources from industrial wastes and development	370	3.2
Land revegetation	170	1.5
Administration and regulation, research and development, education	500	4.3
Maintenance of national parks and reserves	190	1.6
Maintenance of forest resources	1,120	10.0
Capital expenditures		
Air pollution abatement	317	2.7
Water pollution abatement, rational use of water resources	2,091	18.0
Conservation and rational use of land resources[b]	393	3.3
Other	321	2.7

[a]Figures do not add up due to rounding.

[b]Energy, metallurgical, chemical, and forestry industries.

Sources: USSR Goskomstat, *Narodnoe khozyaistvo SSSR v 1988 g.* (Moscow: Finansy i statistika, 1989), p. 252; USSR Goskomstat, *Okhrana okruzhayushchei sredy i ratsional'noe ispol'zovanie prirodnykh resursov v SSSR* (Moscow: Finansy i statistika, 1989), p. 9.

comparison, the U.S. Environmental Protection Agency during this period employed over 15,000 people and had over $5 billion at its disposal.

Despite the increased government activity to protect nature in the late 1980s, total spending, as a share of GNP, did not increase substantially: According to USSR Goskomstat, the amount "practically did not change" during the Thirteenth Five-Year Plan ending in 1990, averaging 1.3 percent annually.[30] By comparison, between 1975 and 1989, public and private spending in the United States on solid waste disposal and air and water pollution abatement alone averaged about 2 percent of GNP.[31]

Finally, data on government spending do not relate the whole picture when examined in the context of the Soviet Union, where the economy was plagued by repressed inflation manifested in widespread shortages. Assessing the overall increase in the government's investment spending in the 1980s, U.S. Sovietologist Boris Rumer noted: "The heightened investment activity is illusory; flows of money did rise, but the quality of physical investment resources (building materials, labor, machinery, etc.) did not. These flows were fed by . . . an increase in government debt and the printing of money."[32] Thus, like the worker who has nothing on which to spend her or his rubles, government agencies and enterprises discovered the critical issue was not access to money but access to goods. In 1989, 3.8 billion rubles were allocated from central government funds for capital expenditures on environmental protection projects—a 21 percent increase from the year before. Yet 545,000 rubles, or more than 14 percent, went unspent, largely for lack of materials to purchase.[33] Thus, as spending increased over the 1980s, the commissioning of pollution abatement systems slowed, by 3 percent for wastewater treatment facilities and 35 percent for air pollution controls.[34] Common technologies, such as catalytic converters, smokestack scrubbers, and wastewater treatment equipment, were rare if not nonexistent on domestic markets. As alluded to in the discussion of water pollution, projects frequently were halted for lack of commonplace items such as piping. Further, a lack of trained environmental engineers and planners meant that an increasing number of projects were slower to get on (not to mention off) the drawing board.

Although the Soviet leadership under Mikhail Gorbachev was successful in breaking up the rigidly controlled command-administrative system, it was unable to replace it with a functioning economic regime. The economic depression in the Soviet and post-Soviet era has been compounded by republics' steps to raise trade barriers in an effort to protect their local economies. The result has been uncertainty, instability, and recession, putting managers in no position to implement required environmental protection measures. Previously, the Soviet economy had difficulty delivering such staples as bread and matches; it is inconceivable that factories' orders for sophisticated pollution control equipment could be filled on time in the current economic chaos. Less than one-half of the government's "most important environmental protection projects" were implemented as planned in 1989[35]; in 1990 the share fell to about one-quarter.[36]

FINANCING ENVIRONMENTAL PROTECTION IN A PERIOD OF ECONOMIC REFORM

Although politicians have been unwilling or unable to allocate government resources needed to pursue comprehensive and aggressive programs of environmental protection and remediation, they have formulated some innovative plans to fund various programs and to encourage environmental protection. In a dramatic departure from the command-administrative methods of the past, many such plans involve market-based mechanisms to protect the environment, the most important of them being the "polluter pays" principle. One of the Gorbachev administration's early economic reform efforts, the 1987 Law on State Enterprises, mandated payments for resources consumed, "full compensation for damage to the environment," and "material responsibility" for violation of environmental protection laws.[37] The 1988 announcement of the founding of USSR Goskompriroda declared that "there must be a resolute move away from administrative to primarily economic methods of managing environmental protection activities."[38] "For environmental protection to be efficient," stated Nikolai Vorontsov in 1990, "it must become unprofitable to harm nature."[39] The appointment of Viktor Danilov-Danil'yan as Russian environment minister in November 1991 also signaled strong support for such an approach by the Russian leadership because he had worked previously as an academic economist studying mathematical models of natural resources management.

Numerous ways to use the market to promote environmental protection goals have been under consideration and are similar to those adopted in the West. Options include direct payments to government agencies for natural resources (either as a concession as in the case of coal or oil or as a usage fee for water); permit fees for air and water emissions; compensation for environmental restoration work; taxes on the production of environmentally hazardous products; fines for violation of environmental laws and norms; fees for mandatory accident insurance based on a firm's potential environmental hazard; tax incentives to support development of environmental protection technologies; and tax incentives and accelerated depreciation allowances for investment in pollution abatement measures.

Because local governments in the Soviet Union traditionally were deprived of an independent source of income, many local governments, backed with popular support, were the first to seize the initiative and turn to local businesses for funds to support local environmental protection programs. One of the most popular methods employed is to charge local enterprises permit fees and punitive fines for the consumption of natural resources and for pollution emissions. The proceeds from such fees, fines, and taxes are then diverted into several different funds: the local government budget designated for environmental management, monitoring, and restoration; special public "environmental funds" to pay for pollution abatement equipment installed on local industries; or enterprise-managed funds earmarked for environmental protection.[40]

As early as 1989 and 1990, experiments in locally financed pollution control efforts already had been undertaken in several regions, including Yaroslavl and Kostroma in Russia and Dnepropetrovsk in Ukraine.[41] Krivoi Rog ranked as one of Ukraine's cities with the greatest amount of air pollution emissions in the 1980s. The city spent 50 million rubles on nature conservation annually; it needed 2 billion rubles. "Where is this money to come from? Where do you expect help from?" a television reporter asked a city official. "No one will help us. We must identify and utilize the [revenue] of our enterprises. This revenue is substantial, but the greater part of it goes to the center [the Soviet government in Moscow]. We have no idea how it is spent." To boost environmental protection in the city, Krivoi Rog created a fund into which the polluting industries must pay money. In the estimate of the reporter, however, the contributions remained "insignificant in view of the scale of the ecological problem."[42]

At the start of 1989, the city government of Grodno began to fine polluting enterprises. The Belarusian city initially charged factories about 17 rubles for every ton of air pollution emitted, and the fee jumped 5-fold for above-norm emissions, building up an environmental protection fund of several million rubles. In November 1989, a local construction materials plant was forced to pay the city 125,000 rubles for shutting off its smoke stack scrubbers. "To restore [nature] requires huge resources. Where will we get them, if not from the guilty parties?" asked a local environmental official.[43] In 1991, the city of Pyatigorsk implemented a 10-ruble toll for trucks traveling through the city. The southern Russian town serves as a major transit junction for road traffic passing through the Caucasus, and local officials hoped to capture revenues to pay for local environmental protection projects.[44] To back up their polluter-pays systems, many local and regional governments have created special enforcement agencies. In the Crimean resort of Yalta, the local government created a special "ecological militia" in 1991. The division's 20 officers were subordinated to the local police department, but their funds were to come from a special fund ostensibly supported with pollution fines.[45]

The polluter-pays programs often have been extended republicwide. In the case of wastewater discharges in Kyrgyzstan, for instance, the government has instituted a base fee for emissions within norms set for each particular firm (based on the type of production) and region. If the concentration of pollutants exceeds permissible norms, the enterprise pays a steep fine ranging from 5 to 10 times the normal emissions fees.[46] Russia likewise instituted a federationwide polluter-pays system at the beginning of 1991 to support a special nonbudgetary fund designed exclusively for environmental purposes.[47] Contributions to the fund come from several sources: permit fees for air and water emissions, waste disposal, and use of natural resources; and fines and court settlements for violation of environmental regulations. Of these revenues, local agencies retain 60 percent; 30 percent is sent to the region's government coffers; and 10 percent is sent to the federal environment ministry. In 1991, such fees totaled 1 billion rubles; in 1992, they were expected to increase 10-fold. According to Russian Minister Viktor Danilov-Danil'yan, the polluter-pays principle has become an essential means of funding environmental protection efforts in Russia during an era of dramatically shrinking government spending.[48]

On paper, the notion of using the market to facilitate environmental protection efforts appears sound, but there are complications. First, the pricing of raw materials poses complex political dilemmas. Political leaders clearly recognize that the discipline of market prices coupled with greater enterprise autonomy would benefit the environment by promoting efficiency in production and resource allocation and, in the long run, relieve the shortages that pervade the economy. Access to cheap raw materials in the Soviet era served as a massive subsidy to enterprises and supported wasteful and inefficient practices. Price reform, or more accurately, price decontrol, however, entails significant social costs, including high inflation, less-equal income distribution, and the potential for widespread unemployment. Government, therefore, will remain under strong pressure to subsidize the prices of raw materials in order to soften the shocks of structural adjustment.

The second problem in incorporating market principles is calculating the levels for the emission fees and fines. If they are too low, as is often the case in the West, they will have no impact on polluters, as firms opt to pay the fines instead of taking costly measures to clean up their operations. Fees and fines in the West typically are set to maximize government revenue (and in particular to support the regulatory bureaucracy) and therefore often do not coincide with the optimal level for enhancing environmental quality.[49] Punitive fees, moreover, may be disadvantageous if they force an enterprise to relocate or shut down. In the current era of government retrenchment, the combination of rising charges for raw material inputs and pollution fees could push many companies into bankruptcy.

Even in smoothly running market economies and with accurate, plentiful information, it is extremely difficult to strike the appropriate and desired balance—as evidenced by the heated debates over revising the U.S. Clean Air Act in the late 1980s. This task will be more difficult with the ex-Soviet economy because the levels of technological development and emissions across regions or within a given industry (or even within an enterprise) vary widely. The iron and steel industry, for example, boasts some of the world's most advanced production facilities (witness its achievements in the aerospace sector), but at the same time, highly inefficient open-hearth mills still accounted for over half of Soviet steel production in the late 1980s.[50] Moreover, the prevalence of monopoly and oligopoly producers in the Soviet economy means that any effort to impose pollution charges or taxes will encourage such firms to restrict output or to pass these costs on to the consumer.[51] The result would not be very different from in the past when enterprises passed on environmental fines to the ministries.

A successful implementation of a polluter-pays system also is threatened by a lack of economic stability and growth. At the time that polluter-pays schemes were being implemented, enterprises started running up massive debts as a result of dislocation and uncertainty due to deepening economic troubles. By 1992, Russian firms alone owed hundreds of billions of rubles to their suppliers, the government, and even their workers. According to the existing system of payment priorities, however, these debts were to be met before those incurred for environment-related reasons. As a result, environmental agencies received only a fraction of the fees and fines they had charged. In the first half of 1992, the Chelyabinsk regional environmental protection agency assessed local firms 50 million rubles in fines and fees, but it had received only one-tenth that sum.[52] In sum, the efficacy of the new market-based approaches to environmental protection being implemented in the region hinges on the successful transition to stable, market-driven economics—a process that, at best, will take many years.

ALL-UNION PARLIAMENTARY
ENVIRONMENTAL POLITICS

For six decades, the USSR Supreme Soviet, the country's highest legislative organ, had functioned as little more than a ceremonial rubber stamp, meeting for a few days a year to unanimously approve decisions taken by the USSR Council of Ministers or the Central Committee of the CPSU. When laws concerning the environment and the use of natural resources were passed by the legislature, their content was dictated by the preferences of the industrial ministries and economic planners, and hence, the Communist Party. When a more democratic USSR Congress of People's Deputies and USSR Supreme Soviet were convened in 1989, the new legislative bodies raised hopes that they would be more successful than Goskompriroda at converting the public's profound concern for environmental problems into effective policy.

Elections to the USSR Congress of People's Deputies were held in spring 1989. Over two-thirds of the 2,250 deputies were chosen in multi-candidate elections, the first such held for national office in the Soviet Union since the 1920s.[53] This contentious and invigorating introduction to democratic politics provided an outstanding forum for amplifying widely felt concerns about deteriorating environmental conditions in the Soviet Union. Given the scale of the environmental problems and their devastating impact on localities and the public's health, many candidates campaigned on platforms that emphasized environmental issues. Those whose focus was on other matters at least felt compelled to pay lip service to the subject. Several prominent environmental activists won election to the Congress, among them Aleksei Yablokov, Sergei Zalygin, and Valentin Rasputin—the latter two writers being famous for their outspoken criticism of the government over the Siberian river diversion scheme. In the Baltic states, many members of the region's established Green movements were elected to the Congress.[54]

The initial two-week session of the Congress of People's Deputies elicited widespread enthusiasm for Gorbachev's efforts to open up the political process. Over 100 million citizens followed the dramatic and unprecedented proceedings on live television, which ran all day, every day. As in the election campaign, environmental concerns figured prominently in the opening session of the Congress. One deputy after another marched up to the podium, many using their precious minutes to catalogue the environmental problems of their beleaguered districts. Many demanded prompt government relief. By the end of the historic meeting, 500 of the over 2,000 deputies had registered some form of environmental complaint.[55] S. I. Konev, a surgeon from Dneprodzerzhinsk, in the heavily industrialized eastern Ukraine, set the tone early on: "The country is approaching an economic and ecological abyss. . . . Our Dneprodzerzhinsk has already gone beyond the permissible limit."[56] As chair of the Congress, Mikhail Gorbachev presented an address on the state of the Union, setting out his legislative priorities. One deputy was not impressed by the speech, likening his home in the Karakalpak Autonomous Republic bordering the Aral Sea to a war zone where the people are "doomed to extinction":

> Esteemed comrade deputies! Mikhail Sergeievich Gorbachev mentioned the imminent ecological crisis as though in passing—that is, among the country's other problems. I should announce that the ecological catastrophe that has taken place and is taking place in the Aral, in terms of its scale and prolonged consequences, is comparable to the latest, large world catastrophes. There are victims, there are people who will be cripples for the rest of their lives. There is poisoned, mutilated land; there are abandoned villages. If you fly over the expanses of the Aral area, you will see white lifeless salt marshes. They have covered the land like snow.
>
> It is dangerous to grow fruits and vegetables in our land today. . . . The land that fed us has been poisoned and destroyed once and for all. Science has not yet been able to purify a single clump of land in Karakalpakia from herbicides, pesticides, and defoliants which have been applied by the ton on each hectare over the past years. If you take the soil into your hands today, it smells no longer like soil; it smells of chemicals. There is a sharp increase in the number of deformed babies. There are also cases of cholera. Disability is constantly increasing. In this situation it is difficult to say with confidence whether there will be a single healthy person left in the Aral area by the beginning of the next century. We have come to this place in life not of our own will but because of the central planning agencies. This is essentially a consequence of the extremely criminal economic policy.[57]

At the end of its first session, the Congress elected 542 of its members to its working subparliament: the USSR Supreme Soviet. The Supreme Soviet had a system of active committees whose members were drawn from both parliaments, and these committees worked while the Supreme Soviet was in session (about eight months of the year). About 100 deputies initially wanted to serve on the Committee on Questions of Ecology and the Rational Use of Natural Resources, but membership was set at 50. The committee elected as its chair Kakimbek Salykov, a longtime Communist Party official from the Karakalpak Autonomous Republic—one of the areas hardest hit by the Aral Sea disaster. The committee created eight subcommittees, each with two or three working groups devoted to specific issues.

Soviet postage stamps commemorate environmental symbols of Lake Baikal (lower left), the Volga River (top), and the Aral Sea, the latter two inscripted with "Region of Ecological Disaster." Photo: RAND.

In addition to being the largest committee in the USSR Supreme Soviet, the Committee on Questions of Ecology and the Rational Use of Natural Resources was one of the parliament's more active bodies. Besides preparing environmental protection legislation, the committee participated in drafting other laws having ramifications for the environment: The committee prepared its own version of the Law on Land in order to ensure that the Supreme Soviet would be aware of the environmental concerns associated with questions of land ownership; reviewed the content of legislation setting income taxes for businesses and individuals; and successfully added an amendment to legislation governing the conduct of Soviet trade representatives abroad, requiring them to inform foreign investors of Soviet environmental regulations and to ensure that imported goods conformed to Soviet standards. The committee also held highly publicized hearings on Chernobyl and on the 1957 nuclear explosion at Kyshtym (Chelyabinsk-40), although these were designed more to further the environmental education of the deputies and the public than to prepare legislation.

One factor limiting the authority and effectiveness of both the ecology committee and the greater parliament was the lack of support services. The USSR Supreme Soviet had fewer than 600 staff workers assisting all 542 legislators, 14 committees, and 8 commissions. Each deputy could call on one or two personal assistants, and the ecology committee employed four full-time staff members. Moreover, staff members often were preoccupied with responding to sundry queries and complaints from deputies' constituents. Finally the essential state of the Soviet economy— with its shortage of telephones, photocopiers, facsimile machines, and most importantly, paper—hampered deputies' efficient work.

During its two and one-half years of existence, the Supreme Soviet was dominated by a large number of basic constitutional and housekeeping issues, and environmental problems barely made the agenda.[58] Despite this, in November 1989, the body passed its first resolution on environmental matters, entitled "On Urgent Measures to Promote the Country's Ecological Recovery."[59] In style and tone, the resolution proved very similar to the array of government and party resolutions passed in the 1960s and 1970s. It set out a broad array of objectives, most of which already were under consideration by the government or had strong support in the public arena. Like its predecessors, the resolution was declarative and did not have the force of law. Among other points, it directed government agencies at all levels to develop long-range plans for environmental protection and resource use. As of 1990, all new development projects would have to be approved by a government commission of ecological experts before receiving public funding. The Ministry of Defense and other agencies were to review options for closing the Semipalatinsk nuclear weapons test site in Kazakhstan and to study effects of testing at the northern Russian test site at Novaya Zemlya. Finally, the resolution called for a series of new laws on nature conservation, nature reserves, protection of plant life, the use of nuclear energy, and safety in the nuclear power industry.

Like the resolution establishing Goskompriroda almost two years earlier, the emergency resolution was good in its intention but too broad, vague, and overambitious. The requirement for all projects to have an environmental impact statement was a case in point; several weeks before the Supreme Soviet passed the emergency resolution, a vice-president of the USSR Academy of Sciences told *The Economist* that scientists under his supervision were so overwhelmed by the number of requests for environmental assessments (under existing regulations) that they lacked the time to evaluate adequately even the most critical projects.[60]

On yet another point, the legislators did not think through the economic implications of their resolution. Within the section on land management, the resolution stated: "Beginning January 1, 1991, overcutting in designated timber areas is prohibited, and beginning in 1990 felling of cedar is banned." This injunction was less warranted by a shortage of cedar trees than by the tremendous waste and destruction caused by the timber industry in search of cedar. Two days before the resolution was to take effect, Soviet Prime Minister Ryzhkov bent to strong pressure from the ministries and ordered a partial rescission of the resolution, contingent on the agreement of the localities involved. Environmental activists in Tomsk oblast, a center of the cedar industry, managed to uphold the original resolution, however. By March, *Izvestiya* reported that three pencil factories were "on the verge of a shutdown" for a lack of feedstock, potentially costing the economy 1.3 billion pencils, 500 million rubles in lost income, and thousands of jobs. A solution remained in the distant future, as the timber and pencil industries needed time and money to obtain less destructive and more efficient equipment. "With time, it's possible for chemists to find a substitute for cedar. But that's tomorrow," the daily noted. "Perhaps it is worthwhile for the Supreme Soviet to 'read through' the simple prohibition in its resolution once more."[61]

ENVIRONMENTAL POLITICS IN REPUBLIC AND LOCAL LEGISLATURES

In early 1990, open elections were held for the parliaments and soviets at the republic and local levels. Unlike the all-Union elections held the year before, the CPSU and other public organizations were not given guaranteed seats in these legislatures. In most cases, then, the local and regional parliaments proved to be more democratic than the all-Union Supreme Soviet. As at the all-Union level, the electorates put many respected environmentalists into their local legislatures, many of whom subsequently assumed prominent positions within environmental committees of these bodies. The result is that parliamentary environmental committees have enjoyed public respect and support not accorded the governmental environment agencies.

Because the republics and their subordinate units inherited similar legal structures, legislative initiatives undertaken at the republic and regional levels have been similar to those of the Soviet parliaments. Thus, environmental politics have centered around rewriting laws on environmental protection and drafting new laws governing foreign investment, private property rights, and the development of market mechanisms. Parliaments also have passed a slate of various decrees, concerning everything from banning the sale of pesticide-contaminated food to declaring regions "ecological disaster zones." As the latter example indicates, most are only declaratory statements of general principles rather than detailed prescriptions for solving environmental problems. A case in point is the comprehensive Russian law "On Environmental Protection," signed by President Boris Yeltsin in December 1991.[62]

The Russian law on the environment was derived from a similar project being pursued in the Soviet parliament but never put to the entire body for consideration. Members of the Russian environmental committee actively worked on the draft; Viktor Petrov, a conservative law professor at Moscow State University, served as principal author. Like its Soviet-inspired antecedent passed in 1961, the 1991 Russian law sets out noble principles—for example, every citizen has the right to a healthy and safe environment. To this end, the law establishes the areas of responsibility of the various levels of government within the Russian Federation, many of which are overlapping. The federal government, for example, is tasked with establishing environmental standards and procedures for setting fees for natural resources use. Governments at the republic level[63] set fees and issue licenses for natural resource use. Regional (krai and oblast) governments issue permits for pollution emissions. Regional and local agencies are responsible for monitoring emissions, and republic- and regional-level agents enforce compliance with federal standards. On this point, the law also stipulates a positive role for individuals and nongovernmental organizations to assist with monitoring and enforcement and guarantees their right to association, their right to information, and their right to seek legal redress for environmental degradation.

In a structure drawn from the USSR Supreme Soviet's emergency legislation, the Russian law mandates environmental impact statements for all development activities. The law sets out the obligations of enterprises with regard to compliance with standards concerning waste management, handling of hazardous materials, air and water emissions, noise pollution, land use and reclamation. Of note, the law extends all regulations to include all military operations on Russian territory, ending the Soviet tradition whereby the military could act independently of the law.[64] In what signals a dramatic departure from the past, the law mandates criminal liability for "environmental damage" as well as "obligation for full compensation" for damages to the environment and also to public health. Finally, the law also contains several novelties, such as mandating "environmental insurance" against natural or manmade disasters and establishing the concept of a "zone of environmental disaster" where all but essential economic activities must be halted in order to restore the environment.

Conversations with legislators and administrators revealed a belief that in its present form, this law will dramatically improve environmental management in the Russian Federation. It will not, for several reasons. First, the law is strikingly similar to its Communist-inspired antecedents; rather than setting out explicit goals and mandating specific programs, the document merely makes declarative statements on the right of individuals to a clean environment. Rafael Vartanov of Moscow's Institute of World Economy and International Relations criticized the lack of specificity regarding the right granted to the public to monitor environmental quality and report violations, arguing it "smacks of useless, bureaucratic scurrying."[65]

Second, the law says little about the reform of and future role for the judiciary, which as Vartanov points out, "was merely window dressing for a totalitarian regime."[66] In the Soviet era, judges were appointed for their credentials as good Communists, not impartial jurists. Moreover, environmental matters were one of the lowest judicial priorities of the Soviet era, and few magistrates and lawyers have experience in the field. Lacking personal motivation to protect the environment and working legal codes and precedents on which to render decisions, judges frequently abstained from hearing cases related to the environment. As a result, enforcement of environmental regulations, when it did occur, was an essentially administrative matter managed by the state. These circumstances have persisted because the judiciary has remained largely unreformed in the post-Soviet era. Petrov, the bill's author, conceded: "In order for this article of the law to be effective, the whole court system should be changed."[67] Thus, creating a judiciary that is responsive to environmental matters will be a long-term task.

Finally, as is evident from the preceding description, the Russian environmental law is an ambitious attempt to regulate everything from electromagnetic radiation to the maintenance of health resorts. The broad array of issues covered in such a short document (four newspaper pages) speaks to the cursory nature with which each issue was treated. As adopted, the law represented a desire by parliamentarians to cover as many areas of environmental protection possible—and as soon as possible—rather than take time to pass detailed and thorough legislation for specific issues, such as air or water pollution, and then leave vast issue-areas essentially unregulated. Thus, the new Russian law sets a long agenda of future legislation to be passed and rules and regulations to be adopted (regarding the environment as well as judicial and economic reform, for example) before the rights and responsibilities stated therein will be enforced.

More autonomous than environmental bureaucrats in government, popularly elected parliamentarians have proved to be outspoken on environmental issues and committed to change—and thus have earned the support of many environmentalists. Despite the interest and activism of the parliaments and their ecology committees, deputies' attention often had been diverted to the more pressing tasks of resolving the structure and fate of society. Pursuant to their avowed goal of turning their countries into "law-based civil societies," legislators have been immersed in the newfound art of writing laws to redefine every aspect of society; crowding the agenda with environmental regulations are bills governing everything from taxes and pensions to property ownership, the structure of government, market reforms, and ethnic relations. The volume of these necessary tasks only increased exponentially with the sudden independence of the Soviet republics. Unfortunately, most parliamentarians tackling the monumental task of rewriting the legal base of their societies are not professional politicians or lawyers but average citizens propelled into their positions through the fast-paced and fluid process of democratization. Politicians and public alike hoped that the election of new representatives and the drafting of new laws would be sufficient to reform Soviet society, but they soon discovered that it was far easier to declare new policies than to implement them.

DECENTRALIZATION OF ENVIRONMENTAL DECISIONMAKING IN THE POST-SOVIET ERA

During its four years of existence, USSR Goskompriroda remained fiscally impoverished, institutionally weak, and perpetually embroiled in bureaucratic struggles. By the time of the demise of the Soviet government at the close of 1991, the all-Union environmental agency failed to sponsor any major environmental legislation or to implement any significant new environmental protection programs. In the end, few seemed concerned about the agency's demise.

Saddled with many new responsibilities, the Soviet successor states also have inherited substantial institutional legacies from the former system: environmental bureaucracies, parliamentary committees, monitoring networks, detailed environmental and public health norms, research institutes, and a system of national parks and wildlife preserves. Finally, there remains a body of standard operating procedures and bureaucratic networks that drive the entire system. Though underdeveloped and often flawed, these institutions offer the Soviet Union's successor states an interim framework on which to base future environmental policies. Given the inheritance of much of Soviet government bureaucracy and technical establishment, environmental policymaking in the Russian Federation is likely to change very little in the near future. Environmental agencies in Ukraine, Belarus, and the Baltic states were created in response to local needs before the 1988 organization of Goskompriroda; as the imposed Soviet uniformity gives way, these republics will devise their own approaches to environmental protection. The Central Asian governments, on the other hand, may see their bureaucracies atrophy entirely because of a lack of trained specialists, equipment, and financing. Indeed, the end of the Soviet era may witness the last efforts at centralized environmental management in poorer regions of Central Asia.

Political leaders and environmentalists alike expect that the decentralization and democratization of the policy process begun in the late 1980s and radically advanced by the demise of the USSR will result in greater responsibility and accountability of government agents toward the management of natural resources—the underlying principle being that local control over natural resources tends to foster a spirit of stewardship. The Soviet government never seriously considered the interests of the republics and their communities, argues Vyacheslav Vashanov, an environmental official from the Russian Federation; rather, "all-Union interests," such as boosting state power, prevailed.[68]

The demise of the Soviet government, however, did not resolve all pressures for decentralization of environmental decisionmaking. Heated disputes centering around natural resources issues continue, most notably in the Russian Federation. In October 1991, for example, the Krasnoyarsk territorial soviet passed a resolution calling on the Russian government to grant the region the status of a republic within the Federation. Deputies objected to the fact that their territory, which is roughly the size of Argentina, had no right of ownership of its vast natural resources and, thus, no ability to capture the wealth of its industry or to shape the path of its future development. "Colonial policies towards Siberia continue to this very day," asserted V. Novikov, chair of the territorial soviet.[69]

A devolution of decisionmaking and funding authority does not guarantee that environmentally sound policies will follow, however. At the heart of the conflict is the surrender or, frequently, the usurpation of executive authority in an era of rapidly declining bureaucratic control from the centers of political power. As noted earlier, in 1992, the Russian government cut all funding to its local environmental protection agencies. To resolve the funding crisis, Danilov-Danil'yan noted: "It was proposed to transfer funding of the local agencies to the oblasts, but the potential implications of such a decision are very clear. These local agencies would be completely dependent on the oblast administrations, which would be able to do whatever they wanted with them." The environment minister went on to point out that many regional administrations were selling rights to log forest land in order to make a quick ruble—"Something they have no right to do."[70] Officials in the Tuva Autonomous Republic which borders Mongolia usurped the authority of the Russian federal government and turned over a section of the autonomous republic's only nature preserve to a local collective farm for reindeer grazing.[71] Local authorities in Turkmenistan permitted hunting in the Krasnovodsk Bay nature preserve, first created in 1932, as well as cattle grazing in the Kugitang reserve.[72]

Three separate scientific appraisals carried out between 1987 and 1989 recommended against the construction of the Katun hydroelectric station located in the Gorno-Altai autonomous oblast of the Russian Federation. Conservationists fear that dislocation caused by the construction of the dam and the rise of a huge reservoir would endanger wildlife in one of the last pristine regions remaining in the Russian Federation. Moreover, the region, which is nestled in the mountains bordering with Kazakhstan and Mongolia, contains deposits of mercury, cadmium, and arsenic that scientists fear could leach from the ground and contaminate the water supply for 3 million people living in the Katun and Ob River basins downstream. In the words of the Social-Ecological Union's Mariya Cherkasova, the project is "a pre-planned catastrophe."[73] Despite a unanimous decision by the Russian Supreme Soviet in September 1990 to cancel the dam, local politicians have sought international support to back their decision to press on with the project.[74]

In the estimate of Danilov-Danil'yan, Russia's environmental agency can be effective only with tight vertical bureaucratic control, which it does not yet exercise. Vitalii Chelyshev, a member of the former USSR Supreme Soviet Ecology Committee, commented: "We recently met with some Americans; they say 'You simply need good laws.' I posit that we also need their normal execution."[75]

INSTITUTIONS OF INTERSTATE COOPERATION IN THE POST-SOVIET ERA

Unlike the forces of decentralization, autarky, and independence, environmental degradation does not acknowledge political boundaries and, indeed, is often exacerbated as a result of them. Thus, there remains a great need for coordination and collective action across newly rising borders. Cooperation to prevent another nuclear power plant disaster at one of the 45 Soviet-built nuclear power units punctuating the landscape is of paramount importance. Each republic also will want to monitor the transfer of hazardous materials—radioactive substances in particular—across its borders. If the Baltic states ever hope to clean up the Baltic Sea, they will need the assistance of St. Petersburg; St. Petersburg meanwhile suffers from air pollution streaming in from power plants in northeast Estonia. Industrial pollution from Belarus affects drinking water supplies in Latvia. Russia receives air pollution from Ukraine. Ukraine and Russia must coordinate their activities to save the Azov Sea. Four republics plus Iran pollute the Caspian Sea. The five Central Asian republics share in the fate of the Aral Sea.

Environmental cooperation in the former Soviet region has become more problematic, however, as the newly sovereign states must negotiate and concur on every point at hand. As is characteristic of most international agreements concerning the environment, negotiations among the Soviet successor states are likely to be drawn out, appeal to the lowest common denominator, contain minimal binding commitments, provide few mechanisms for effective enforcement, and be threatened by free-rider interests that resist accepting their share of responsibility.[76] Unfortunately, the demise of the USSR brought increased political stresses among the Soviet successor states. Conflict has been sharpest in the military and economic spheres, as states seek to enhance their strategic position vis-à-vis each other. Although issues like rising barriers to trade and the fate of the Soviet military have predominated, recent developments also indicate increased tension with regard to environmental affairs.

In the wake of a serious turbine fire that crippled the number 2 unit at Ukraine's Chernobyl nuclear power plant, the Supreme Soviet of Belarus passed a resolution calling for immediate notification in the case of accident at the nuclear power plants located in neighboring Lithuania, Russia, and Ukraine. The document noted that the Chernobyl plant, which is located close to the Belarusian border, "presents great danger" to the region and to the world. Moreover, the parliament called for an agreement detailing states' "full ecological and economic responsibility" for damage caused by a nuclear accident.[77]

In January 1992, the Krasnoyarsk territorial government announced that it would no longer accept spent fuel rods coming from nuclear reactors located in Ukraine. According to media reports, Krasnoyarsk officials were angry that Ukraine had not fulfilled existing contracts to supply sugar, vegetable oil, and other goods to the region, and that

Ukrainian authorities had refused to renegotiate barter contracts for the future.[78] The storage facility reportedly was the only such site in the former USSR designed to store the fuel rods, and Krasnoyarsk officials apparently were looking to strike a more advantageous deal with the newly independent republic. "It's difficult for us to explain our one-way partnership [with Ukraine] to our inhabitants," said a local official. "If we receive radioactive wastes for storage, then we must receive appropriate compensation. And our decision is the final argument in favor of equal economic cooperation."[79] As mentioned in Chapter 5, the Russian parliament called for the banning of all radioactive imports, suggesting that the conflict over waste disposal might be long-term.

Despite these obstacles, many observers in the former Soviet Union continue to advocate a limited role for some interrepublican institutions and agreements concerning such areas as elaboration of environmental regulations, coordination of environmental monitoring and research, and oversight of safety at nuclear power installations. Until the final days of the USSR, the Soviet minister of the environment, Nikolai Vorontsov, argued adamantly for the maintenance of some form of interrepublican environmental organization, warning that the collapse of all-Union institutions may result in environmental "chaos."[80] On the issue of air pollution in the Baltic region, for example, Vorontsov asked, "Is it possible to declare the 'independence' of the atmosphere?"[81] Some of the Soviet successor states have attempted to continue cooperation and to preserve some basic environmentally related functions of the former regime, at least within their own geographic region. In October 1991, water resources ministers from Kazakhstan and the Central Asian republics gathered at Tashkent to pen an agreement recognizing the region's water resources as derived from a "common basin," and calling for coordinated water use in the region.[82]

At the February 1992 meeting of members of the Commonwealth of Independent States (CIS) in Moscow, participants (with the notable exception of Ukraine) signed the interrepublican agreement "On Cooperation in the Area of Ecology and Environmental Protection."[83] In the agreement, the participant states recognized that "borders between governments do not coincide with natural-ecological and basin boundaries," adding that economic activity in one state "must not cause damage to the environment, the public's quality of life, or economic activity of other states." To this end, the parties resolved among other points to coordinate and cooperate on the drafting and enforcement of environmental legislation and regulations, monitoring and assessing environmental quality (in part, by maintaining the former Soviet meteorological service), preserving wilderness areas and biodiversity, and pursuing joint environmental research. Moreover, they agreed to form an interstate ecological council composed of the environment ministers of the participating states to oversee cooperative ventures, to settle disputes, and to render disaster assistance.[84]

The fact that environmental issues appeared on a crowded political agenda at such an early stage in the CIS negotiation process is encouraging. The thrust of the agreements illustrates a desire to maintain a "common regulatory space" with regard to the environment, which not only will help the region avoid environmentally destructive economic competition but also will make the regulatory environment more comprehensible to potential foreign investors. In the case of the Central Asian republics, the desire for cooperation also may reflect a recognition that they are unable to pursue their own policies and programs, given a lack of expertise and resources.

The agreements to date represent a low-cost attempt to save the most basic and effective elements of the Soviet regime. Under Soviet rule, for example, each state followed a common body of environmental standards and regulations, and states' environmental laws, many of which were developed independently over the past few years, remain similar in form and content as well. Thus, many of the pledges already characterize the status quo and do not mark a significant departure from past priorities and practices. Nevertheless, like all of the documents on cooperation penned by members of the CIS, agreements to date regarding the environment are broad statements of good intention backed up by few specifics and minimal commitments.

The test of any cooperation will come in the application. Because all states now are equal competitors on the world market, the possibility exists that they may pursue beggar-thy-neighbor policies as poorer states seek advantages in attracting foreign investment and trade by relaxing environmental regulations. Similarly, competition for finite resources—such as water for irrigation in Central Asia or fishing rights in the Black and Caspian seas—will be keen, tempting governments to free ride on an agreement. Meanwhile, the potential for conflict over the environment has increased dramatically, a function of increased economic competition in the region as well as a rise in international stress overall. States will be less likely to cooperate on environmental issues if relations among them are strained—a significant possibility, given the large number of territorial, military, and economic disputes that are pitting people and republics against each other. Sergei Karaganov of Moscow's Institute of Europe set the Kremlin's new priorities in perspective: "The real agenda of Russian foreign policy is avoiding war. Not war with the United States, but war within our Commonwealth."[85]

Notes

1. Eric Green, *Ecology and Perestroika* (Washington, DC: American Committee on U.S.-Soviet Relations, 1990), p. 8.

2. USSR Goskompriroda, *Sostoyanie prirodnoi sredy v SSSR v 1988 g.* (Moscow: VINITI, 1989), pp. 2–4.

3. Other agencies involved were USSR Gidromet, USSR Gosplan, and the USSR Council of Ministers State Committee for Science and Technology.

4. Barbara Geddes, "Building 'State' Autonomy in Brazil, 1930–1964," *Comparative Politics,* January 1990.

5. *Komsomol'skaya pravda,* July 18, 1989, pp. 1, 4.

6. *Pravitel'stvennyi vestnik,* No. 17, 1989.

7. Green, *Ecology,* p. 9.

8. *Sobesednik,* No. 3, 1990, p. 9.

9. Vladislav Larin, "Opasnoe neponimanie," *Energiya: Ekonomika, tekhnika, ekologiya,* No. 4, 1990, p. 6.

10. Mikhail Dubrovskii, "Zashchita Vorontsova," *Poisk,* No. 28, 1989, p. 4.

11. Petr I. Poletaev, "Vosstanovit' garmoniyu prirody i cheloveka," *Zdorov'e,* No. 6, 1989, p. 1. The experience of Goskompriroda has a precedent in Soviet history: Shortly after the October revolution in 1917, the Bolshevik government was forced to call back many of the deposed imperial government's bureaucrats whom the new regime had summarily fired. The revolutionaries did not know how to manage a government.

12. Rafael and Hamida Yernazarov, staff members, Kazakh Ecological Fund, personal communication, Los Angeles, April 1992.

13. *Sovetskaya kul'tura,* March 10, 1990, p. 5.

14. Yevgenii Gol'tsman, "Vremya vypolnyat' zakon," *Energiya: Ekonomika, tekhnika, ekologiya,* No. 4, 1988, p. 3.

15. *Izvestiya,* August 6, 1990, p. 3.

16. *Trud,* January 18, 1990, p. 1.

17. *Sovetskaya kul'tura,* August 5, 1989, p. 4. This point was made by Viktor Akovetskii, a member of the Collegium of USSR Goskompriroda.

18. Green, *Ecology,* p. 11.

19. *Economist,* April 27, 1991, p. 20.

20. Dubrovskii, "Zashchita Vorontsova," p. 4.

21. In 1978, Izrael' was appointed chief of the then USSR State Committee for Hydrometeorology and Environmental Control. With the creation of Goskompriroda in 1988, it was changed to the USSR State Committee for Hydrometeorology, with Izrael' retained as its head.

22. See, for example, *Komsomol'skaya pravda,* April 26, 1991, p. 2.

23. Gol'tsman, "Vremya vypolnyat' zakon," p. 3.

24. Green, *Ecology,* p. 11.

25. *Molodezh Moldavii,* August 2, 1990, p. 2, translated in JPRS-UPA-90-056, p. 68.

26. *Kuranty,* March 12, 1992, p. 4.

27. Discussion about government spending is complicated by the fact that the value of the ruble declined rapidly in recent years, whereas prices, which were state-set and very stable, rose sharply with economic reform. Nevertheless, spending figures are useful for comparing the level of funding on environmental protection in recent years.

28. *Vestnik statistiki*, No. 4, 1991, p. 21; USSR Goskomstat, *Press-vypusk*, No. 226, June 7, 1990.

29. The shortage of funds was particularly severe when it came to managing the region's 190-odd nature preserves and national parks; in 1988, the Soviet government allocated just 44.6 million rubles to this endeavor. Vorontsov referred to the parks as "completely indigent organizations" and described the people who work in the parks as "simply devotees." N. V. Uspenskaya, "Nuzhna polnaya ekologicheskaya glasnost'!" *Priroda*, No. 11, 1989, p. 5.

30. USSR Goskomstat, *Press-vypusk*, No. 226, June 7, 1990. According to accounting by Vorontsov, environmental spending during the Eleventh Five-Year Plan (1981–1985) averaged 1.23 percent of gross national income *(valovoi natsional'nyi dokhod)*. Uspenskaya, p. 5.

31. In 1988, U.S. spending for abatement, regulation, and research and design pertaining to air and water pollution and disposal of solid waste in the nonagricultural sectors totaled $86 billion, or 1.9 percent of a GNP of $4.9 trillion. Government spending accounted for 22.5 percent of this amount. U.S. Bureau of Census, *Statistical Abstract of the United States: 1991* (Washington, DC: Government Printing Office, 1990), pp. 213, 431.

32. Boris Rumer, "Investment in the 12th Five-Year Plan," *Soviet Studies*, Vol. 43, No. 3, 1991, p. 455.

33. *Vestnik statistiki*, No. 6, 1990, p. 39; USSR Goskomstat, *Press-vypusk*, No. 226, June 7, 1990. In 1989, 2.2 billion rubles were allocated for capital investment on water pollution control; 15 percent went unspent. The figures for air pollution control in 1989 were 404,000 rubles and 24 percent, respectively.

34. USSR Goskomstat, *Okhrana okruzhayushchei sredy i ratsional'noe ispol'zovanie prirodnykh resursov v SSSR* (Moscow: Finansy i statistika, 1989), pp. 151–152. See also Stanislav Shatalin et al., *Perekhod k rynky: Kontseptsiya i programma* (Moscow: Arkhangel'skoe, 1990), p. 179. Between 1981 and 1985, an average of 5,367 wastewater treatment facilities were commissioned per year nationwide; in 1988, the number was 5,196. The corresponding figures for air pollution controls were 40,000 and 25,820, respectively.

35. USSR Goskomstat, *Press-vypusk*, No. 76, February 21, 1990. In 1989, 73 projects across the USSR were commissioned as planned; 77 were not. Broken down by sector, the completion rate was 50 percent for water pollution control projects and 56 percent for air pollution control. USSR Goskomstat, *Press-vypusk*, No. 226, June 7, 1990.

36. *Ekonomika i zhizn'*, No. 5, 1991, p. 11.

37. "O gosudarstvennom predpriyatii (ob"edinenii)," *Vedomosti Verkhovnogo Soveta Soyuza Sovetskikh Sotsialisticheskikh Respublik*, No. 26, 1987.

38. *Pravda*, January 17, 1988, p. 2.

39. Novosti Press Agency, *Perestroika Panorama*, No. 38, 1990.

40. "Gosudarstvennaya programma okhrany okruzhayushchei sredy . . .," *Ekonomika i zhizn'*, No. 41, 1990, insert pp. 3-4. Discussion of the efficacy of economic levers for environmental management was not a product of perestroika but had been a topic in Soviet academic literature since the 1970s. For recent discussion, consult, for instance, Konstantin G. Gofman and Nikolai P. Fedorenko, "Ekonomicheskaya zashchita prirody," *Kommunist*, No. 5, 1989; N. Bystritskaya and V. Baranova, "O sisteme platezhei za vodnye resursy," *Planovoe khozyaistvo*, No. 12, 1989; Nadezhda V. Pakhomova, "Okhrana okruzhayushchei sredy: Perekhod k ekonomicheskim metodam upravleniya," *Vestnik Leningradskogo Gosudarstvennogo Universiteta: Seriya ekonomicheskaya*, No. 5, 1990; *Ekonomicheskaya gazeta*, No. 41, 1989; *Ekonomika i zhizn'*, No. 4, 1990.

41. *Ekonomicheskaya gazeta*, No. 52, 1989, p. 18.

42. Central Television, "Vremya," September 3, 1990.

43. *Pravda*, April 19, 1990, p. 2; TASS, November 25, 1989.

44. *Pravda*, January 7, 1991, p. 3.

45. *Krasnaya zvezda*, March 22, 1991, p. 4.

46. Anatolii Grebenyuk, deputy chair, Committee on Ecology, Kyrgyz Supreme Soviet, personal communication, Moscow, 1991.

47. In 1990, an experimental polluter-pays system was implemented in 49 oblasts. The federationwide system was outlined in the 1991 law on the environment. *Rossiiskaya gazeta*, March 3, 1992, pp. 3–6.

48. *Kuranty*, March 12, 1992, p. 4.

49. Robert W. Hahn, "Economic Prescriptions for Environmental Problems: How the Patient Followed the Doctor's Orders," *Journal of Economic Perspectives*, Spring 1989.

50. Green, *Ecology*, p. 21.

51. James M. Buchanan, "External Diseconomies, Corrective Taxes, and Market Structure," *American Economic Review*, March 1969, pp. 174–177.

52. Vasilii A. Bakunin, Chair, Chelyabinsk Oblast Committee for the Protection of Nature, personal communication, Chelyabinsk, August 1992.

53. The other one-third of the deputies were nominated to the Congress by "social organizations" such as the Communist Party of the Soviet Union, trade unions, the military, and the USSR Academy of Sciences—a device contrived by Gorbachev to maintain control over the body.

54. For a discussion of two candidates' positions on environmental affairs, see Matthew Sagers, "News Notes," *Soviet Geography*, October 1989, pp. 680–685.

55. "Jerusalem Environmental Conference" (no author), *Environmental Policy Review*, January 1990, p. 13. The count was made by Yurii Shcherbak.

56. *Izvestiya*, May 29, 1989, p. 5.

57. *Izvestiya*, June 1, 1989, p. 7.

58. During the USSR Supreme Soviet's first session in the summer and autumn of 1989, the environment was the last of 34 items on the agenda. Larin, "Opasnoe neponimanie," p. 5.

59. For the text of the resolution, see *Izvestiya*, December 3, 1989. For a more detailed review of its contents, see DJ Peterson, "Supreme Soviet Passes Environmental Resolution," *Report on the USSR*, No. 49, 1989; and William

Freeman, "Environmental Issues in the USSR Supreme Soviet," U.S. Information Agency, Research Memorandum, January 25, 1990.

60. *Economist*, November 4, 1989, p. 26.

61. *Izvestiya*, March 9, 1990, p. 2.

62. *Rossiiskaya gazeta*, March 3, 1992, pp. 3–6. For a copy of a similar law adopted by Turkmenistan, see *Turkmenskaya iskra*, December 5, 1991, pp. 2–3.

63. This level includes autonomous oblasts and autonomous okrugs.

64. The potential impact of this clause was stressed by Kristen Suokko, National Resources Defense Council, telephone communication, April 1992.

65. Rafael Vartanov, "A Response to the New Russian Law on Environmental Protection," trans. Scott D. Monroe in *CIS Environmental Watch*, No. 2, Spring 1992, p. 24.

66. Ibid.

67. Douglas Stangin, "Toxic Wasteland," *US News and World Report*, April 13, 1992, p. 45.

68. Presentation at conference on Democratic Federalism and Environmental Crisis in the Republics of the Former Soviet Union, Moscow, August 1991.

69. *Izvestiya*, February 25, 1992, p. 2. See also *Izvestiya*, November 22, 1991, p. 2. For more on national resources issues in Siberia, see Andrew R. Bond, ed., "Panel on Siberia: Economic and Territorial Issues," *Soviet Geography*, June 1991.

70. *Kuranty*, March 12, 1992, p. 4.

71. *Izvestiya*, May 8, 1991, p. 8.

72. Steve Raymer, "Cash Needs Precede Forests in Poverty-Stricken Russia," *National Geographic News Feature*, April 1992, p. 5.

73. "The State of Soviet Ecology: An Interview with Maria Cherkasova" (no author), *Multinational Monitor*, March 1990, p. 25.

74. Andrei Ivanov-Smolenskii, coordinator for nature protection and biodiversity, USSR Social-Ecological Union, personal communication, Los Angeles, October 1991.

75. Central Television, "TSN," October 21, 1991.

76. Peter H. Sand, "International Cooperation: The Environmental Experience," in Jessica Tuchman Matthews, ed., *Preserving the Global Environment* (New York: W. W. Norton, 1991), pp. 236–279.

77. *Izvestiya*, November 28, 1991, p. 2.

78. Radio Moscow, January 8, 1992; Central Television, "Informatsionnaya programma," January 11, 1992.

79. TASS, January 15, 1992.

80. *Moscow News*, No. 44, 1990, p. 3.

81. *Sel'skaya zhizn'*, October 29, 1991, p. 3.

82. UzTAG-TASS, October 11, 1991. For an extensive review of water resource issues in the region, see Gregory Gleason, "The Struggle for Control over Water in Central Asia: Republican Sovereignty and Collective Action," *Report on the USSR*, No. 25, 1991.

83. TASS, February 9, 1992.

84. Various CIS member states have signed other protocols, including agreements to cooperate on preserving the Aral Sea and on the Chernobyl

cleanup (TASS, December 30, 1991), and to preserve fish stocks in the Caspian Sea (*Rossiiskaya gazeta*, January 1, 1991, p. 2).

85. *Los Angeles Times*, January 30, 1992, p. A12.

7

The Environmental Movement and Environmental Politics

An ecologist is a healthy guy in boots who lies behind a knoll and through binoculars watches a squirrel eat nuts. We can manage quite well without these bums.
—Nikita S. Khrushchev

The people's growing ecological environmental awareness is one of the manifestations of the democratization of society and a key factor of perestroika. . . .
We must welcome this in every way possible.
—Mikhail Gorbachev

Like a steady wind fanning a forest fire, the revelations of eco-glasnost in the 1980s fed the rage of a public long suppressed by the communist regime. In response to the state's inaction, citizens formed hundreds of environmental organizations to take matters into their own hands. The political impact of environmental interest groups has been augmented by the demise of centralized authority and the natural affinity between environmental and ethnic issues in the former Soviet context. As a result, environmental groups have evolved into an important catalyst for change in the Soviet and post-Soviet era. In a society where the state once attempted to organize and control virtually all social activities, the rapid mobilization of independent nongovernmental organizations (NGOs) is remarkable and indicates the rise of a "civil society" in the former Soviet Union.

Nevertheless, numerous obstacles remain: The dead hand of bureaucracy discourages citizens' initiatives, and authorities, threatened by the
rise of independent and powerful voices, often put up obstacles to their
newfound challengers. Moreover, poor communications facilities thwart
interaction among groups, and their relative poverty prevents their undertaking any large-scale programs. Finally, the stresses of economic reform and upheaval draw attention away from ecology. The effect is that
environmental groups have been slow to evolve beyond movements of
opposition into the types of grassroots self-help organizations that have
been so effective at promoting local development and environmental
protection in the United States, Latin America, Asia, and elsewhere
around the world.

THE MAGNITUDE OF CONCERN ABOUT
THE ENVIRONMENT

With the revelations of glasnost, citizens became acutely aware that
environmental conditions in their neighborhoods were far from favorable. Though crude by Western standards, local public opinion polling
has revealed the magnitude of concern about the environment.[1] In a 1989
USSR Goskomstat survey, 1 in 10 people surveyed said the environment
was the country's most serious problem. Of twelve major problems
enumerated, cleaning up the environment was listed fourth, behind food
supply problems, poor housing conditions, and inflation. Surprisingly, it
surpassed such pressing and visible issues as ethnic tensions, social injus-
tice, poor healthcare, and crime.[2] In 1990 and 1991, official surveys reported by USSR Goskomstat revealed that almost one-half of the urban
population polled considered environmental conditions in their neighborhoods to be "unsatisfactory."[3] In July 1991, the Russian state statistical agency reported that of those polled in another study, three-quarters
considered environmental conditions in their hometown "intolerable."[4]
In a survey conducted in the Moscow region in spring 1990,
environmental degradation was ranked as the most important social
problem. Of those polled, 98.1 percent rated the issue "important" or
"very important." Less pressing issues, by comparison, were crime (94.7
percent), food shortages (94.4 percent), and consumer goods shortages
(93.4 percent).[5] In a 1989 survey conducted in Ukraine, environmental
problems were "the main concern" of 26 percent of the population, behind economic problems (44 percent) but well ahead of political and
cultural issues.[6]

Of all environmental issues, citizens are most strongly antinuclear; so
powerful is their aversion, that the mood aptly has been labeled

"radiophobia." Two nonbinding, unofficial referendums conducted in 1990 illustrate the level of sentiment against nuclear power.[7] In February, voters in the small Ural Mountains city of Neftekamsk went to the polls to decide the fate of the Bashkir Atomic Energy Station, located 30 kilometers away. The referendum, organized by the Neftekamsk (population 109,000) city government along the lines of a regular election, attracted an 80 percent turnout of voters—a stunning 99 percent of whom voted to halt construction of the plant immediately.[8] Three months later in the Russian city of Voronezh (population 895,000), a local group calling itself Ecological Initiative prodded the city government into holding a referendum on the fate of a nuclear-powered citywide heating system. Of the 82 percent of the voting-age population who went to the polls, 96 percent turned down the scheme.[9]

The environmental movement has garnered great respect from the public, in part as a result of its efforts to discover the truth about ecological conditions. In the spring 1990 survey of Muscovites previously mentioned, the Green movement had earned the trust of over 54 percent of the population. Only the Russian Orthodox Church (64 percent) and the military (56 percent) scored better. Far down on the list was the CPSU (39 percent), the official trade unions (37 percent), and the government (28 percent).[10] Anatolii Panov, vice-president of the Zelenyi Svit (Green World) environmental association, claimed his organization enjoyed the highest trust rating of any group in Ukraine in 1991.[11]

THE RESPONSE OF THE GOVERNMENT TO THE ENVIRONMENTAL MOVEMENT

The best way to gauge the strength of the environmental movement is to examine its impact on the government policy process. Responding to the public's concern, many politicians make a point of showing their awareness of environmental problems and their desire to resolve them. Officials and politicians frequently visit ecological hot spots to render some measure of political first aid. For example, in August 1990, Boris Yeltsin, recently elected chairman of the Supreme Soviet in the Russian Federation, took advantage of this traditionally quiet period in Soviet politics to make a three-week tour of Siberia and the Far East; he wanted to assess environmental conditions. "I received a very strong sense of colossal problems on my trip," he told Radio Moscow.[12] One year later, campaigning for the Russian presidency, Yeltsin again made a point of visiting ecological hot spots such as Chelyabinsk oblast and Sakhalin Island.

Citizens protest heavy pollution in the central Siberian city of Kemerovo, heart of the Kuznetsk industrial basin. Photo: Novosti Press Agency from Sovfoto.

Obsessed with bolstering its public image, even the KGB took pains to demonstrate its environmental awareness. In October 1990, the Soviet news agency TASS noted that the KGB had prepared a report to challenge the military's plans to use a nuclear device to create an underground storage facility for high-level radioactive wastes near the Ural Mountains city of Chelyabinsk.[13] On the occasion of the agency's seventieth anniversary two months later, Soviet television screened a program illustrating the KGB's environmental consciousness. The agency was so bold as to claim partial responsibility for the government's decision in 1986 to cancel the Siberian rivers diversion project. Although conceding the impact of scientific and cultural figures working in opposition to the scheme, Major-General Eduard N. Yakovlev of the KGB's analytical department added: "We spoke from an objective, unbiased position."[14]

Local as well as national officials often turn to environmental groups for expertise and input. Sometimes the relationship goes beyond this; many environmental officials consider the public a helpful ally in bureaucratic battles against industry. Thus, although Ukrainian industries were required to submit an environmental impact statement (EIS) for development projects, they also were able to pressure the Ukrainian environment ministry to waive its standards and to accept their plans. According to one official at the environment agency, independent EISs conducted by environmental groups along with public pressure were welcomed as an aid to the beleaguered agency in enforcing its regulations.[15] A deputy of the Latvian environmental agency told a local paper that his agency "must make a major effort to consolidate the various movements and organizations of the Greens."[16] The general director of Moldova's environmental agency went much further: "We will utterly and completely support any movement to protect the environment, including through rallies, strikes and picket lines." Said I. I. Deyu, formerly a professor at Moldova State University, "We are trying to do it in a way that people trust us."[17]

Evidence of a growing alliance between government environmental officials and the environmental movement also can be seen in the plethora of ecology-oriented newspapers that have sprung up. By jointly publishing newspapers, environmental groups can gain access to state publishing facilities, and officials seek to tap into the popularity and respect earned by these organizations. In 1991, the Moldovan environmental agency announced that it was publishing an ecological newspaper, *Abe natura*, jointly with the Moldovan Green movement.[18] The Kurgan oblast Committee for the Protection of Nature joined with the local branch of the All-Russian Society for the Protection of Nature to publish *Ekologicheskaya gazeta* (The Ecological Newspaper). The RSFSR environmental agency teamed up with the Ekopress information and publishing association to put out *Zelenyi mir* (Green World).

ENVIRONMENTALISM STRIKES THE ECONOMY

Rising protests in the 1980s had a strong impact on the region's economy, as environmentalists began to demand a rapid solution to pollution problems in their neighborhoods. In all, over 1,000 production units either were closed or had their output scaled back in 1989 for "violation of environmental protection laws," USSR Goskomstat reported (see Table 7.1).[19] In the city of Moscow alone, 72 plants and production lines were closed.[20] A trade union leader pointed out that over 100 plants in the chemical industry were idled around the country in mid-1990 because of demands from the communities in which they were located to be "dechemicalized."[21] In 1990, output sacrificed was projected to total 5.2 million tons of fertilizer, 951,000 tons of soda, 400,000 tons of cellulose, 387,000 tons of methanol, 500,000 tons of polymers, and over 250,000 tons of synthetic rubber, among other goods, and leading econ-

TABLE 7.1 Selected plant shutdowns for violation of environmental protection regulations, 1989

Enterprise (location)	Number of Days Closed[a]	Reason Cited
Yenakievo Metallurgical Factory (Ukraine)	178	Air pollution control equipment not started up
Dzhambul Superphosphate Factory (Kazakhstan)	128	Ineffective air pollution equipment
Azot Production Association (Novgorod, Russia)	125	Lacking air pollution control equipment
Belgorod Vitamin Kombinat (Russia)	115	Exceeded atmospheric emissions standards
Zaspensk Starch Factory (Belarus)	84	Delays in installing wastewater treatment equipment
Titan Production Association (Crimea, Ukraine)	79	Exceeded atmospheric emissions standards
Crimea Soda Factory (Ukraine)	77	Ineffective air pollution equipment, exceeded atmospheric emissions standards
Taganrog Fish Combine (Russia)	60	Delays in installing wastewater treatment equipment
Nisporeni Wine Factory (Moldova)	60	Released wastes in protected watershed

[a]Closure involved only specific production unit where the environmental infraction occurred.

Source: USSR Goskomstat, Press-vypusk, No. 136, April 4, 1990.

omists were worrying that the ecological movement would deal a fatal blow to the already failing economy.[22] Indeed, in his report on the performance of the Soviet economy during the first quarter of 1990, USSR Goskomstat chair Vadim Kirichenko blamed a sharp downturn in economic performance, among other causes, on the closing of factories for not meeting "basic ecological demands."[23] Most of these plants were shut down only temporarily as a form of sanction, it must be pointed out, but in many cases, the closure was intended to be permanent.

Energy is one sector in which the public virtually has dictated policy. Media reports suggest that not one nuclear power plant has been safe from opposition as the public has been gripped by radiophobia. In the fallout from the Chernobyl accident, public pressure had forced the abandonment of 60 projects by January 1991, including the much-disputed Crimea, Rostov, Tatariya, and Bashkiriya atomic energy stations (AESs), and expansions at the Smolensk, Khmelnitski, Tver (Kalinin), and Zaporozhye stations. The generating capacity of these plants was projected to total 160 million kilowatts.[24] The fates of numerous others remain uncertain as officials have been forced to undertake a complete reappraisal of nuclear energy development plans. As if to beat a dying horse, one week after its inauguration in the summer of 1990, the popularly elected Supreme Soviet of the Russian Federation voted to issue a moratorium on nuclear projects beginning in 1991.[25] One month later, the Supreme Soviet of Ukraine passed a five-year moratorium on all nuclear projects in that republic,[26] and after a turbine fire at Chernobyl's power unit No. 2 in October 1991, the Ukrainian parliament voted to decommission immediately the crippled reactor and the two other units (1 and 3) still operating on the site by 1993.[27]

With less nuclear power on which to rely in the future, the region will have to turn more to oil, coal, gas, and hydroelectric resources. These options are limited as well, however, as environmental pressure mounts against the diversion of water and the submersion of land for hydroelectric projects and against the continued use of aging and dirty coal-fired power plants. In one of its first actions, the first democratically elected Moscow city council voted in May 1990 to scrap construction of the Severnaya station—planned to be the largest gas-fired heat and power plant in Europe.[28] Opponents, led by the Moscow Green Party, collected 300,000 signatures against the plant, arguing that it was not necessary. Instead, they pointed out that massive heat losses in the distribution network, estimated to average 25–40 percent, could be reduced with the improved insulation of heating pipes and the construction of small, local heat and power cogeneration facilities.[29] On the other hand, Vasilii Selyunin, a prominent radical economist and government critic, warned: "It is not possible now to stop even one, even the tiniest, power station because of the shortage of electricity."[30]

Unexpectedly, environmental activism has also had an effect in the area of pharmaceuticals. Much of the region's drugs are produced by the metallurgical and chemical industries—two sectors of ill ecological repute. Environmental protests halted production of pharmaceuticals at the infamous Azot (nitrogen) production enterprise in Kemerovo, at Yerevan's Nairit, and at the Kirovgrad copper smelter. In some cases, Radio Moscow reported, these plants were the only ones in the USSR producing certain essential medicines.[31] According to USSR Minister of Health Igor Denisov, the domestic pharmaceuticals industry was able to meet 39 percent of the Soviet Union's demand for drugs in 1990, down from 52 percent five years earlier. Denisov predicted that domestic production would fall to 30 percent of demand in 1991.[32]

In preparation for the Second USSR Congress of People's Deputies in December 1989, the USSR Supreme Soviet Committee on the Protection of Public Health also looked into the medicine crisis; the head of the USSR Ministry of the Medical and Microbiological Industry (Minmedprom) reported that local opposition had prevented the siting of new plants to produce pharmaceuticals, including those to produce disposable syringes, desperately needed to avoid the spread of AIDS.[33] Construction had been halted in Arkhangelsk, Kursk, and Saratov oblasts and in Novosibirsk, the Mari Autonomous Republic, Latvia, and Uzbekistan.[34] Of the 36 Minmedprom pharmaceutical projects slated for the 1986–1990 plan, 21 had yet to be initiated because local forces had refused to allocate any land to the ministry.[35] Public opposition stemmed from Minmedprom's reputation as an inveterate polluter, an example being its petroleum-based livestock supplement operations at Kirishi, outside St. Petersburg. The labor daily *Trud* noted pessimistically that the pharmaceuticals industry was "falling apart with even greater speed" than the rest of the Soviet economy.[36] "Until we convince the population that our production units can be safe—and there are already some that are—we will not move the sector forward," gravely testified Minister Valerii Bykov. "'Green' extremism will not let the pharmaceuticals industry take a breath."[37] "We have already seen cigarette shortages," concluded *Trud.* "Should we prepare for aspirin shortages?"

ENVIRONMENTAL OPPOSITION TO THE MILITARY

Even before the demise of the Soviet Union the prestige of the military was suffering. There were retreats from Afghanistan and Eastern Europe, criticism at home, budget cuts, draft evasion, and ultimately, the collapse of the USSR. Under the Soviet regime, the military was allowed to pollute the environment egregiously by appealing to the imperative of national security. Nevertheless, in the late 1980s and early 1990s the prerogative of the military to act regardless of public opinion was checked by a growing environmental movement. The defense industry accounted for a very large share of the Soviet economy, and there were correspondingly many objects of public opposition. In 1990, for example, the defense sector came under strong criticism after the Navy was implicated in the massive death of sea life in the White Sea near Arkhangelsk and after industrial accidents at its explosives plant in Gorlovka in eastern Ukraine and at a nuclear materials facility at Ust-Kamenogorsk in eastern Kazakhstan. These and many other clashes show that public opposition to the military, especially to military activities that posed a threat to the environment, was forceful and widespread.

Speaking at an international conference on arms control in Paris in January 1989, Foreign Minister Eduard Shevardnadze announced that the USSR unilaterally would begin destroying its stocks of chemical weapons at an undisclosed facility the government was about to open. Upon hearing that a top-secret site twenty kilometers from their city was this facility, the citizens of Chapaevsk (population 97,000) were stunned. Shock quickly turned to outrage at the fact that the Ministry of Defense would dare to build the plant in their heavily populated region close to the Volga River without studying the potential impact on the environment and without the public's consent. A spontaneous and vociferous protest campaign led by the group Initsiativa focused on safety issues and the already severe pollution problems of the region, caused by local chemical plants. An expert commission designed to placate the protesters concluded that the plant's equipment was safe, "provided there are no accidents."[38]

Needless to say, the community was displeased with such findings. With 60,000 signatures in hand and frequent pickets at the plant site, Initsiativa convinced city and oblast leaders to oppose the commencement of operations at the plant (they too were unaware of its purpose apparently) and forced Moscow to appoint another commission to study the project.[39] In August 1989, the commission, led by Nikolai Laverov, chairman of the USSR State Committee of Science and Technology, recommended against opening the 50-million-ruble facility, citing public unrest and the existing pollution problems in the region. The government finally agreed and decided to convert the plant to a training center.[40] Soviet officials, however, were left with the problem of finding the means to comply with the treaty signed in June 1990 by Presidents Gorbachev and Bush in which they pledged to begin destroying stocks of chemical weapons by 1993.[41]

In April 1990, Radio Kiev announced that a government commission headed by academician Yevgenii Velikhov had recommended scrapping a ballistic-missile early warning station near the town of Mukachevo in western Ukraine.[42] The radar, under construction since 1985 at a cost of 100 million rubles, was one of nine large, phased-array radar systems being built across the Soviet Union and expected to be operational by the mid-1990s. For two years, local residents protested the radar's construction on grounds of the health hazard from electromagnetic radiation and because of the large volume of water the installation would use for its cooling systems; 700,000 citizens signed a petition calling for its closure. In January 1990, the movement gained strength when the oblast soviet backed the public's demands. Nevertheless, residents complained that the military had accelerated construction, with work proceeding at the site day and night. Though the Velikhov commission sided with the environmentalists, stating that their concerns were "well founded," the military's construction brigades pressed on throughout the spring. Frustrated by the military's refusal to comply with its order, the oblast soviet posted police officers at the site to prevent the delivery of construction materials. In August, Moscow finally acceded to the local demands and ordered the dismantling of the site and the restoration of the territory to its original state.[43]

THE CASE OF NUCLEAR WEAPONS TESTING AT SEMIPALATINSK

The greatest impact of the environmental movement has been on the military's nuclear weapons testing program at Semipalatinsk and Novaya Zemlya. The Soviet Union conducted its first test of an atomic device at Semipalatinsk on August 29, 1949. Since then, over 300 nuclear explosions are known to have been conducted at the site, located on the hilly steppe of eastern Kazakhstan. Before the signing of the Limited Test Ban Treaty in 1963, almost all tests at Semipalatinsk were conducted aboveground.[44] Although the military routinely evacuated residents from the area before a test (albeit with little warning or explanation), many people have spoken of witnessing the blinding flashes and mushroom clouds. After a test, soldiers would pass through the villages to repair damage resulting from tremors—some settlements were located as little as thirty kilometers from the seat of the explosion.[45] A local teacher, a Volga German exiled to Kazakhstan on Stalin's orders during World War II, told a correspondent of *The European*:

> When a test was about to be carried out, we were driven from our houses to the riverside, even at night, and told to push wool into our ears. The light was so bright you could see a needle on the ground. I saw the yellow and red mushroom clouds and felt the earthquakes. Once my father was sitting near a window and the window smashed and cut his face. During the last blast aboveground, in 1963, the door flew off the oven and fire was thrown into the room, almost blinding my younger brother. On another occasion, the roof fell in and crushed to death a young woman.[46]

Atmospheric testing stopped in 1963, and the 1974 Threshold Test Ban Treaty limited the explosive yield of the nuclear explosions to 150 kilotons. Nevertheless, the frequency of tests remained steady; according to research by the National Resources Defense Council, Semipalatinsk averaged about one blast per month between the mid-1960s and late 1980s.[47]

Abandoned instrument towers used for atmospheric testing at the Semipalatinsk nuclear weapons test range. Photo: James Lerager.

By the 1990s, half a million people were living in the immediate vicinity of the Semipalatinsk test range. In response to public demands, a government commission was dispatched to the region to examine public health conditions as well as to survey medical archives. The commission determined that as many as 10,000 people living in several regions adjacent to the test range had been contaminated during the course of atmospheric tests; the researchers also noted that indicators of health in the region had shown a decline during the period of testing but since then had recovered to the national average.[48] Numerous anecdotal reports, however, speak of continuing high rates of cancer, miscarriage, infant mortality, hair loss, skin disorders, depression, and suicide among the region's population, conditions many doctors have labeled collectively "Semipalatinsk AIDS."[49] *Izvestiya* compared problems at Semipalatinsk to the disasters at Chernobyl and the Aral Sea and noted that the average life span in the region declined by three years between 1970 and 1990.[50] Comparisons in the type and frequency of cancers have been drawn to the epidemiology of the populations of Hiroshima and Nagasaki.[51]

The Soviet government impeded thorough epidemiological studies of the region by maintaining tight control over health data. Military and government officials countered the allegations of abnormal health conditions by repeatedly stating that radiation levels in the region were normal and that any health problems there could not be attributed to radiation from the test range.[52] After visiting the site as a member of a USSR Supreme Soviet delegation organized by the conservative Soyuz faction, Colonel Nikolai Petrushenko stated that the area was "absolutely safe," and a Soviet defense ministry spokesman stated categorically that "no local residents had suffered from radiation sickness as a result of a nuclear test."[53] Ultimately, linking the region's public health problems to nuclear testing at Semipalatinsk may prove impossible, given the traditionally poor monitoring and recordkeeping practices by Soviet officials. On this point, the government commission asserted that persistent health problems could be traced to the region's poor air quality and to groundwater contamination by pesticides and by runoff from livestock farms.

An environmental lobby was slow to appear in Central Asia, but as the case of the Nevada-Semipalatinsk antinuclear testing movement illustrates, once it was organized, public interest exploded. This opposition organization finally came into being after an accident at the site in which gas was vented during a test in February 1989. Within a year, the organization, whose name was intended to stress the international ramifications of nuclear testing, had collected over 1 million signatures calling for the Semipalatinsk test site to be closed and had enlisted as its leader the popular Kazakh poet and member of the USSR Supreme Soviet, Olzhas Suleimenov. The group's primary tactic was to stage large street demonstrations in various cities and towns around the republic, including Alma-Ata, the capital. The Nevada-Semipalatinsk movement also maintained close contacts with Moscow through other sympathetic parliamentarians, such as Yurii Shcherbak, and received favorable press coverage, most notably in the government newspaper *Izvestiya*. By 1991, Nevada-Semipalatinsk had become the largest and most influential public organization in Kazakhstan, drawing its support from a broad range of people—from the intelligentsia to the working class.[54]

In response to the growing pressure, Soviet Prime Minister Nikolai Ryzhkov announced in November 1989 that further tests at the site would be halted until the end of that year. One week later, the USSR Supreme Soviet called for a study on closure of the range as part of its resolution of emergency environmental protection measures.[55] The moratorium was extended until the end of March 1990, when Deputy Prime Minister Igor' Belousov told the USSR Supreme Soviet that the government had decided to postpone indefinitely all tests at Semipalatinsk until "new measures" were taken to safeguard the people living there. By that time, the government had also made known its intent ultimately to close the site.[56]

The defense ministry countered with a proposal to conduct up to 27 tests during "a transitional period" before closing the site permanently in 1993.[57] Local opposition, however, was intent on thwarting these plans. Soon after it convened, the first democratically elected Kazakh Supreme Soviet called on Moscow to stop nuclear testing and in October 1990 banned testing outright in the republic as part of its declaration of state sovereignty. The parliament reiterated its call in December 1990, with added demands that Moscow improve social services in the region and compensate victims of the tests.[58] The Semipalatinsk city and Karaganda oblast governments likewise asked Moscow to end testing, and in October 1990 the Semipalatinsk oblast soviet banned further testing at the range.[59] The mayor of Kurchatov, a once-secret city of 12,000 residents, most of whom worked at the test range, countered in the military press that "the situation around the test site is such that the continuation of tests appears to be out of the question."[60]

The conflict over Semipalatinsk climaxed in 1991. By spring, the Ministry of Defense and its ally, the USSR Ministry of Atomic Power and Industry, had reduced their demand to three tests: two 20- and one 0.05-kiloton explosion to occur before closing the site permanently in 1992.[61] Apparently bowing to pressure of the military, Mikhail Gorbachev announced his support of the tests during a June visit to Kazakhstan. Kazakh President Nursultan Nazarbaev refrained from taking a prominent stand in the debate as he attempted to balance the opposing pressures coming from both Moscow and from his constituency in what Vladimir Yakimets, science adviser to Olzhas Suleimenov, described as "just a terrible struggle."[62] For their part, local officials raised the pressure on Moscow by demanding compensation payments to those living in the area around the test site. According to Yakimets, the USSR Ministry of Defense originally offered Kazakhstan 250,000 rubles for the three explosions to be carried out in 1991. By June, the military raised the offer to 1 billion rubles, as the devices were already in the ground, and time for preparations and for notification to the United States (according to treaty obligations) was growing short.[63] In July, Suleimenov reported that the military had agreed to compensation of 5 billion rubles for just two tests, or about 2,500 rubles for every inhabitant living in the three oblasts bordering the test site.[64] However, no payments were ever made: With the failed coup attempt of August 19–21, 1991, the closure of Semipalatinsk became a reality. On August 29—the day an explosion was scheduled to have taken place—President Nazarbaev issued a decree formally closing the site. The USSR Ministry of Defense in Moscow agreed.[65]

The closure of Semipalatinsk would not necessarily have represented a major setback for the military's nuclear weapons testing program. Resources could be shifted to Novaya Zemlya, an archipelago along the eastern edge of the Barents Sea, which from 1958 to 1963 served as the primary Soviet test facility. Between 1954 and the signing of the Limited Test Ban Treaty in 1963, many tests of very large-yield weapons were conducted aboveground and underwater at Novaya Zemlya. After 1964, the site served as the USSR's secondary test range and was used for its largest nuclear weapons tests. According to Western observers, an average of 1–2 tests have been held there annually since 1965, compared with about 12 per year at Semipalatinsk.[66] After several years of silence at the site, a test was conducted at Novaya Zemlya in October 1990, probably as a result of the political troubles to the south. However, because of its remote location and harsh climate, conditions for the military at Novaya Zemlya are not as propitious as at Semipalatinsk.[67]

The political climate in the north also has grown somewhat unfavorable; opposition to testing at Novaya Zemlya grew rapidly after the government's original decision to halt testing temporarily at Semipalatinsk. Several peace and environmental groups banded together to form the Novaya Zemlya–Nevada and For Novaya Zemlya movements, and the governments of Arkhangelsk oblast and the Russian Federation have expressed their opposition to testing there.[68] The Norwegian government also has weighed in with its opposition to nuclear testing in the Arctic. A decision to close the range, argued Vladimir Burakov of the Russian Peace Committee, "is no less radical than that made with regard to Semipalatinsk."[69]

After the closure of Semipalatinsk, President Boris Yeltsin issued a decree in October 1991 banning testing for one year at Novaya Zemlya. To the dismay of environmentalists, however, he subsequently issued another decree claiming Russian jurisdiction over the site and granting the military the right to prepare for up to 2–4 tests per year, when and if he decided to lift the moratorium.[70] Moreover, Yeltsin chose as his minister of atomic energy (the post responsible for Novaya Zemlya) Viktor Mikhailev, former head of the USSR's nuclear weapons program and a staunch advocate of continued weapons testing.[71]

THE DIVERSITY OF THE ENVIRONMENTAL MOVEMENT

Despite major successes like that at Semipalatinsk, most proenvironment groups are loosely organized, small, and often short-lived. In April 1990, the co-chairman of the Leningrad Green Party counted approximately 60 "ecological organizations" in that city, most of which had fewer than a dozen members.[72] Environmental groups usually focus on a single issue in their own locality. As elsewhere in the world, the rallying cries are numerous, and groups span the ideological spectrum, ranging from fiercely nationalist organizations to apolitical bird-watching societies. *Sovetskaya Rossiya*, the staunchly conservative Russian newspaper, sponsored the Committee to Save the Volga, whereas the Committee to Save the Ob is based in the scientific research center of Novosibirsk. Reflecting its constituency, the latter group announced plans to conduct research and environmental impact studies on all developments threatening the Ob and Irtysh river basins.[73] Founded in October 1989, the Chernobyl Union, with member chapters throughout the former Soviet Union, aims to serve as a support and legal advocacy group for victims of the nuclear accident as well as the 600,000 people it estimates have participated in the cleanup operation, 50,000 of whom reportedly have become unable to work.[74]

Although each group has its own eclectic agenda, many express similar principles and objectives—ecological glasnost, comprehensive environmental monitoring and assessment, public education, grassroots cleanups, and direct political action. For example, environmental NGOs often spend a large share of their resources to establish themselves as alternative and credible sources of information. Although government agencies have made major strides in bringing environmental information into the public domain, much remains hidden or unknown. "A lot of interesting information is out there," says Sheryl Belcher, coordinator of Greenpeace International's "Children of Chernobyl" project based in Kiev: "[Environmental groups] need to access it."[75] Thus, environmentalists persistently lobby for full disclosure of government data. Paradoxically, however, they and the public at large remain highly suspicious of much official data that are released, arguing that accurate data would indicate problems so severe as to be too risky politically to be made public.[76] Such a situation lies in stark contrast to that in the United States, where environmental groups rely heavily on access to official government data through the Freedom of Information Act, for example, to pursue their objectives, including challenges to the government.

Where reliable data are either lacking or unavailable, groups have sought to acquire their own monitoring equipment and to conduct independent studies. Using a battery of radiation monitoring devices, Vladimir Mikheev of Krasnoyarsk's Green World association, conducted several informal surveys revealing high radiation levels in the Yenisei River north of the Krasnoyarsk-26 nuclear facility. Often environmentalists turn to their counterparts in the West for monitoring equipment as well as information that is considered independent and credible. Greenpeace's "Children of Chernobyl" project, for example, imported a special truck outfitted with diagnostic equipment to travel around Ukraine and sample environmental conditions. Because membership in NGOs frequently includes highly qualified scientists, groups often aim to serve as an independent source of expertise for policymakers and the public. The Chelyabinsk Ecological Fund, for instance, retains several medical and scientific specialists to assess and to inform the public about environmental conditions.

Similarly, many environmental groups place a strong emphasis on educating the public, especially the youth, about ecology and the environment. Activists often describe the general public as being "ecologically illiterate"—a consequence of the Soviet government's low priority on raising environmental consciousness and teaching ecology in public schools, its suppression of information, and its hostility to independent thought. Anatolii Grebenyuk, a parliamentarian from Kyrgyzstan, stressed the legacy of Soviet environmental education thus: "We have been taught since kindergarten that we have no ecological problems, and that we can live for millions of years with no concerns. Today we see this is not so. It is very difficult to change people's opinions, to make them realize the severity of our situation."[77] To correct this attitude, many groups have opened environmental libraries (with donations often coming from abroad) and educate the public through their own publications, the mass media, and the schools.

THE TACTICS OF ENVIRONMENTAL GROUPS

Despite the liberalization of politics in much of the former Soviet Union, democratic politics remain in a nascent and tentative stage. Democratic institutions and instruments such as referendums, public opinion polling, parties, lobbyists, public hearings, fundraising and advertising are still in the early stages of development. The lawsuit, the mainstay of environmentalists in the United States, is not an effective or realistic option in the newly independent republics, given that environmental laws remain weak and often unenforceable. This problem is compounded by an often unsupportive judiciary. As a result, organizing traditional mass demonstrations—with attendance frequently numbering in the tens of thousands—has been the most visible and popular tactic of environmental groups and has served to send the most potent messages to the authorities about the legitimacy of their public's demands.[78]

Environmentally concerned individuals need not form organized groups to be effective participants in the policy process. Scientists, for

Over 3,000 people participated in a four-day bicycle race in Estonia in June 1989 to draw attention to severe pollution problems in the northeast of the republic. Photo: TASS from Sovfoto.

example, with their high prestige in society and privileged access to information, have formed effective lobbies, as was the case with the relatively unorganized yet successful campaign against the Siberian rivers diversion plan. Physicists and writers formed a strategic alliance to oppose successfully the development of nuclear power, most notably in Ukraine: The physicists were able to disseminate their authoritative information and forebodings about the government's plans, exploiting writers' access to such media as the influential newspapers *Literaturnaya Ukraina, Komsomol'skaya pravda,* and *Moscow News.*[79]

Analysis of the political agendas of various ecological groups makes clear that not all "green" organizations are what they appear to be. The Russian ultranationalist group Pamyat' has been charged with creating the innocuous-sounding All-Union Ecological Society in an attempt to use environmental issues to add a veneer of legitimacy to its less benevolent pursuits (e.g., its harassment of Jews and non-Russians). Leaders of the Social-Ecological Union (SEU) have leveled similar charges against the Committee to Save the Volga.[80] In addition to political opportunists, the environmental movement also attracts people and institutions motivated by material impulses, and their actions may not bode well for nature. Environmentalists have accused Communist Party *apparatchiks* of founding or supporting front organizations, such as the Green Party of Leningrad, to draw support away from real opposition groups.[81] In Chelyabinsk oblast, conservative interests put forth the Green Party, while the "real Greens" in the region are said to be represented by the Democratic Green Party.[82] Similarly, leaders of the SEU have accused the Green movement of being a tool of the Communist Party and agro-industry: "The one who pays the piper calls the tune," they write.[83]

Some ministries also have formed their own environmental front organizations much in the way U.S. industries form political action committees with ecologically correct-sounding names. The Ecological Foundation, a group that announced its intention to establish a bank that would finance purchases of environmental technology, reportedly is controlled by the oil and chemical industries' ministries. Acquisitive individuals are also seeking to profit from widespread concern about the environment. It is relatively easy for an organization to open a bank account and solicit donations by publicizing the account number, but there is no mechanism to ensure that the money collected is spent on environmental improvement.[84]

THE POLITICS OF THE GREEN MOVEMENTS

Practically all Soviet successor states have some form of Green party or political organization. This process of creating Green movements has been most advanced in the Baltic states of Estonia, Lithuania, and Latvia; the first Green Party was formed in Estonia in spring 1988. The Baltic region's Greens scored remarkable successes in early elective politics: Juhan Aare of Estonia and Vaidotas Antanaitis of Lithuania, running as official Green candidates, won election to the USSR Supreme Soviet in March 1989.[85] Both served on the USSR Supreme Soviet's Ecology Committee before withdrawing from the parliament in 1990 in recognition of their republics' political sovereignty. In the 1990 republican elections, the newly created Green Party of Lithuania won three seats in the state's Supreme Council.[86]

Georgia's Greens movement is described as a "public-political organization" and bases its action on the following principles: ecological safety, democracy, and nonviolence.[87] Leaders of the Armenian Union of Greens conceive of their movement as one of human rights, such as fighting for the right to breathe clean air. As a result, they decided not to create a Green party because they hoped to count a large number of people and political parties in their movement without making a bid for power.[88]

By far the most politically significant Green movement to have developed in the former Soviet region is Ukraine's Zelenyi Svit (Green World). In the late 1980s, Communist officials at the regional and local levels, sensing the strength of environmentalism and Zelenyi Svit, cooperated with environmentalists to oppose the construction of potentially harmful enterprises.[89] After democratic elections held in 1990, Zelenyi Svit counted 7 of its adherents among the 105 members of the Ukrainian parliament.[90] In June 1989, members of Zelenyi Svit created the Ukrainian Green Party. The success and popularity of the Ukrainian environmental movement can be attributed in part to the high visibility and close proximity of environmental threats: from Chernobyl and the numerous other nuclear power plants in the republic, from wide-scale devastation in the Donets Basin, and from the ecological decline of the beloved Crimea and the Black Sea. Success may also be attributed to the symbiotic relationship between the movement and its leader Yurii Shcherbak: The popular writer, doctor, and scientist brought a great measure of visibility and respect to Zelenyi Svit and to the Ukrainian Green Party; the movement, in turn, provided him with a strong group of supporters and a vehicle with which to further his political ambitions and, ultimately, to propel him into the government as minister of the environment in 1991.[91]

THE ENVIRONMENT AND LABOR

One of the most significant changes as a result of perestroika during the Soviet era was the reemergence of an independent and insurgent labor movement after decades of being smothered by an official labor bureaucracy that was ultimately loyal to the Communist Party and government instead of the workers. Strikes and other labor actions became commonplace, if not ubiquitous, attesting to a high level of worker dissatisfaction. Protests centered around traditional economic issues such as pay and benefits, work rules, and autonomy of their enterprises. Many strikes were organized with purely political goals or as part of nationalist and ethnic protests. Quality-of-life issues such as food supply, housing, and the environment also figured high on strikers' agendas. According to official reports, almost two-thirds of all strikes in 1990 centered around economic demands, 15 percent had a political nature, and about 4 percent were called to protest environmental conditions.[92]

Improved working conditions have been one demand of labor. This is understandable because the workplace is exceedingly dangerous: In the late 1980s, about 14,000 workers were killed while on the job, 20,000 were maimed, and an estimated 10,000 suffered from work-related maladies every year. More than 9 million people were forced to work under harmful conditions, such as excessive noise, vibrations, and dust. According to one state study, 20 to 38 percent of all illnesses in the Soviet Union were believed to have been "connected with conditions in the workplace."[93] Conditions have only deteriorated under the rigors of economic reform, as new constraints have prompted managers to divert funds away from occupational safety.[94] According to one specialist on the issue, such economizing was "a very widespread problem." Commented Dr. E. Petrosyants: "The following is occurring at many enterprises: Having received the right to distribute a portion of their profits [managers are] releasing funds to boost wages and bonuses. Simultaneously, they reduce investment in occupational safety down to nothing." Thus, managers pay their workers more to put up with deteriorating conditions. Asked *Rabochaya tribuna*, "Is it worth the price?"[95]

Labor's support for environmental cleanup was strongest in the late 1980s and early 1990s. Workers at the Volga Automobile Works, the former Soviet Union's largest car factory, for example, attempted a strike in September 1989; in addition to pay increases and more vacation time, the workers demanded improved working conditions and a cleanup of their city of Tolyatti, which also has been polluted by chemical factories.[96] In the Bashkir capital of Ufa, workers held a three-hour warning strike on May 21, 1990, paralyzing the city. They were protesting a chemical spill at a local chemical plant that left 600,000 residents—over half the city's population—without safe running water for a fortnight.[97] In Karaganda, Kazakhstan, 12,000 coal miners joined with Nevada-Semipalatinsk to call for a halt to nuclear testing at Semipalatinsk, 350 kilometers east of their city.[98]

The strength and anger of labor were most clearly demonstrated in the wildcat strikes that paralyzed the coal industry and sent the Soviet government into a state of crisis for over two weeks July 1989. After an initial walkout at one mine in the Kuznetsk Basin (Kuzbass) in central Siberia, strikes spread to other mines in the region as well as in Kazakhstan and the Donets Basin in Ukraine, the largest mining region. Throughout decades of centralized planning, the government packed these areas with large heavy industrial complexes to make use of the local coal. As a result, all of these areas still rank high as being environmentally distressed; Kemerovo oblast in the Kuzbass is arguably the worst. "I was in the Kemerovo region where the strikes took place," says Aleksei Yablokov. "People were walking around with masks because you couldn't breathe the air."[99] After the strike ended, *Pravda* examined conditions there. The state of people's health was "critical," concluded the newspaper: One-half of all workers in the oblast suffered from chronic ailments, and 87 percent of all children were born with "mental and physical anomalies."[100] The problem stems in part from the poor working conditions of women. Health workers in the city of Kemerovo report that there are "practically no healthy women" working in industrial enterprises, and 99 percent of all expectant mothers have been classified as "at risk." "If these trends continue," noted *Argumenty i fakty,* "by 2000 not one single infant will be born healthy."[101] Said Vladislav Stergilov, a local environmental activist: "Only with the strike did people really become aware of the environmental crisis."[102]

In its economic platform, the Kuzbass Union of Workers, an independent union set up by the coal miners, placed ecology at the top of its list of social concerns:

> Several industrial centers in the Kuzbass are located on the verge of ecological disaster. Illnesses, caused by a polluted environment, victimize oblast residents not only at work but also at rest. The ministries, oblivious to the region's interests, commit ecological crimes. The Kuzbass Union of Workers declares as its objective to work for legislation which will protect oblast residents from environmental degradation and which will create such an economic mechanism as to make dangerous production unviable. We reproach the oblast's previous management structure for allowing an unbalanced and rapacious approach towards natural resources and the interests of the Kuzbass population; we will demand a program of ecological recovery for the oblast, environmental assessments of construction projects, [and] for the provision of the population with reliable instruments for the monitoring of chemical and other forms of pollution of the environment and foodstuffs.[103]

Still, for most blue-collar workers, the environment is a nonissue. Most are willing to discount their future in favor of immediate material gains, especially if that means holding onto a job—a growing concern as economic reform threatens tens of millions of workers in the 1990s. Conditions in the Arctic mining and metal refining region of Norilsk (population 250,000) provide a case in point. On most days, a sickly yellow-grey pall of sulfur dioxide, nitrogen oxides, carbon monoxide, phenol, and chlorine from the region's light metal smelters settles over the region. One can literally taste the sulfur in the air. Air and water pollution has poisoned local lakes and scorched the fragile tundra: "It's like Hell," summed Andrei Ivanov-Smolenskii of the SEU.[104] Most residents do not live past the age of 50.

After decades of rapid immigration and growth, the city's population decreased by 8,000 people between 1987 and 1990—attesting to increased dissatisfaction with the quality of life in the far north. By 1991, however, outmigration slowed and many workers began to return to Norilsk in search of their old jobs; in the south, economic reform had boosted the cost of living sharply and good-paying jobs had disappeared. In contrast, miners' wages in Norilsk stood at 40,000–50,000 rubles per month in the summer of 1992, while the local minimum wage (including a premium for hardship conditions in the far north) was approximately 10,000 rubles. By comparison, the average monthly wage in Moscow stood at about 6,000 rubles.

Vladimir Shishkov, a manager at the Volga Automobile Plant in Tolyatti, related the following story to *Moscow News* about a trip to Chelyabinsk to negotiate supply contracts for his firm: "At the shop producing lead-containing products, I saw men almost naked to the waist and without respirators. I asked how I could help them: with working clothes or protective means? They answered: if we could just have at least 50 cars [to sell to] our employees each year."[105] The Odessa city government, under heavy pressure from environmental groups, decided in the summer of 1990 to shut down a local chemical plant. The city's leaders, in turn, quickly found themselves in conflict with the plant's employees, who challenged the measure in order to save their jobs. Higher-ups in the chemicals ministry ignored the city's order.[106] The city resorted to a public referendum on the plant "as the last means" to resolving the impasse. The result was that 83 percent of voters were in favor of the plant's closing.[107]

In the Soviet era, industrial ministries perfunctorily absorbed the cost of fines for pollution from their enterprises as a routine business matter. With the transition to free-market relations and the rise of private and collective ownership, enterprises now are forced to pay these fines out of their own revenues and profits, hence impinging on their social benefits and wage funds. The result has been predictable: Miners striking on Sakhalin Island demanded, among other things, that fines assessed against their enterprise for polluting the environment be lifted.[108] In October 1990, oil and gas workers in the Tyumen region threatened to shut down their pipelines unless the government lifted pollution fines assessed on employees of the firm; accidents had garnered the west Siberian concern 26 lawsuits for violation of environmental regulations. *Moscow News* commented:

> The oil workers found themselves unprepared for the demands of the oblast procuracy and committee for the protection of nature recently created in the oblast. For decades, oil poured onto the ground from the active pipelines; for decades, an indulgent system meticulously protected the guilty parties. And suddenly . . . popular concern, new people in the soviets, million-ruble suits against enterprises, criminal cases, fines.[109]

The Tyumen workers were dismayed at being held responsible for the pipelines, which were laid through swamps and were shoddily built by other firms. In addition to the removal of the fines, the workers demanded that their enterprise be permitted to keep more of the hard-currency earnings it produced. Radio Moscow pointed out that the workers were not intending to pocket all of the money; instead, they planned to use much of it to purchase new drilling equipment and to renovate the pipelines, which were in "a dangerous condition."[110]

ENVIRONMENTALISM, NATIONALISM, AND NATIONAL MOVEMENTS

Parallel with the rise of environmental awareness, the Soviet Union witnessed a dramatic upsurge in nationalism. Yet the distinction between rising environmentalism and ethnic or nationalist sentiments often blurred, and during the 1980s and early 1990s, the two causes frequently proved mutually reinforcing. "The degradation of natural areas," an official in the USSR Council of Ministers wrote in 1989, "which people identify with their national dignity, aggravates relations between ethnic groups."[111] In some regions, such as the Baltic states of Lithuania, Estonia, and Latvia, environmentalism often was couched in a broader anti-Russian feeling. Everywhere, even inside the Russian Federation, environmentalism frequently turned anti-Soviet and anti-Moscow as activists attempted to break the grip of the center's "environmental colonialism." Everywhere the combination was explosive.

In February 1990, Mikhail Gorbachev sent paratroopers into the Tajik capital of Dushanbe to thwart an attack by young rioters on the republic's Communist Party headquarters and to prevent the victory of "narrow egotistical aims."[112] According to Soviet press reports, however, the protesters' goals were not so narrow: In addition to demanding the ouster of party and government leaders in the republic, the deportation of Armenians (already refugees from recent pogroms in Azerbaijan), and the repatriation of profits from the sale of local cotton, protesters also demanded the closing of the Tajik Aluminum Plant—an inveterate polluter of the region. The following April, 150,000 people gathered in Yerevan to protest the accidental release of chloroprene gas from the Nairit plant, which caused 100 people to be hospitalized and many more to fall ill. The meeting was organized by the Union of Greens, the Ecological Union, and the Armenian National Movement to demand the resignation of Prime Minister Vladimir Markayants, who had been resisting the parliament's order to close Nairit at the end of 1989. After the demonstration, a group of about 1,000 youths marched to the republic's

KGB headquarters shouting "provocative calls to liquidate the KGB" and laid siege to the building with homemade bombs and flare guns, causing heavy damage.[113] Later that month, youths broke away from an ecological meeting in Kiev shouting "anti-Soviet and anti-Socialist slogans" and vandalized a statue of Lenin and a monument commemorating the Bolshevik revolution.[114]

Interestingly, it was environmental issues that first ignited many of the movements for national identity, which ultimately destroyed the foundation of the Soviet state. To many citizens, the destruction of nature in their homelands epitomized everything that was wrong with Soviet development, the Soviet economy, and the Soviet state itself, and these great injustices against nature were obvious and easy focuses for action. Nature became a medium for social change. In the early days of perestroika, government officials tolerated environmentalists' activity because it was seen less as a political threat and more as a catalyst for their style of change. One victory after another—the cancellation of the Siberian rivers diversion project in summer 1986 being the most symbolic—boosted the morale and aspirations of the "informal movement," as it was called for years.

Events quickly ran out of officials' control, however. In Latvia, a series of articles appeared in the local press in 1986 and 1987 criticizing Moscow's plans to build a hydroelectric dam on the Daugava River. Dainis Ivans, an author of the articles, eventually was elected deputy chairman of the Latvian parliament and leader of the Latvian Popular Front, the movement that led the republic's drive for independence.[115] Janis Peters, another founding member of this group, boldly declared at the First USSR Congress of People's Deputies that only republic sovereignty "now can lead us out of our political, economic, ecological, and national crisis."[116] At about the same time, concern over oil-shale and phosphate mining precipitated the formation of the People's Front in Estonia. In Georgia, protests against the Transcaucasus Main Railway led to the creation in April 1988 of the Ecology Association under the auspices of the All-Georgia Rustaveli Society, the forerunner of the movement that asserted Georgian independence.

The experience of the Baltic environmental movement epitomized the synergy between environmental and ethnic issues. Having been forcibly incorporated into the Soviet Union in 1940, the Baltic people became convinced that their predominantly Russian rulers in Moscow were systematically destroying their economies, cultures, and natural resources. In a briefing issued to participants at the October 1989 Conference on Security and Cooperation in Europe (CSCE) meeting on the environment held in Sophia, the Lithuanian Greens argued that besides a lack of pollution control equipment, the republic suffers "a lack of control over its production and resources." In the document, the authors went on to accuse Soviet occupiers of turning the republic into "a colonial industrial dump site producing goods and services far beyond the needs of its own inhabitants."[117] Given such language, it is clear the Baltic environmentalists had more on their agendas than planting trees. Apart from improving air and water quality, the Greens expressed a desire to cleanse the political, mental, and even ethnic environment of their republics. In one statement, the Estonian Greens associated environmental problems with immigration into their republic, namely by Russians: "The suffocating overpopulation afflicts ever more our space of living and culture. We are becoming a minority in our own country."[118] Opposition to Lithuania's Ignalina nuclear power plant was based, in part, on the desire to force the predominantly Russian work force at the plant to leave the republic.[119] Many Estonians considered the values espoused by the German Green Party—renunciation of economic growth, antimilitarism, and strict protection of the environment—a perfect antidote to problems created by what they referred to as the "Soviet occupying forces." Their party proposed to reduce the number of resource-intensive industries situated in Estonia, to transfer land ownership from federal to republican or local levels, and to end in-migration from other republics. These demands, considered by many to be outlandish when they were first expressed, quickly became obtainable.

"We believe that the ultimate resolution of all problems is possible only after full restoration of state independence," stated Zurab Zhvaniya, spokesman for the Georgian Green Party in 1990. "Georgia . . . must always exist independently, in a situation of real equality."[120] In Ukraine, the Green Party was one of the republic's strongest supporters of sovereignty and independence, and its leaders figured prominently in emotional celebrations when the Ukrainian bicolored flag was raised for the first time over Kiev's city hall in the spring of 1991. The Green movements in Moldova and Belarus also developed in concert with national independence movements.

The interaction between environmental issues and nationality relations in the former Soviet Union can be viewed in a broader context as stemming from an ongoing struggle for control over resources. Nowhere have such pressures been greater than in Central Asia, which is presently in the midst of a population boom. In June 1989, communal violence broke out between native Uzbeks and Meskhetian immigrants in the Fergana Valley; over 100 people perished, 1,500 were injured, and 17,000 eventually were evacuated as a result of the bloody pogrom, largely precipitated by disaffected Uzbek youths. "Fergana can be seen as a direct result of a demographic explosion," asserted demographer Mark Tol'ts.[121] Moscow's pressure on the region to produce cotton had led to a fall in the availability of food in the region, and heavy chemical and pesticide use had contaminated the water supply.[122] Competition for jobs, water, and land is keen as a result of the skyrocketing population of Uzbeks in the valley. "There's a feeling of competition, and it creates a feeling of resentment against the minority," Tol'ts added.

As part of the effort to improve the social and economic situation in the Fergana Valley, Uzbekistan's Goskompriroda in 1989 announced the closure of a chemical plant in the city of Kokand. The plant, which had recently been completed, was situated over the valley's largest freshwater aquifer, and the republic's prosecutor had opened an investigation to determine responsibility for this "gravest mistake."[123] One month after tempers subsided in Fergana, a territorial dispute erupted nearby, this time in the towns of Bakten and Isfara, which straddle the Kyrgyzstan-Tajikistan border. Noted *Pravda:* "The basis of the conflict" between the two nationalities was "a shortage of land and a deficit of water."[124]

ENVIRONMENTALISM IN RUSSIA

The formation of a unified environmental movement in Russia has been much slower than in other states of the former Soviet Union. First, political cleavages in many parts of the Russian Federation have not produced the same situation found in the other republics, where ecology, nationalism, and anti-Moscow sentiments reinforced each other. Politics in the Russian republic have been generally far more complex than the "us versus them" attitude that has dominated politics in the non-Russian republics. Although many people like Valentin Rasputin have tended to blame bureaucrats in Moscow for problems in the countryside, the differences with Moscow have not been so great as to warrant secession. Rather, environmental interests in the Russian Federation have opted for more autonomy and control over the resources and industries of their region—a popular position given the spate of declarations of autonomy by numerous local and regional governments in the Russian Federation in 1990 and 1991. However, many of the center/periphery cleavages between the former Soviet government and the republics have been replicated in the minority ethnic regions of the federation in the post-Soviet era. Tatarstan and Bashkortostan, for example, have challenged the authority of Boris Yeltsin's Kremlin on national resources issues.

Second, geography has presented a major obstacle. The size of the federation and the lack of a reliable communications network have prevented the development of links between organizations. Environmental groups in neighboring cities, for example, often are unaware of each other's existence. Other Soviet successor states are small enough that the "backyard" metaphor accurately describes how citizens relate to their national territory. Russians feel equally strongly about their homeland, but Russia is not a backyard by any stretch of the imagination. Moscow residents want to eat rice; distance makes it more difficult to be concerned about the fact that fertilizer runoff from rice farms in Krasnodar is killing the Azov Sea, 1,200 kilometers away, especially when Muscovites are forced to contend with radioactive waste in their own city parks. This situation is an extension of the think-locally-act-locally model; environmental groups have formed in response to local needs. An overarching worldview or philosophy has yet to arise to unite these diverse groups spread across the Eurasian continent.

Third, as in the West, the environmental movement in the Russian Federation has been ideologically disparate and has attracted people from all points on the political and social spectrum. Journalist Viktor Yaroshenko noted that the Soviet Union in 1989 had "left-greens, right-greens, eco-socialists, and even eco-fascists." This is particularly true of Russia.[125] The case of Valentin Rasputin illustrates the strange and often incompatible bedfellows that Russian environmentalism brings together. Rasputin, one of contemporary Russia's most talented and famous writers, has been a longtime defender of the Siberian wilderness. As a native of Irkutsk oblast, he has been a vocal critic of the government's feeble efforts to protect Lake Baikal. Rasputin also has been associated with Pamyat', the staunchly Russian nationalist society that often has been accused of anti-Semitism.

Several large umbrella groups nonetheless have emerged that loosely link citizens associations from across the Russian Federation and the former Soviet Union. These NGOs, all based in Moscow, have achieved some measure of influence on policymaking and have successfully cultivated contacts with environmental groups abroad. The largest umbrella group is the Social-Ecological Union, with over 100 affiliated organizations, clubs, and societies drawn from virtually all former Soviet republics.[126] Formed at a national congress of environmentalists in December 1988, the SEU's goal is to serve as an effective counterweight to government. In its founding charter, the SEU calls for "the liquidation of the monopoly State Ministries and Departments maintain on receiving and disseminating information, and on elaborating plans and projects."[127] In April 1991, the Soviet Ministry of Justice issued a new charter to the SEU, giving the organization the same legal basis as a political party and granting it the right to monitor the enforcement of environmental protection legislation. The group thus became the first non-governmental organization in the Soviet Union with such privileges.

As its name suggests, the SEU's activities have extended beyond environmental protection per se in regions of particularly severe environmental degradation such as the Volga delta, where the group has expanded its agenda to include public health issues. Hence, its programs range from grassroots work educating the public about nitrate residue in foods to furnishing expert information to the former USSR Supreme Soviet Ecology Committee. The SEU does not have a centralized leadership, but international support has enabled the group to employ ten full-time coordinators responsible for diverse programs covering issues from the creation of nature preserves in the Pamir Mountains and Taimir Peninsula to the independent monitoring of radioactivity in Chelyabinsk oblast (the site of the Kyshtym disaster) and the creation of a pediatric "ecoclinic" in St. Petersburg. One of the SEU's leaders, Svetaslav Zabelin, is a close adviser to Aleksei Yablokov, who in turn serves as Boris Yeltsin's adviser on the environment.

Another group, the Ecological Union, was formed at the same time as the SEU as the result of a disagreement among organizers at the founding congress of the SEU. The Ecological Union differs from the SEU in that it focuses more on the science—as opposed to the politics—of environmental protection. Its motto reflects this technocratic approach: "High professionalism in solving ecological problems; less emotion and more work." Its leader remarked in an interview that he opposes "ecological hysteria." Said biology professor Nikolai Reimers: "One must be a realist. Now it is time to roll up our sleeves and prepare our own cadre of experts."[128] The Ecological Union has conducted studies on Lake Baikal, on economic development in the Altai region of Siberia, and on preserving the Black Sea. Like the SEU, the organization does not accept individual members; its approach is to form alliances with local environmental groups and to supply them with scientific support.

CHALLENGES FOR THE ENVIRONMENTAL MOVEMENTS

Despite their successes, the environmental organizations have encountered serious obstacles. Because organizing independent associations was forbidden for so long by the Soviet Union and is still discouraged in many regions, environmental groups must spend a considerable share of their energy working merely to establish themselves, thus diverting them from actual environmental activities. Having trouble being accepted as legitimate participants in civil society, most groups find themselves battling on two fronts, ecological and political. Over decades of rule, Communist Party authorities became quite accustomed to running things without interference from the public. Similarly, it will take decades of democratic experience to eradicate dictatorial tendencies that continue to pervade the political cultures of the newly independent republics. Although he himself was once a dissident, Zviad Gamsakhurdia quickly began to demonstrate dictatorial tendencies shortly after being elected president of Georgia in the spring of 1990. Similarly, popularly elected officials like St. Petersburg's Mayor Anatolii Sobchak and Russian President Boris Yeltsin have been accused of flouting democratic principles and practices in their haste to consolidate power.[129]

Bureaucrats on the whole still do not accept the idea that citizens groups can make substantive contributions to the formulation and implementation of environmental policy. Although welcoming the public's support, many environmental officials (like those elsewhere in the world) do not want NGOs monitoring their every move, criticizing them, or offering unsolicited advice. The deputy chairman of Kazakhstan's Goskompriroda, Boris Mishariakov, admonished local groups for demanding too much too soon and labeled them "dilettantes" unqualified to take an active part in environmental policy. "They don't understand that resolving ecological problems requires time. They say, 'No, we want it now, it must be done now.'"[130]

Officials have obstructed citizens groups from registering as independent organizations; often it is only through official registration, however, that a group can obtain office space, telephones, and other basic resources that Western NGOs take for granted. The bureaucracy can frustrate any initiative. It took an act of the Ukrainian parliament to secure three cramped rooms in a Kiev hotel for Greenpeace International's "Children of Chernobyl" project, and organizers had expected to spend another year fighting the bureaucracy and shortages to obtain, renovate, and outfit a simple storefront office.[131]

Negative attitudes toward environmental groups (indeed, toward the democratic movement as a whole) are shared by many people in post-Soviet society. With increasing troubles besetting the region's economy, many have begun accusing environmentalists of blocking or slowing economic recovery and growth. Under a September 1990 front-page headline, *Izvestiya* queried "Are the Greens always right?" and alleged that the "Green offensive" was implicated in shortages of everything from cigarette filters, washing powder, and fabric dyes to photographic film and eyeglass lenses.[132] Alluding to the shortage of aspirin in Ukraine, *Rabochaya gazeta* attacked the popular Ukrainian environmental movement Zelenyi Svit, writing that "people literally have headaches from environmental problems."[133] Commentary in the liberal *Literaturnaya gazeta* accused Greens of acting with "a Red fury" and detailed how environmentalists had sought to shut down worthy enterprises and to assign guilt for transgressions. In a search for a resolution to the country's environmental problems, the newspaper criticized environmentalists for victimizing well-meaning enterprise directors, when the real culprits were the "achievements" of Soviet development—the polluting factories themselves.[134]

To charges of economic sabotage, environmentalists counter that they unfairly have been made scapegoats for the failures of the Soviet economy; they claim that not all factories were closed or projects abandoned solely for environmental reasons. Many operations were shut down because they were outdated or simply were no longer needed. Many projects, like the famous Siberian rivers diversion scheme and those concerning nuclear power, were shelved after impartial commissions concluded they were economically unfeasible or based on questionable technological merit.[135] However, it is true that the success of environmental groups came primarily in their vociferous opposition to ecologically hazardous projects rather than in abatement of pollution from an enterprise or in remediation of existing damage. Having demonstrated its power of opposition, the environmental movement must now provide credible alternatives to the status quo.

Much of the early environmental debate in the former Soviet Union was conceptualized in terms of "us" (the localities) versus "them" (Moscow and the ministries), engendering a "not in my backyard" mentality that became reinforced by sentiments for political autonomy and economic autarky. Environmentalists are aware of global problems such as climate change, ozone depletion, and acid rain, but the alarming conditions citizens must confront in their backyards everyday force them to concentrate on the more proximal dangers. As already noted, large distances between population centers, a shortage of communications equipment, and an underdeveloped telecommunications infrastructure prevent NGOs from spreading their message more widely and making contacts with each other.

In part, the local focus also can be attributed to the movement's youth and inexperience. Even the most successful groups, such as Ukraine's Zelenyi Svit, have at most a few paid or formally trained staff members. Despite the devotion and vigorous activity of their supporters, many groups are poorly organized, do not know how to obtain information or use what is available to support their positions, and become overwhelmed by the intricacies and arbitrariness of the legal system.[136] Even when groups have access to equipment like telephones, faxes, computers, and photocopying machines, they do not always use them to their full advantage. With support from U.S. foundations and the Institute for Soviet-American Relations, a Washington, D.C.–based nongovernmental organization, the SEU set up an electronic mail network to link environmental groups with each other as well as with the West. Although international communications have proved popular, few messages beyond the occasional greeting have been exchanged among groups within the former Soviet Union. This can be attributed in part to the lack of networking skills among environmentalists in the former USSR—a legacy of policies designed to atomize society over the decades of Communist Party rule.

In contrast to the pattern in other regions, particularly favorable local conditions were one reason for the Baltic Greens' early organizational and political successes. With the inception of perestroika and glasnost, the Baltic people (and governments quickly thereafter) were the first to adopt the goal of developing pluralist political structures. Moreover, they were quick to embrace the concepts of economic autonomy (i.e., control over the republics' resources and industry) and eager to promote the region's agriculture and to develop cleaner high technology and service industries. In addition, with official sanction, Baltic environmentalists were able to take advantage of a relatively well-developed (by Soviet standards) communications infrastructure. In the early 1990s, over 130 independent newspapers were published in Lithuania alone, for example, and local governments improved public access to local radio and television facilities.

Furthermore, international contacts, facilitated by the region's proximity to Scandinavia, proved crucial as a source of information and organizational support. During the Soviet era, the Estonians were able to receive Finnish television, allowing them to monitor events in that country and the West at large. Moreover, Baltic environmentalists were able to strengthen contacts abroad through their extensive participation in regional conferences, such as those concentrating on the cleanup of the Baltic Sea. Finally, the independence and environmental movements were supported by an energetic émigré community, particularly in the United States, where they had as advocates several members of the U.S. Congress. In recognition of these links, Vaidotas Antanaitis of Lithuania and Vello Pohla of Estonia were invited to testify before that body in October 1989. The Environmental Protection Club, one of the largest citizens organizations in Latvia, received computers, photocopiers, and Geiger counters from members of the organization's chapter in the United States.[137] Using office equipment donated from the West, many

Baltic environmental groups began to exploit electronic mail and facsimile machines much earlier than their counterparts elsewhere in the Soviet Union. These advantages organizations in the Baltic states had are significant when compared with the situation of other groups in distant Siberia or even in neighboring St. Petersburg.

A lack of accomplishment by some environment activists also may be attributed to extreme and uncompromising positions they hold as well as to a marked lack of trust in their opposition. Although many environmental officials and politicians have made overtures toward environmental NGOs, the latter often consider any cooperation with government or industry tantamount to violating their principles and sacrificing their independence. Konstantin Ryabchikhin of the Leningrad International Center for Environmental Law disagrees with this stance. Whereas he feels the "radical environmental movement" is effective at influencing public opinion and political discourse, working with the government and, in particular, the judiciary is more effective at achieving concrete results.[138]

Similarly, one of the striking features of the overall environmental movement is its divisiveness—groups operating in the same arena seem to trust each other as little as they trust government officials. Despite the advances of democratization, many environmentalists remain in the mold of *Homo Sovieticus*, says Sergei Pomogaev, a prominent environmental organizer in St. Petersburg.[139] Environmental leaders often profess ignorance of other groups' activities, either local or national; when they do mention others, they frequently express little toleration for their perspectives and opinions—a reflection of the political polarization and disaffection of post-Soviet society. As for government bureaucracies, access to resources and information for NGOs—especially that coming from abroad—is critical to obtaining a measure of power, and groups often appear disinclined to share. Relations can even approach enmity between NGOs, as was the case between the SEU and the Ecological Union after their split. SEU leaders portrayed environmental specialists in the Ecological Union as unsophisticated moonlighters conducting research "in their free time for an extra ruble."[140] Such frictions thwart cooperation, but they are not unique to the former Soviet Union: Similar cleavages mark relations among peak organizations, science-based groups, and grassroots activists in the United States. Like their counterparts elsewhere in the world, the environmental movements of the former USSR must learn to respect the diversity of opinions among their ranks to capitalize on the breadth of the movement and to learn from the experiences of others.

ENVIRONMENTALISM IN A PERIOD OF FLUX

Despite the surge in environmentalism witnessed in the 1980s, environmental leaders were admitting by 1991 that public concern and activism on behalf of the environment had dropped off significantly. Some have attributed the public's newfound apathy to the fact that the shock and indignation about the extent of environmental degradation revealed during the early days of glasnost has dissipated. Realizing that little can be done in the near future to resolve the staggering environmental problems, people once again have become resigned to living with them. This trend has been compounded by the fact that economic hardship has diverted attention and energy away from environmental concerns, as more time is devoted to obtaining the necessities of life.

In a society where citizens spend a large share of their earnings and free time trying to obtain the most basic of necessities and services, people, particularly women, have little time or energy left to labor on behalf of the environment. A report carried by *Izvestiya* in 1991 indicated that as a result of economic reform, individuals had even less free time to spare—presumably because of the longer time spent waiting in lines and working to make ends meet.[141] On this point, committed environmentalists frequently complain that their fellow compatriots show too little interest in protecting nature. In October 1990, for example, a group of academic, religious, and ecology figures organized the "Vozrozhdenie" (Rebirth) boat excursion down the Volga River to dramatize the river's precarious fate. When their boat, the *Konstantin Smirnov*, pulled into Cherepovets, no one was at the dock to greet them, even though a demonstration had been planned. Instead, local citizens reportedly were standing in lines trying to cash in their ration cards for the previous month's allotment of sugar.[142]

Change in the political discourse since the inception of reform in the 1980s also has affected the nature of environmental activism. Environmentalism played a significant role in the early democratization of political life in the Soviet Union. In the first days of perestroika, before Communist Party officials sanctioned independent political activity, environmental degradation served as an issue around which people could organize and vent their frustration with the status quo in Soviet society. Environmentalism provided the issues and space around which other political movements could coalesce. Ironically, nuclear power stations, noxious chemical plants, and hazardous waste disposal sites provided the first safe political space in which individuals could organize and work against the Communist regime, because these targets of protest often were distant from the centers of political power and thus were not considered a direct and visible threat to the political leadership.[143]

As these environmental movements evolved, experiences in them afforded emerging national political leaders valuable organizational skills and public exposure they could then transfer to other initiatives. Thus, many of the region's major political figures—Gennadii Fil'shin and Valentin Rasputin from Russia, Vaidotas Antanaitis of Lithuania, Yurii Shcherbak of Ukraine, and Olzhas Suleimenov of Kazakhstan—achieved political prominence through their work on environmental issues. As previously noted, movements of ethnic awareness or national revival in Russia, Armenia, Ukraine, Lithuania, Georgia, and elsewhere can trace their roots to the early environmental movements. But glasnost and democratization broadened and deepened the discourse by incorporating more issues spread over a larger political spectrum. In turn, many political entrepreneurs transferred their investment of time and effort from their narrower environmental focus to agendas of more broadly based political and ethnic movements in their ascendancy. According to Zurab Zhvaniya, spokesman for the Georgian Green Party, local politicians "speculated" on the environment in their bid for power. For example, opposition to the construction of the Transcaucasus Main Railway and the Khudon hydroelectric project in Georgia helped cement the opposition to the local Communist leadership. Once they came to power in 1990 and 1991, however, the same individuals who had challenged the projects as leaders of the opposition began to champion them as essential to Georgian national development and independence.[144]

Thus, although in many regions, Green parties were among the first overt de facto political parties to form in opposition to the Communist Party, they quickly were eclipsed by more conventional mass political parties and organizations, particularly those oriented around nationalist platforms.[145] One observer commenting on the rocky start of the Latvian Green Party noted that "people feel rather skeptical about forming new parties at a time when all should act as one to achieve the supreme objective—a free and independent Republic of Latvia." When they officially did form a party in January 1990, the Latvian Greens decided to nominate candidates for the republic's Supreme Soviet to run under the banner of the Latvian Popular Front (which was acting as an umbrella group for all proindependence candidates) rather than to support environmental candidates in their own right.[146] The decline in the visibility of environmental concerns has been most noticeable in the non-Russian republics, where the issue was once strongest because of the affiliation of ecology with national and ethnic causes.[147] In an interview with the *Los*

Angeles Times, Janos Tamulis, a leader of the Lithuanian Greens and a member of the Lithuanian parliament, asserted, "The Green movement here is weaker than it was two years ago, that's for sure."[148] Ukraine's *Rabochaya gazeta* went so far as to describe the situation as a "profound crisis in the Green movement."[149]

The early 1990s indeed brought a decrease in public activism, but environmental issues are not disappearing entirely from the political agenda, and environmentalism continues to shape the region's evolving political culture. Eliza Klose of the Institute for Soviet-American Relations argues that the early movement was like "a large-scale rebellion" carried by emotion and the newfound immediacy of environmental problems, as portrayed by the press. "The time for that is over."[150] As in the West, mainstream political parties and movements have made significant efforts to incorporate ecological issues into their platforms, and the environmental movement must compete with them for the public's support. Svetaslav Zabelin of the Moscow-based Social-Ecological Union expects support for the environmental movement in the former Soviet Union ultimately to settle at levels seen in the West—about 10 percent of the population.[151] In place of mass movements, many environmental organizations are becoming professionalized with full-time scientists and staffs. Having supplanted Communist Party bureaucrats who traditionally managed environmental matters, the new NGOs have attracted the attention and support of international environmental organizations. Despite their lower profile, environmentalists in the former Soviet Union "are working harder than ever, and the quality of the effort has been enhanced on both sides," asserts Klose.

The scale of environmental deterioration in the former Soviet Union, however, requires costly steps to ameliorate the situation. A severe lack of resources dictates that a political compromise be struck. To reach a satisfactory compromise between the goals of protecting the environment and improving the population's material well-being, a democratic society must comprehend the consequences of its actions—both for the economy and for the environment—and develop a quality-of-life ethic that reconciles differences and meets these needs. Thus, the environmental movement has a prominent role to play in the deepening of democracy in the post-Soviet societies through the promotion of public awareness about the value of an unpolluted and healthy society. In this light, the environmental movement has registered success, concludes Aleksei Yablokov: "The consciousness of the people is growing. The people are starting to think."[152]

Notes

1. For reviews of problems in Soviet public opinion research, see Amy Corning, "Recent Developments in Soviet Public Opinion Research," Radio Free Europe/Radio Liberty Soviet Area Audience and Opinion Research, AR 6-89, October 1989; Ronald Pope, "Public Opinion Research in the Soviet Union: A Firsthand Account," *Report on the USSR*, No. 43, 1990; and William E. Freeman, "Soviet Telephone Survey Methods," U.S. Information Agency Research Report, R-13-89, August 1989.

2. USSR Goskomstat, *Press-vypusk*, No. 226, June 7, 1990. In the Goskomstat survey, 46 percent of those questioned replied that the state of the environment gave them cause for concern.

3. *Vestnik statistiki*, No. 4, 1991, pp. 20–21; TASS, September 26, 1991.

4. Radio Rossii, July 1, 1991, translated in JPRS–TEN–91–015, p. 63.

5. *Moskovskie novosti*, No. 22, 1990, p. 7. The survey was conducted jointly by the USSR Academy of Sciences Institute of Sociology, a major institution involved in public opinion research, and the University of Houston.

6. Vladimir Paniotto, "The Ukrainian Movement for Perestroika—'Rukh': A Sociological Survey," *Soviet Studies*, Vol. 43, No. 1, 1991, p. 179.

7. The referendums were nonbinding because at the time they were held, there was no legal mechanism in the USSR for conducting such a poll.

8. Radio Moscow, February 27, 1990. For a report on the Neftekamsk referendum, see *Izvestiya*, March 1, 1990, p. 3. In another issue on the ballot, 98 percent voted against raising the level of the Nizhnekamsk Reservoir.

9. Radio Moscow, May 15, 1990; *Izvestiya*, May 17, 1990, p. 2. *Komsomol'skaya pravda*, May 24, 1990, p. 2, reported a slightly higher share (97.9 percent) against the scheme.

10. *Moskovskie novosti*, No. 22, 1990, p. 7.

11. Personal communication with Anatolii Panov, Kiev, July, 1991.

12. Radio Moscow, August 12, 1990.

13. TASS, October 26, 1990.

14. *Pravda*, December 20, 1990, p. 8. Interestingly, Yakovlev reported that his agency's position was based on research on global fresh-water resources that the KGB had obtained from Western intelligence services.

15. Anatolii Andrienko, public relations specialist, Ukrainian Ministry of Environmental Protection and Rational Use of Natural Resources, personal communication, Kiev, July 1991.

16. *Sovetskaya Latviya*, January 1, 1990, p. 4, cited in JPRS-UPA-90-012, p. 75.

17. *Molodezh Moldavii*, August 2, 1990, p. 2, translated in JPRS-UPA-90-056, p. 69.

18. Novosti Press Agency, July 30, 1991, reported in Radio Free Europe/Radio Liberty (RFE/RL) Daily Report, August 1, 1991.

19. USSR Goskomstat, *Press-vypusk*, No. 136, April 4, 1990.

20. *Vechernyaya Moskva*, December 23, 1989, p. 2.

21. *Pravitel'stvennyi vestnik*, No. 41, 1990, p. 6.

22. K. Malakhov, "Material'no-tekhnicheskoe obespechenie narodnogo khozyaistva," *Planovoe khozyaistvo,* No. 10, 1989, p. 7.

23. TASS, April 20, 1990.

24. *Izvestiya,* January 26, 1991, p. 3. In a July 1990 appeal to President Gorbachev and the all-Union and republic Supreme Soviets, physicists under the aegis of the USSR Ministry of Atomic Energy and Industry noted that "under public pressure, the design, survey, and construction work to build nuclear power plants with a total capacity of more than 100 million kilowatts has been discontinued," and that trained work collectives are "falling apart." TASS, July 17, 1990.

25. *Sovetskaya Rossiya,* June 28, 1990,.p. 1.

26. *Pravda Ukrainy,* August 8, 1990, p. 2

27. TASS, October 29, 1991. Earlier in the year, the Ukrainian Supreme Soviet had voted to close the reactors by 1995.

28. Central Television, "Vremya," May 6, 1990. For a scathing critique of the project, see *Moskovskaya pravda,* January 11, 1990, p. 3.

29. Anatolii Stepanov, Yulii Petrovich, Aleksandr Gusev, Moscow Green Party, personal communication, Moscow, June 1991.

30. *Sotsialisticheskaya industriya,* December 31, 1989, p. 2.

31. Radio Moscow, February 6, 1990.

32. *Trud,* August 30, 1990, p. 1.

33. *Meditsinskaya gazeta,* December 10, 1989,p. 3.

34. *Pravda,* November 9, 1989, p. 2.

35. *Meditsinskaya gazeta,* December 10, 1989, p. 3.

36. *Trud,* August 30, 1990, p. 1.

37. *Meditsinskaya gazeta,* December 10, 1989, p. 3.

38. *Izvestiya,* June 13, 1989, p. 6; *Sovetskaya Rossiya,* August 30, 1989, p. 2.

39. For more on Chapaevsk and the USSR's plans to destroy its chemical weapons, see *Pravda,* February 10 and August 22, 1989; *Izvestiya,* May 13, 1989; *Komsomol'skaya pravda,* October 18, 1989; *Svet,* No. 2, 1990; and *Khimiya i zhizn',* No. 6, 1990.

40. Radio Moscow, August 28, 1989; *Izvestiya,* August 30, 1989, p. 1.

41. In July 1991, Aleksei Yablokov commented that the Soviet government had not yet elaborated any program to destroy its chemical weapons. Radio Moscow, July 10, 1991.

42. Radio Kiev, April 2, 1990; Radio Moscow, April 4, 1990.

43. Radio Moscow, August 13, 1990. For more on Mukachevo, see *Trud,* February 25, 1990; *Pravda Ukrainy,* March 21, 1990; *Pravda,* April 1, 1990; *Izvestiya,* April 26, 1990; and Central Television, "Television News Service," June 11, 1990.

44. Natural Resources Defense Council, *Nuclear Weapons Databook,* Vol. 4 (Soviet Nuclear Weapons) (New York: Harper & Row, 1989), pp. 355, 375 (hereafter NRDC, *Databook*).

45. *Izvestiya,* March 11, 1990, p. 4.

46. *European,* June 1–3, 1990.

47. NRDC, *Databook,* pp. 375–376.

48. *Pravda,* February 12, 1990, p. 4.

49. For example, Dr. Maira Zhangelova, a medical researcher and chair of the Semipalatinsk Oblast Peace Committee, and Dr. Boris Gusev, head of the USSR Radiology Research Institute, have separately argued that as many as 500,000 people were contaminated by tests in the course of 40 years, with 100,000 succumbing to cancer-related deaths. Agence France Presse, November 1 and 13, 1990; see also, *Stuttgarter Zeitung*, November 3, 1990; Reuter, October 1, 1990; *Kazakhstanskaya pravda*, January 28 and May 25, 1990; *Izvestiya*, March 11 and October 20, 1990; and Central Television, July 23, 1989. For an extended view of life and conditions around Semipalatinsk, see Kanat Kabdrakhmanov, "Lyudi na poligon," *Znamya*, No. 5, 1990.

50. *Izvestiya*, March 11, 1990, p. 4.

51. Ibid. Similar comments have been made by Saim Bamlukhanov, deputy director of the Kazakhstan Ministry of Health Institute of Oncology and Radiology. Novosti Press Agency, *Voennyi vestnik*, No. 18, 1989.

52. See, for example, *Sovetskaya Rossiya*, July 21, 1989; *Krasnaya zvezda*, July 17, 1990.

53. TASS, June 11, 1990. Petrushenko, a local deputy, was a vocal supporter of continued testing at Semipalatinsk. For instance, see his comments in *Krasnaya zvezda*, November 29, 1990; *Rabochaya tribuna*, September 14, 1990; and *Nedelya*, No. 35, 1990.

54. Bess Brown, "The Strength of Kazakhstan's Anti-Nuclear Lobby," *Report on the USSR*, No. 4, 1991, pp. 23–24; Bess Brown, "Semipalatinsk Test Site Finally Closed," *Report on the USSR*, No. 37, 1991, pp. 15-16.

55. TASS, November 27, 1989; *Izvestiya*, December 3, 1989, p. 3. The last test held at Semipalatinsk was in October 1989.

56. Central Television, March 6 and 28, 1990.

57. TASS and Radio Moscow, March 7, 1990; RFE/RL Daily Report, March 8, 1990. The military's plan was put forth by Colonel General Vladimir Gerasimov. The military apparently scaled back its proposed program to 18 blasts, according to comments by USSR Minister of Defense Dmitrii Yazov on December 19, 1990. Novosti Press Agency, December 20, 1990.

58. TASS, May 23 and December 6, 1990.

59. TASS, October 1, 1990; Radio Moscow, December 14, 1990.

60. *Krasnaya zvezda*, April 1, 1990, p. 2.

61. The experiments were billed not as tests of nuclear weapons but as calibrating explosions to test verification methods that would allow the USSR to meet treaty obligations, only after which could the site be shut down.

62. Personal communication with Vladimir Yakimets, Moscow, June 1991.

63. Ibid.

64. Interfax, July 13, 1991, cited in FBIS-SOV-91-137, July 17, 1991, p. 74.

65. Brown, "Semipalatinsk Test Site Finally Closed," p. 15.

66. NRDC, *Databook*, pp. 375–376.

67. According to the NRDC, most underground tests at Novaya Zemlya have been conducted in September and October, with a few being held in August, November, and December. Ibid., p. 336.

68. TASS, April 23 and November 1, 1990; *Izvestiya*, October 26, 1990, p. 2, and November 13, 1990, p. 2.

69. TASS, October 14, 1991.

70. Ukaz Prezidenta Rossiiskoi Federatsii, "O poligon na Novoi Zemle," No. 194, Moscow, February 27, 1992.

71. Dr. Paula Garb, Program on Social Ecology, University of California, Irvine, telephone conversation, April 1992.

72. TASS, April 1, 1990. Apparently, ecologically oriented groups make up a large portion of citizens organizations in St. Petersburg. According to a sociologist studying the St. Petersburg political scene, there were about 150 "groups and organizations" in the city. This figure was not based on official data but on a count of groups that had "to one extent or another an expressed public orientation." E. Zdravomyslova, "'Neformaly' trebuyut," *Leningradskaya panorama*, No. 8, 1989, p. 18.

73. Radio Moscow, October 9, 1990.

74. TASS, April 8 and April 20, 1990. For reports on the Chernobyl Union's first congress, see Central Television, "Vremya," June 15, 1990, and *Sovetskaya molodezh*, June 20, 1990, p. 1.

75. Personal communication with Sheryl Belcher, Kiev, July 1991.

76. According to a 1990 government survey, only 23 percent of the general public canvassed expressed partial or complete confidence in the government's information; 50 percent expressed no trust at all. *Pravitel'stvennyi vestnik*, No. 24, 1991, p. 10.

77. Anatolii Grebenyuk, presentation at conference on Democratic Federalism and Environmental Crisis in the Republics of the Former Soviet Union, Moscow, August 1991.

78. In May 1987, the first officially reported environmental demonstration was held in Tartu, Estonia. Between then and the end of 1989, 182 environment-related public demonstrations were reported in the official media. Mark Beissinger, University of Wisconsin, personal communication, Phoenix, Arizona, June 1992.

79. Jane Dawson, "Intellectuals and Anti-Nuclear Protest in the Soviet Union," unpublished manuscript, University of California, Berkeley, 1991.

80. Svetaslav Zabelin, Mariya Cherkasova, and Andrei Ivanov-Smolenskii, "Informal Ecological Movements in Moscow," unpublished manuscript, August 1991, p. 9.

81. This fact was conveyed by Jane Dawson, an observer of the Soviet environmental movement (telephone communication, December 1990), and reiterated in conversations with representatives of environmental groups in the USSR in June 1991.

82. Natal'ya Mironova, deputy chair, Chelyabinsk Ecological Foundation, personal communication, Moscow, June 1991.

83. Zabelin et al., *Informal Ecological Movements*, p. 7.

84. See, for example, *Izvestiya*, March 27, 1989.

85. Of the remaining 40 people's deputies elected to the USSR Supreme Soviet from the Baltic region, 33 were members or sympathizers of the popular front movements, which had platforms similar to the Green parties.

86. B. Yastrebov and A. A. Nelyubin, "Obshchestvenno-politicheskie organizatsii, partii, i dvizheniya v Litve," *Izvestiya TsK KPSS*, No. 3, 1991, p. 97.

87. *Zarya Vostoka*, February 20, 1990, p. 4.

88. Valerii Papanian, consultant to Union of Greens of Armenia, personal communication, Kiev, July 1991.

89. See David Marples, "The Ecological Situation in the Ukraine," *Report on the USSR*, No. 3, p. 23; and David Marples, "Ecological Issues Discussed at Founding Congress of 'Zelenyi svit',"*Report on the USSR*, No. 2, 1990, p. 21.

90. Anatolii Panov, vice-president, Green World, personal communication, July 1991.

91. Sergei Kurykin, member of coordination council of the Ukrainian Green Party, personal communication, Kiev, July 1991.

92. *Vestnik statistiki*, No. 4, 1991, p. 21.

93. *Argumenty i fakty*, No. 15, 1990, p. 1. The data were supplied by the All-Union Central Scientific Institute for Occupational Safety.

94. TASS, May 8, 1990; *Trud*, October 7, 1989, p. 1.

95. *Rabochaya tribuna*, April 18, 1991, p. 1.

96. *Financial Times*, October 6, 1989.

97. TASS, May 22, 1990.

98. *Argumenty i fakty*, No. 31, 1990, p. 5.

99. Elizabeth Shogren, "Reds Go Green," *Moscow Magazine*, October 1990, p. 42.

100. *Pravda*, August 21, 1989, p. 3.

101. *Argumenty i fakty*, No. 30, 1989, p. 8.

102. *Independent*, November 17, 1989. For more on the issue, see Theodore H. Freidgut, "Ecological Factors in the July 1989 Mine Strike," *Environmental Policy Review*, January 1990.

103. "Ekonomicheskaya platforma Soyuza Trudyashchikhsya Kuzbassa" (no author), *Voprosy ekonomiki*, No. 2, 1990, p. 86.

104. Personal communication with Andrei Ivanov-Smolenskii, Los Angeles, October 1991.

105. *Moscow News*, No. 9, 1991, p. 9.

106. Radio Kiev, August 25, 1990, translated in FBIS-SOV-90-166, p. 102.

107. Radio Kiev, December 17, 1990, translated in FBIS-SOV-90-243, pp. 96–97; *Izvestiya*, December 23, 1990, p. 6. For more on the controversy, see *Rabochaya gazeta*, October 5 and 6, 1990.

108. N. V. Uspenskaya, "Nuzhna polnaya ekologicheskaya glasnost'," *Priroda*, No. 11, 1989, p. 6.

109. *Moskovskie novosti*, No. 42, 1990, p. 6.

110. Radio Moscow, October 6, 1990. For more on the incident, consult Reuter and *Financial Times*, October 19, 1990.

111. A.Tsygankov, "Gde ugodno, tol'ko ne u nas," *Pravitel'stvennyi vestnik*, No. 20, 1989, p. 9.

112. United Press International (UPI), February 14, 1990.

113. *Los Angeles Times*, April 16, 1990, pp. A1, A14.

114. TASS, April 28, 1990.

115. *Surviving Together*, Summer 1990, p. 22.

116. Central Television, June 2, 1989.

117. Lithuanian World Community and Lithuanian Green Movement, *The Degradation of the Environment in Lithuania*, briefing to the Conference on Security and Cooperation in Europe, Sophia, October 1989, unpublished manuscript, p. 4.

118. *Maaleht*, May 26, 1988, as translated in Eric Green, *Ecology and Perestroika* (Washington, DC: American Committee on U.S.-Soviet Relations, 1990), p. 39.

119. *Los Angeles Times*, October 2, 1991, p. A1

120. *Zarya Vostoka*, February 20, 1990, p. 4.

121. *Baltimore Sun*, June 19, 1989.

122. For more on the problems of the region, consult Ann Sheehy, "Social and Economic Background to Recent Events in Fergana Valley," *Report on the USSR*, No. 27, 1989.

123. Radio Moscow, July 7,1989.

124. *Pravda*, July 19, 1989, p. 6. For more on the nexus between environmentalism and nationalism, see "Panel on Nationalism in the USSR: Environmental and Territorial Aspects," *Soviet Geography*, June 1989.

125. Green, *Ecology*, p. 42.

126. Andrei Ivanov-Smolenskii, program coordinator, Social-Ecological Union, personal communication, Los Angeles, October 1991.

127. *Ustav Sotsial'no-ekologicheskogo soyuza*, Moscow, 1988, translated in Green, *Ecology*, p. 44.

128. *Sotsialisticheskaya industriya*, November 4, 1988. For more on Reimers and the Ecological Union, see *Sobesednik*, No. 3, 1990, p. 9.

129. See, for example, Carla Thorson, "The Collapse of the Constitutional Order," *Report on the USSR*, No. 42, 1991.

130. *Izvestiya*, May 19, 1990, p. 2.

131. Sheryl Belcher, coordinator, Greenpeace International "Children of Chernobyl" project, personal communication, Kiev, July 1991.

132. *Izvestiya*, September 17, 1991, p. 1.

133. *Rabochaya gazeta*, January 30, 1991, p. 2.

134. *Literaturnaya gazeta*, No. 30, 1990, p. 11.

135. According to the Social-Ecological Union, about one-half of the nuclear projects scrapped were the result of environmental protests. *Rossiiskaya gazeta*, June 14, 1991, p. 4.

136. Many of these points were raised by Kristen Suokko, staff member, National Resources Defense Council, telephone communication, January 1991.

137. *Surviving Together*, Summer 1990, p. 22.

138. Personal communication with Konstantin Ryabchikhin, Leningrad, June 1991.

139. Personal communication with Sergei Pomogaev, Leningrad, June 1991.

140. Zabelin et al., *Informal Ecological Movements*, p. 10.

141. *Izvestiya*, July 3, 1991, p. 8. According to survey results, men spent an average of just 7 minutes per day on "meetings, visits, games, [and] entertainment." Women allocated just 3 minutes to such activities. In comparison, 1 hour 47 minutes by men and 50 minutes by women were devoted to television watching. The lower figures for women reflect the "triple burden" (profession, housework, and childcare) that taxed women particularly heavily in the Soviet Union.

142. Central Television, "Television News Service," October 17, 1990.

143. Examples are two early protests waged in Yerevan in 1987. On Saturday, October 17, a crowd of 2,000 people gathered at the Nairit Scientific Production Association on the edge of the city to protest pollution problems associated with Nairit. Attendees included many prominent party and government officials. The police were in force, but they only observed the proceedings. The following day, a crowd of 1,000 people gathered in the city center to protest the persecution of Armenians in the Nagorno-Karabakh enclave in neighboring Azerbaijan. The protesters set off for the republic's Communist Party headquarters, but got into scuffles with the police and were dispersed. *Literaturnaya gazeta*, October 28, 1987, p. 9; Agence France Presse, October 17 and 19, 1987, translated in FBIS-SOV-87-203, p. 63. The author thanks Michael Schlitzer, RAND/UCLA Center for Soviet Studies, for his insights on this case.

144. Personal communication with Zurab Zhvaniya, Kiev, July 1991.

145. According to Dr. Peter Hardi, executive director of the Regional Environmental Center for Central and Eastern Europe, a support agency for nongovernmental organizations working on environmental issues, a similar trend occurred in Eastern Europe, most notably in Bulgaria. Before the democratizations of 1989, dissident and opposition figures gravitated toward various environmental movements that either had semiofficial status or were at least tolerated by the government and, therefore, enjoyed a modicum of political independence. With the opening of democracy, many leaders dropped the environmental movement for mainstream political parties. Personal communication with Peter Hardi, Los Angeles, February 1991.

146. *Atmoda* (in English), No. 4, 1990, p. 2.

147. For more on this issue, see DJ Peterson, "Environmental Protection and the State of the Union," *Report on the USSR*, No. 12, 1991.

148. *Los Angeles Times*, October 2, 1991, p. A8.

149. *Rabochaya gazeta*, January 30, 1991, p. 2.

150. Telephone communication with Eliza Klose, May 1992.

151. Personal communication with Svetaslav Zabelin, Los Angeles, April 1991.

152. Shogren, "Reds Go Green," p. 40.

8

The Environment and Economic Transition

In the face of hunger and cold . . . one can forget all other problems.
—Vitalii Chelyshev, USSR Supreme Soviet environment committee

Your dirt is our dirt and our dirt is your dirt.
—Mariya Cherkasova, chair, Social-Ecological Union

As the states of the former Soviet Union have grappled with the most wrenching social and economic upheaval since the Bolshevik revolution and civil war, political leaders and environmentalists have been attempting to change radically how their societies affect their natural surroundings. The restructuring of environment and resources management outlined in the previous two chapters illustrates the most visible changes taking place. Regardless of the accomplishments of glasnost, democratization, and legal reform, the fate of the environment in the post-Soviet era depends to the greatest extent on the results of the third component of reforms: economic restructuring.

As Mikhail Gorbachev and his successors have discovered, government bureaucracy, entrenched political and economic interests, the pain of cruel choices, and the fear of social upheaval all work as a powerful brake on the reform impulse. Thus, the traditional emphasis on industrial development and the exploitation of natural resources continues to threaten nature, while state-controlled prices promote neither efficiency nor conservation and hamper efforts to regulate pollution through market mechanisms. Meanwhile, funds for environemntal protection remain scarce, poor technology and an overworked infrastructure slow the cleanup process, and structural characteristics remaining from the former Soviet economy slow the transition to market-oriented principles. Finally, with the Union broken up and the economy broken down, policymakers and legislators are forced to overlook the environment while the disruption upsets any well-intentioned environmental plan.

As the post-Soviet societies choose their development paths and decide the fate of their natural environments, they will encounter complex issues, such as pegging the cost of remediation, establishing the social value for a clean environment (often conceived of as a tradeoff between jobs and the environment), choosing development options, determining the appropriate role of technology, and clarifying the implications of foreign investment.

ESTIMATING THE SCALE OF A LONG-TERM CLEANUP

The uncertainty of the process of economic reforms under way makes estimating the cost of a future cleanup impossible. Though hampered by the distorted prices of the Soviet economy, predictions made in the late Soviet era give an estimate of the scale of the financial burden left for the successor states. What is clear is that vastly more resources will be required in the future to make a noticeable improvement in conditions.

According to the 1990 long-range environmental program presented to the Soviet government by USSR Goskompriroda, environmental spending, if continued at the heightened levels of the late 1980s (about 1.3 percent of GNP), was sufficient only to maintain the status quo, or the same rate of degradation experienced before—a condition the agency labeled its "pessimistic forecast." In contrast, decisively reversing environmental problems would require spending on the order of 7 to 9 percent of GNP—the "optimistic but unreasonable" scenario.[1] Nikolai Vorontsov personally advocated spending on the order of 5 percent of GNP.[2] Government planners settled on boosting spending substantially to bring it in the range of 3–4 percent of GNP—Goskompriroda's "moderately optimistic" forecast—and targeted government-backed capital investment for the program at 132–146 billion (pre-price reform) rubles between 1991 and 2005. This worked out to about 9 billion rubles a year (presumably in constant rubles), or about 2.5 times higher than investment levels in 1990. Aleksandr Tsygankov, deputy chairman of the Commission on Emergency Situations that oversaw the program's development, said that planners aimed at stabilizing environmental conditions by 1995 and bringing pollution down to a "tolerable level" by the end of the century. From then on, the planners envisioned a general improvement in conditions.[3]

Although never implemented, the aforementioned program would have claimed over 10 percent of the government's dwindling capital investment budget. In the summer of 1990, however, the team of economists under Stanislav Shatalin (commissioned jointly by Mikhail Gorbachev and Boris Yeltsin) issued their blueprint for rapid economic reform, concluding that the government's environmental remediation program would have required the added conversion of defense industries to producing pollution control equipment amounting to 2 billion rubles a year—a doubtful prospect given the poor performance of the conversion program. Moreover, the financial requirements for retooling Soviet industry to bring it in line with environmental standards would have exceeded all of the government's other social programs, and required "the public's recognition of the expediency of substantially faster progress in the ecological sphere than in other priority areas of socioeconomic development," such as education, health care, and social security.[4]

As the Shatalin team suggested, the pressure to limit spending on the environment to fund these other needs will be fierce. In the years before its demise, the Soviet government assumed new commitments to upgrade the pension system, to increase benefits to handicapped persons and war veterans, and to provide job retraining to displaced workers. These responsibilities have fallen to the republics. Need remains to upgrade the region's neglected healthcare and education systems. The Soviet successor governments also must provide relief to citizens living in poverty; at least one-quarter of the Soviet population lived at or below the poverty line in 1991, even before the imposition of radical economic reforms.[5] These pressing needs come at a time when the region's new states are facing the rigors of the market and global competition, and politicians are under pressure to maintain subsidies to uncompetitive industries to prevent massive unemployment. Finally, economic recovery eventually will demand massive resources to rebuild the region's dilapidated infrastructure—roads, telephones, and viable water systems. With the breakup of the Union, each individual republic now is responsible for funding its own environmental and social programs. As everywhere in the world, political leaders will have to make some difficult decisions about the allocation of resources and the fate of environmental quality—decisions made even more pressing by the rigors of economic restructuring.

ECONOMIC CHALLENGES IN THE POST-SOVIET ERA

During the Cold War, the Soviet Union ranked as a superpower in international politics, but domestic conditions in many parts of the USSR resembled those of less-developed nations. Environmental problems outlined in Chapters 2 through 5 reflect this dual image: The region must confront problems common in advanced industrialized nations as well as those of Third World countries. As officials contemplate ways to dispose of toxic wastes from high-technology industries and to manage fallout from nuclear disasters at Chernobyl and Kyshtym, they also must find the tremendous resources necessary to extend more basic but essential communal services such as garbage collection and sewage treatment. A tragic aspect of environmental policy decisions in the former Soviet Union is that the debate is not simply one of aesthetics—for many communities, the environmental crisis has reached the scale of a health crisis. In 1990, 4 million people in Belarus, Ukraine, and the Russian Federation lived in areas contaminated by Chernobyl; 5 million inhabitants of rural Uzbekistan did not have running water.[6]

The response to environmental degradation in the post-Soviet world will vary, determined largely by the ability of each successor state to foot its own bill. For most republics, the collapse of the central government resulted in an immediate loss of financial resources, as they were net recipients of investment and subsidized raw materials. Although the polluter-pays systems adopted as part of the overall transition to market economies have helped fund some environmental protection efforts, the high costs of the task combined with the political imperative to cut government spending as part of structural adjustment have hurt overall environmental protection efforts in the post-Soviet era. As a consequence, many republics have been forced to slash even the meager environmental programs they had under the Soviet regime.

Before the demise of the Soviet government, for example, the government of Kyrgyzstan expected to fund three-quarters of its 1992 budget with money from Moscow; by May of that year, it was asking an already strapped Kremlin for a handout.[7] As his republic lost funds coming from Moscow in December 1991, Tajik President Rakhman Nabiev called for "a large-scale effort" to cut government employment by up to 40 percent across the board.[8] Despite severe environmental problems in Ukraine and the great personal prestige of the republic's environment minister, Yurii Shcherbak, the Kiev government sharply curtailed funding for environmental protection in Ukraine in 1992 as a result of budget cutting. The Russian government under Prime Minister Yegor Gaidar also threatened to cut its funding for the environmental protection bureaucracy by one-half, and none was allotted to environmental protection agencies below the federal level.[9]

The total cost of the Chernobyl cleanup for Belarus was pegged at 16 billion rubles in early 1992, more than half the republic's annual national income produced.[10] Ukraine also will be hard-pressed to tackle the fallout from Chernobyl as well as the devastation in the Donets Basin in the east and pollution in its rivers and along its coast. The Central Asian republics, because of their large, unskilled labor forces, underdeveloped infrastructure, and poor social services, will struggle to achieve rates of growth that exceed their birthrates. In such a situation, they will have little to spare for environmental protection; collectively, they will look abroad for help. In the Russian Federation, moneys for the already-impoverished system of nature preserves were slashed by 80 percent in 1992, leading officials to approach the World Bank and the U.S. government for emergency funding.[11]

Indeed, with costs mounting and funds drying up, officials in all of the new republics are in search of outside aid. Admitting that millions of their citizens were condemned to live in contaminated regions with no hope of evacuation or adequate medical care, officials from Ukraine and Belarus were forced to turn to the United Nations and the international community at large for assistance. "There never has been in the history of mankind a technological disaster so destructive and so unprecedented in its consequences for the health and lives of present and future generations and for the state of the environment," read a 1990 appeal from the Ukrainian government to the United Nations.[12] The same year, Belarus asked the UN for assistance in relocating 2 million of its citizens still living in 27 cities and almost 2,700 villages contaminated by the Chernobyl accident: "[W]e have no energy, no transportation, no communications" in the affected regions, said Belarusian ambassador Viktor Borovikov.[13] In a special address to the UN General Assembly, the head of the Belarusian government requested that the republic be reclassified from a donor country to a recipient of technical assistance.[14]

THE DILEMMA OF ECONOMIC PRODUCTION VERSUS ENVIRONMENTAL PROTECTION

Regardless of the volume of foreign aid or domestic spending on the environment, a significant improvement in environmental quality in the Soviet successor states only can be obtained by closing down the thousands of inefficient, dated, and dirty industrial enterprises that are the legacy of Soviet economic development. Given their economic predicaments, however, many republics will be pressured to fall back on the factors of production with which they were endowed by the past regime, regardless of the environmental consequences. For Turkmenistan and Uzbekistan, this may mean continuing to produce huge quantities of cotton; for Kazakhstan uranium and fertilizers; for Estonia shale oil–generated electricity.

One reason Soviet enterprises are unlikely to be abandoned quickly is the "monopoly problem": Many goods produced in the former Soviet economy are supplied by only one factory.[15] Unlike Western economies, the ex-Soviet region's economy lacks surplus production capacity in most sectors and therefore is unable to compensate for plant shutdowns by shifting production to less controversial facilities. Severe shortages of hard currency compounded by an underdeveloped transportation system and large distances to Western markets prevent the rapid replacement of domestic production with imports. The concentration of production also means that the closure of a single enterprise can have a devastating impact on the economy of localities. Large population centers have sprung up around single industries often in isolated and remote locations. Migration in search of jobs is an option for few in the near term because most of the former Soviet Union suffers from an acute housing shortage and an undeveloped housing market and enterprises threaten to shed millions of workers to cut costs.

In September 1990, an explosion at the Ulba Metallurgical Plant in eastern Kazakhstan sent a poisonous cloud of beryllium and beryllium oxide gas over the neighboring town of Ust-Kamenogorsk. In response to public anger, the oblast soviet declared the region an "ecological disaster zone" and voted to close the plant. Yet Ulba reportedly was responsible for 80 percent of Soviet production of rare metals such as beryllium and tantalum, as well as fuel for nuclear power plants.[16] "This is unrealistic," said the plant's chief engineer about the decision to shut down the facility. "We have obligations to thousands of enterprises in the Union, not to mention consumers abroad. They cannot get by without beryllium. From an economic point of view, it will be cheaper to build the city in a new location."[17] After the explosion at Ulba, *Izvestiya* noted: "From a town of 30,000 inhabitants in the 1940s, Ust-Kamenogorsk became an oblast center of 300,000, thanks to its factories. Today the enterprises that gave rise to the city are killing it. The situation is deadlocked and typical of many of the country's cities."[18] The massive Bratsk aluminum processing complex exports 40 percent of its output, produced with cheap hydropower generated from the Angara River. "Bratsk has been declared an ecological disaster zone," noted Vyacheslav Vashanov, a Russian en-

The Nadezhda plant at the Norilsk Mining-Metallurgical Combine is one of Russia's largest and most modern light metal smelters and a major hard-currency-earner for the Federation. For the foreseeable future, Nadezhda (which means "Hope" in Russian) will continue to play a major role in the economic development and environmental degradation of the Russian north. Photo: DJ Peterson.

vironment official, of the city of a quarter million residents. "The local population pays with their health."[19]

The breakup of the USSR also radically changed the external economic relations of the region; with the notable exception of the Russian Federation, most of the republics will find themselves in a less advantageous trading position in world markets than they enjoyed in the Soviet system.[20] One potential source of hard-currency income for many republics is the development and sale of natural resources. Governments will be under great pressure to increase the exploitation of nature rather than to promote conservation. Several scientists writing in *Izvestiya* in 1990 warned that economic autonomy without sufficient provisions for environmental protection threatened "a clearance sale on nature." The scientists noted that in Central Asia, valuable plants, animals, and minerals already were being sold abroad through official as well as illegal channels. "In the race for hard currency," officials had issued licenses for the export of tons of antelope antlers obtained illegally outside of their territory.[21] Many local governments in Siberia and the Russian Far East have circumvented Russian environmental codes to negotiate deals directly with Asian companies. Speaking of one deal permitting clear-cutting north of Vladivostok, Aleksei Yablokov claimed that the Kremlin was "virtually powerless to prevent the Koreans from cutting every last tree in Siberia."[22] Although many point to the vast mineral wealth of Russia as a sustaining factor, efforts to boost rapidly exports of gas, oil, timber, and metals have depressed global markets for many of these commodities, diminishing returns. During the last years of its existence, the Soviet Union held a virtual clearance sale on its mineral reserves, depressing world prices for zinc, aluminum, gold, platinum, mercury, and other metals.[23] "Our society is in the middle of a revolution," says Yablokov, "and our natural resources are caught in the middle."[24]

HARD CHOICES: THE CASES OF LITHUANIA, UKRAINE, AND ARMENIA

For aspiring politicians, campaigning on behalf of the environment in the late 1980s was a no-lose strategy; environmentally troublesome enterprises in many of the Soviet republics were censured as evidence of "ecological colonialism" by Moscow. Asserting they were autonomous from the center, local governments responded to public pressures and shut down polluting enterprises in record numbers. The collapse of the USSR foisted new economic and political responsibilities on the successor states, however, changing the priorities of political elites and environmentalists alike. In many cases, nature looks to be the loser. A new attitude is apparent in republican and regional politics that frequently paints nature as a fungible good to be exploited when the economy or national interest is at stake.

In the 1980s, Lithuanian environmentalists, backed by the Lithuanian national movement Sajudis, challenged the operation of the Ignalina Atomic Energy Station, pointing out that the two operating reactors at the station were of the same design as the one that exploded at Chernobyl in 1986, only 50 percent larger. Antinuclear forces also pointed out that Ignalina lacked automated safety systems found on reactors in the West, that it was subject to frequent fires, and that it was built on unstable soil, causing the foundation of one reactor to subside. In addition, thermal pollution from water used to cool Ignalina's reactors had destroyed wildlife in adjacent Lake Druksiai.[25] With support from local authorities, the antinuclear movement forced Moscow to agree to halt construction of reactor No. 3 at Ignalina in 1988, and the movement pressed on with its demands that the plant's two operating reactors be decommissioned.

Attitudes in the republic changed, however. In March 1990, the Lithuanian parliament declared the republic's independence from Moscow. In retribution for this act, Mikhail Gorbachev, newly empowered as president of the Soviet Union, cut off the republic's supply of oil and gas flowing in from Russia. Transport quickly ground to a halt and factories shut down, but the lights kept burning. Suddenly, Ignalina became a pillar and symbol of Lithuania's independence. The plant was not so bad after all: Ignalina produced the equivalent of 30 percent of all electricity consumed in Lithuania. In addition, a share of the energy produced by the plant was exported.[26] "The Ignalina problem is still here," an environmentalist told the *Los Angeles Times* in October 1991, one month after Moscow formally handed over control of the nuclear plant to the newly independent Lithuanian government. Said Janos Tamulis, a leader of the Lithuanian Greens and a member of parliament: "It's impossible to shut down [Ignalina] now because the electricity it produces serves Latvia, Belarus, and Kaliningrad. In 1988, that would have been Moscow's problem. Now it's a problem between Lithuania and other countries." Vytautas Statulevicius, founder of the Lithuanian Green movement, put it another way to the same newspaper: "When Lithuania was in the Soviet Union, it was one thing. But now it belongs to us."[27]

A similar shift of attitude appeared in Ukraine. In the 1970s, Moscow laid out ambitious plans to develop nuclear power in Ukraine to help meet the voracious demands for electricity created by the heavy industries of the republic as well as the Soviet Union's Warsaw Pact allies to the west. As illustrated in Chapter 7, public opposition in the aftermath of the Chernobyl disaster effectively thwarted the Kremlin's nuclear power development plans in the republic. In August 1990, the popularly elected Ukrainian Supreme Soviet bowed to public pressure and passed a five-year moratorium on all nuclear development projects in the republic. After a turbine fire in the No. 2 power unit at Chernobyl in October 1991, the Ukrainian parliament voted to decommission immediately the disabled unit and called for the two reactors still operating at Chernobyl to be shut down by 1993. Yet despite the republic's tribulations with harnessing the atom, many in Ukraine continue to see nuclear power as an essential energy supply option.

On the eve of Ukraine's independence, nuclear power accounted for over one-quarter of electricity generated in the republic. Ukraine could meet just 30 percent of its electricity needs with domestic fossil fuel resources, the most important of these being high-sulfur coal.[28] To fill the large gap in domestic supplies, the republic relied on imported energy— namely, oil from Russia and natural gas from both Russia and Turkmenistan. When Ukraine was a member of the Union, the wholesale price it paid for a ton of oil purchased from Russia averaged 70 rubles in 1991, about the market price of a pack of imported cigarettes.[29] In the wake of the collapse of the USSR, Ukraine has had to pay world market prices for its energy imports coming from its unreliable and rather hostile neighbors. As a result of a trade dispute that cut supplies of natural gas coming in from Turkmenistan, Ukraine was forced to turn to domestic supplies of low-quality fuel in the winter of 1991–1992.[30]

To help meet domestic needs, the Ukrainian government decided to halt electricity exports to Eastern Europe by 1994, sacrificing a valuable source of hard currency pegged at $1.5 billion annually.[31] Another option for the republic is to build more coal-fired power plants. But obtaining Ukrainian coal is difficult, dangerous, and expensive—many of the republic's mines are over 100 years old—and the product is dirty. Burning vast new increments of high-sulfur coal, not to mention the disruption caused by increased coal extraction, would devastate an already stressed environment. The republic faces bleak options: "In terms of ecological damage and human casualties, the current cost of the Donbass coal fields outstrips that of the nuclear industry, even taking into account the effects of the accident at Chernobyl," argues David Marples, a Canadian specialist on Ukrainian environmental affairs.[32] In 1991, the Ukrainian first deputy prime minister and energy minister both began to say that new nuclear power plants might be needed.[33]

Like Lithuania and Ukraine, Armenia faces hard development choices having significant environmental repercussions. After four years of efforts to reduce emissions from Yerevan's Nairit Scientific Production

Association, the Armenian Supreme Soviet ordered the plant to cease operations at the end of 1989. The production of chloroprene-based rubber and latex at Nairit (the only such site in the Soviet Union) had resulted in the yearly release of 3,500 tons of noxious gases into the air over the Armenian capital (1990 population of 1.2 million). Similar topographically to Mexico City, Yerevan is surrounded by tall mountains and is subject to thermal inversions resulting in some of the highest levels of dust, sulfur dioxide, carbon monoxide, nitrogen dioxide, low-level ozone, chloroprene, and lead officially reported in the former Soviet Union.[34] Nairit had been the target of protesters who cited official data indicating drastic increases in the rates of cancer, cardiac and respiratory diseases, birth defects, and leukemia. Invoking images of genocide, many opponents of Nairit linked the fate of the plant to the fate of the Armenian nation.[35]

The closure of Nairit in early 1990 resulted in the lost production of thousands of tons of chloroprene, ammonia, fertilizer, and caustic soda. Moreover, Nairit was a monopoly producer of inputs for various lines of heart medicines, painkillers, and vitamins, many of which disappeared from store shelves across the Soviet Union. Soon after the plant shut down, however, critics began to charge that the closure was responsible for a sharp deterioration in the Armenian economy, including the worsening of food shortages: Armenia had lost an important source of export revenue, and other republics had begun retaliating with trade sanctions for the breaking of supply contracts. Given the difficulty of quickly renovating the plant (its technology dates back to 1941) or raising capital to build a new factory, Armenians have found themselves in a terrible dilemma: Do they threaten their health in order to earn money providing others with essential life-enhancing drugs?

As members of the anti-Communist opposition, many parliamentarians had voted in 1989 to shut down the plant because of its poor environmental record. After the opposition came into power in democratic elections the following year, however, opinions about Nairit changed rapidly.[36] During the debates to reconsider its decision, Levon Ter-Petrosyan, chair of the Supreme Soviet, noted that when the parliament had decided to close the plant, "Nairit wasn't ours, we received nothing from it but hell and insignificant compensation; all else went to the Union." Ter-Petrosyan noted that the decision to halt production was made in an effort to coerce the Soviet government into taking a more favorable position on Armenia's dispute with Azerbaijan over Nagorno–Karabakh. This tactic failed—and in the process, the republic sacrificed one of its major exporting industries. The decision had turned Armenia into a "beggar" to the Union with nothing to offer in return, said Premier

Vazgen Manukian. "If we are going to be a nation, we must think about morality and national dignity."[37]

As protesters chanted "Traitors! Traitors!" in the streets outside, the Armenian Supreme Soviet voted in April 1991 to overturn its decision and to reopen Nairit. In the decision to restart Nairit, the Armenian parliament indicated its intention to take over control of the plant from the all-Union government, implying that it would be better managed under local control.[38] Despite assurances that strict measures would be implemented to minimize pollution when the plant was restarted, environmentalists contended that Nairit's performance only had deteriorated as a result of the plant standing idle for over one year.[39]

Another Armenian plant once closed may also be reopened. In January 1989, the two reactors at the Armenian nuclear power station at Medzamor were decommissioned; the plant had been built in a seismic zone, and the Spitak earthquake one month before had convinced officials in Moscow of the possibility of another nuclear disaster. Plans were under way to convert Medzamor to burning natural gas. In 1990, Armenia began suffering severe energy shortages as neighboring Azerbaijan cut off its fuel supplies in an economic boycott; the two republics virtually were at war over the fate of Nagorno-Karabakh. Frequent brownouts forced the closure of schools and factories in Armenia, and electricity had to be diverted from Georgia and southern Russia, regions experiencing their own energy shortages.[40]

Not only is the Medzamor plant located in a seismic zone, but international experts have declared its two VVER-440 reactors the most dangerous Soviet commercial type because they lack basic safety equipment. Nevertheless, calls for Medzamor to be recommissioned soon could be heard: "The decision of the Armenian and Soviet Union governments to halt the Armenian nuclear power station was hasty, not thought out, and, to say directly, not correct," wrote A. Petrosyants, an Armenian academician. Before Medzamor was closed, the plant's output equaled 40 percent of the republic's electricity needs, and power was exported to Georgia and Azerbaijan. Petrosyants called not only for the two existing reactors to be restarted but for more to be built in the republic: "A sovereign Armenia cannot exist without its own supply of energy."[41]

As with the opposition to Nairit, images of genocide have been conjured up by many in Armenia when they speak of the potential threat from a nuclear accident. In response to such a heated debate, the Armenian Supreme Soviet passed a resolution declaring that Medzamor would not be started or any new plants be built in the small republic without a national referendum.[42] But in an interview published in June 1991, an official at the Soviet Union Ministry of Atomic Power indicated that Armenia already had requested Moscow to restart the plant on "a temporary basis." "Their proposal . . . seems strange to me," said N. Yermakov. "It's unrealistic and not serious. A nuclear power station is not a samovar [in which] you boil water, drink a little tea, and shut it off."[43] When power outages the following December forced all enterprises in Armenia to grind to a halt, an official announced that the government was going ahead with its plans to recommission Medzamor by the end of 1992, adding that the original decision to close the plant was "mistaken and not thought out . . . made under the influence of emotions."[44]

THE POTENTIAL BENEFITS OF ECONOMIC REFORM

Despite the hardship presented by the upheavals of political and economic change, the news is not all bad. A transition away from the Soviet model of economic development, if executed, could result in a radical restructuring of the region's emerging economies. In meliorating the ills of the Soviet economic legacy, reform also presents the potential for improvement of many types of environmental problems. It is impossible to predict the pace of change and the nature of the region's economy in the future, but one can outline broad trends that are likely to ensue.

For the short term, the impact of radical economic reforms and the ensuing structural adjustment of the region's economy will have some positive effects on the environment. As mentioned in Chapter 2, economic downturn was responsible for a sharp improvement in atmospheric emissions from stationary sources beginning in 1990. Idle factories also will ease the pressure on the region's overworked, outdated, and under-maintained power plants—thermal, nuclear, and hydroelectric. Thus, the environment benefits from an immediate depression dividend. Eventually, the region's economy will rebound, but many former Soviet enterprises are likely to be closed permanently, and this will have long-term implications for the environment. There are several reasons why.

First, the introduction of scarcity-based prices for goods and the end of state subsidies to industries will reduce enterprises' insatiable appetite for inputs like steel and energy. As illustrated in Chapter 5, the inefficiency of the Soviet economy was manifest in the massive generation of waste; accordingly, the value of a conservation dividend in the former Soviet economy cannot be underestimated. An example of the potential gains to be made from increasing efficiency is demonstrated by the case of energy consumption. Although accurate figures are elusive, the gist of the argument is undeniable: In 1987, the CIA estimated that the Soviet economy produced $253 of GNP for every barrel of crude-oil equivalent consumed; the corresponding figures for the United States, West Germany, and Japan were $341, $420, and $604, respectively.[45] Thus, the Soviet Union used one-third more energy to produce the same amount of GNP as the United States, another country with a reputation for inefficient use of energy.[46] Other estimates put the energy intensity of the Soviet economy at 50–70 percent above the rate of the United States, or twice that of Western Europe.[47] Therefore, the less energy consumed, the less pollution goes up the stack. In addition, lower rates of energy consumption translate into less environmental disruption, because less coal, for example, must be extracted, transported, and processed to meet the needs of the economy.

Second, market mechanisms and exposure to international competition will force local producers to improve the quality of their output, thereby ending the propensity in the former Soviet economy to produce high volumes of shoddy output. The shoe industry is an example. In 1989, Soviet factories produced 827 million pairs of shoes, enough to provide every Soviet citizen with three pairs.[48] Nevertheless, Soviet footwear sat on store shelves, while citizens queued up for days just for the opportunity to purchase one of the 150 million pairs imported that year.[49] Given the notoriously sad state of Soviet footwear design and quality, one wonders: Who needed so many bad shoes? The higher the shoe quality, the fewer shoes discarded prematurely. The same was true for the 160,000 tons of steel, 143,000 metal-cutting machines, and 532,000 tractors poorly produced in 1989.

Third, the future may see entire economic sectors bankrupted because of their inability to compete on the world market without access to state subsidies and artificially cheap raw materials. As already mentioned, the technology employed in many Soviet enterprises dates back to World War II and before; many firms simply will be unable to compete in the world marketplace. Moreover, research in the West has pointed out that the largest heavy industrial enterprises had become the most reliant on state subsidies under the Soviet regime, and, thus, grew the least efficient.[50] Just as the U.S. rustbelt saw its aged steel mills put out of business in the 1970s, many of the open-hearth steel mills of the Donets and Kuznetsk basins will be rendered unprofitable when confronted with cheap imports of steel (from the Pacific Rim, for instance).

Fourth, the output of many enterprises will be rendered superfluous for a lack of consumers. The end of the Communist-inspired forced-pace industrialization and the end of the arms race mean that the region's economy no longer will require vast quantities of domestically produced steel, aluminum, petroleum, plutonium, and practically everything else produced by the Soviet economy. Examples of the peace dividend are

numerous: In 1990, the Soviet government shut down the last of five reactors producing fissile material for nuclear weapons at the notorious
Mayak plant in Chelyabinsk-40. Military reactors at Tomsk-7 and Kras-
noyarsk-26 also have been decommissioned. Nuclear weapons testing
was halted at Semipalatinsk in 1991. Cuts in the military's procurement
budget resulted in a 66 percent reduction in the output of tanks in 1991,
with tank factories in Kharkov and Nizhnii Tagil being shut down.[51] In
1992, the military's High Command revealed that it was planning an
"urgent program" to decommission up to 100 obsolete nuclear submarines.[52] Thus, the environmental impact of the peace dividend will be
tremendous; Western estimates pegged the share of total economic
output accounted for by the defense sector at up to 25 percent in the
1980s. Moreover, as illustrated by the case of Chelyabinsk-40, defense-
related activities proved to be some of the most destructive to the
environment. As the ex-Soviet economy deindustrializes and de-
militarizes, one can expect to see the development of lower-polluting
service and high-technology industries.

Finally, structural adjustment should produce a resurgence of the
agricultural sector as higher food prices and the privatization of land
create incentives for increased production and investment in the countryside. Price reform will erase distortions in the economy central planning caused, such as incentives to farmers to bury fertilizer as well as the
massive waste that claimed up to 40 percent of agricultural output. As
pointed out in Chapter 4, farmers began to decrease their use of agricultural chemicals in the late 1980s as a result of reforms designed to increase economic accountability. With time, Russia and Ukraine once
again could become major food exporters, using less land and fewer inputs per hectare.[53]

NEW THREATS OF POST-SOVIET DEVELOPMENT

Although the heavy industrialization drive of the Soviet period
proved disastrous for the environment, the postponement of the mass
consumerism and living style of the West minimized the damage in
many ways. As mentioned in Chapter 5, Soviet-style development, for
better or for worse, produced few consumer goods and, therefore, little
domestic waste. As a result, the region largely has been spared the bur-
geoning landfills of the advanced industrialized nations and the littered
landscapes of many Third World countries. On a per capita basis, U.S.
citizens generated three times as much trash as their Soviet counterparts
in the 1980s.

The concentration of industrial development in a relatively small number of large complexes created hot spots of intense environmental degradation, but such development also left vast corridors of territory relatively unscathed to serve as refuges for wildlife. Strict security measures also have left broad swaths of undeveloped land along international boundaries and sensitive coastlines.[54] Despite the encroachment of poorly managed development, cities remain ringed by greenbelts, and bioindicators like bears, moose, and storks remain common sights, even near urban centers. Many cities obtain their heat and electricity from the same facility (the principle of cogeneration). Urban planners were able to site these plants where needed (often near residential neighborhoods) because there was little "not-in-my-backyard" opposition during the Soviet era. With the application of the latest Western technology, such as combined-cycle turbogenerators, the thermal efficiency of these cogeneration facilities could be raised well above the world average.

Although the Soviet government boosted car production in the 1970s, the private automobile remains rare in the post-Soviet era: In 1987, there was only 1 car for every 22 Soviet citizens compared with 1 car for every 1.8 persons in the United States. As a result, urban landscapes remain uncluttered by ribbons of freeways and acres of paved parking lots. In place of the automobile, city dwellers have benefited from the most extensive public transportation systems available in the world. In 1989, Moscow's aging subway system carried over 2.7 billion passengers, and Muscovites relied on passenger cars for less than 5 percent of their trips.[55]

A successful economic reform, however, if not mediated by effective environmental protection controls, could spell a second onslaught against nature. Like developing nations in Latin America and Africa, the Soviet successor states are poised to see an explosion in their generation of solid waste, an issue they have not adequately managed in the past. A proliferation of cars would not only choke the existing system of roads and highways but boost levels of urban smog. Economic development is associated with increased energy consumption and, hence, higher emissions of greenhouse gases. Referring to the pent–up demand for consumer goods like large refrigerators, washers, and dryers, the National Resources Defense Council (NRDC) has warned:

> If . . . perestroika increases these products' availability, energy consumption in the residential and commercial sectors could explode. For example, from the end of World War II to 1973, US electricity consumption for residences grew at an average annual rate of 9 percent. The challenge will be to establish a large-scale conservation effort that can reduce or hold energy use constant in this repressed sector in the face of growing wealth.[56]

As the newly industrializing nations of Asia are discovering, an economy growing rapidly at the expense of environmental quality does not guarantee a higher standard of living or ensure long-term prosperity. Reducing environmental degradation is essential to improving public health, reducing the burden on the region's overtaxed healthcare system, and increasing worker productivity. And, as many in the West now argue, the "get rich fast, first" development argument does not hold in the long run, as the cost of remediation of environmental damage often proves more expensive and problematic than does pollution prevention.[57]

The temptation to borrow wholesale the development experience of the West is great—if indeed it is made available. Yet this approach could prove to be as misguided as the Soviet government's wholesale purchases of car plants, oil refineries, chemical plants, and cattle farms in the past. Many commentators in the former Soviet Union consider the West to have solved its pollution problems—despite decades of being told that capitalism spelled the devastation of nature. Indeed, the Soviet media often have painted images of conditions in the West as far more favorable than reality would dictate. Officials express familiarity with the concept of *ustoichivoe razvitie* (sustainable development), but few demonstrate a commitment to its principles. The chair of the Moldovan environmental protection agency represents one of the few policymakers to demonstrate that they are looking beyond the Western experience:

> The entire world, the United States, and France, and the FRG, and Japan, and other countries included, are making a fatal mistake today: they are spending intellectual efforts and material resources for purification structures rather than for no-waste technologies, and from the standpoint of preventive measures, that is altogether unpromising. We are trying not to repeat that mistake.[58]

THE ROLE OF THE INTERNATIONAL COMMUNITY

The former USSR, on the one hand, accounts for over one-sixth of the earth's landmass and almost one-quarter of its forest resources, most of which remain virgin, old-growth stands. A vast wilderness of wetlands, tundra, and Arctic coastline supports summer populations of migratory birds from Europe, Africa, and Asia and provides a year-round home to indigenous rare and endangered species like the Siberian tiger, sable, and the snow leopard. The territory includes treasures such as Lake Baikal, the world's deepest fresh-water lake, and the Ob, Asia's longest river. It is in everyone's interest that these resources be sustained. On the other hand, in the mid-1980s, the Soviet economy accounted for 10 percent of the world's production of chlorofluorocarbons and produced almost 1 billion tons of carbon annually, 18 percent of global anthropogenic emissions. It is in everyone's interest that these emissions not be sustained.

Businesspeople, government officials, and environmentalists traveling and working in the former Soviet area are struck by the great interest expressed in acquiring Western environmental technology as well as know-how in environmental economics and public policy. Indeed, government officials and the public alike see a leading, if not commanding, role for the West in cleaning up the destruction wrought by Soviet rule. This mind-set is characteristic of an attitude that dates back to the time of Peter the Great and represents a lack of faith in the ability of the domestic economy, the technical establishment, and the political system to remedy the situation. Belief in the correctness of things foreign, says Sheryl Belcher of Greenpeace's "Children of Chernobyl" project, is powerful, a view maintained by the notion that "transplanted technology and skills will solve everything." Indeed, when the international organization opened an office in Kiev, many Ukrainians expected Greenpeace to create a new environmental protection agency for the republic.[59] Ominously, the mood often dips into a paralyzing resignation to the environmental status quo or the desire simply to escape the predicament. As implied by Aleksei Yablokov (see Chapter 1), the notion of an environmental refugee has gained currency.[60]

The lack of confidence in the domestic scientific and engineering establishment—a sector held in the highest esteem in the Soviet period— stems, in part, from such misguided and poorly applied adventures as the Chernobyl-type RBMK nuclear reactor, methods to produce cattle feed supplements from petrochemicals, and the St. Petersburg flood-control dam. Blatant untruths told by scientific officials such as Yurii Izrael' of the Soviet meteorological service only served to further erode the level of citizens' trust. The general public has not, however, lost faith in science and technology and consequently has frequently demanded that foreign expertise be brought in to assess environmental problems in an earnest desire to get at the "objective" truth. In autumn 1988, for example, over 100 children in the western Ukrainian city of Chernovtsy began suffering from sudden hair loss as well as other disorders. The Soviet and Ukrainian governments commissioned several investigations of the matter, but their findings were inconclusive and disputed.[61] Protesting what they said was officials' lack of concern, troubled mothers went on a hunger strike.[62] As the problem persisted, the public demanded outside help: "The inability of medical personnel and Soviet officials to definitely identify the source of the problem . . . has the local population in a near panic," noted one doctor visiting from the United States.[63] Two doctors from the World Health Organization were brought in, but again their findings were inconclusive.[64]

Similarly, officials have turned abroad in search of expertise to back their agendas. To help cool the fever of radiophobia after Chernobyl, officials have sponsored and publicized international inspections of many nuclear plants. Studies of Lithuania's Ignalina plant and the Nizhnii Novgorod (formerly Gorkii) nuclear-powered city heating station, for example, both returned favorable results.[65] Eugene Yeremy, a member of the team visiting the Nizhnii Novgorod plant, pointed out that the Soviet government had invited this international commission in an attempt to calm the "severe negative public reaction" of local residents to the project.[66] The effort was not very successful; the Nizhnii Novgorod city and oblast soviets subsequently voted to scrap construction. Although international expertise is welcomed, local critics have pointed out that such a tactic is often used by the government to find "obliging consultants" when projects are opposed by the domestic technical community.[67]

The potential impact of international organizations is illustrated by the case of Chernobyl. In October 1989, the Soviet government asked the International Atomic Energy Agency (IAEA) to conduct the first independent analysis of public health in those regions contaminated by the Chernobyl accident. The IAEA agreed, noting that its goal was to corroborate data already collected by Soviet experts and to restore the trust of people still living in the affected areas.[68] When the report was released in May 1991, it was not surprising that the agency, a strong advocate of nuclear power, downplayed the impact of the accident. To the dismay of Ukrainians, Belarusians, and Russians affected by the disaster, the IAEA stated that the Soviet government had overestimated radiation exposures and contended that the accident had not caused widespread illness as assumed.[69] Criticizing the IAEA for not examining all populations at risk and accusing the organization of a "cover-up," Ukraine's Zelenyi Svit environmental group complained that the study had "compromised the efforts of Ukrainian governmental and nongovernmental organizations to effectively bring international aid to the victims of the Chernobyl disaster."[70] Ukrainian officials also protested, calling the report "too optimistic"[71] and accusing the IAEA of "deliberately undermining international efforts to eliminate the consequences of the Chernobyl disaster."[72]

For some functions, such as the disposal of weapons of mass destruction and the cleanup of the defense complex, Western assistance is crucial. This is the intent of the U.S. pledge of $400 million in 1992, $25 million of which was dedicated to a new nuclear technology center in

Russia: "We want to help you find new projects . . . applying your skills to the cause of science and peace, rather than forging the weapons of war," proclaimed U.S. Secretary of State James Baker to a group of scientists assembled in the secret city of Chelyabinsk-70.[73] The West will have to contribute much more money and technology to the cleanup. As Viktor Mikhailev, director of the Soviet military's nuclear weapons program, commented, without the financing and skills needed to erase the legacies of the cold war, Russia could become "one big Chernobyl."[74] "They have a hell of a mess on their hands and don't have any good way to clean it up," concluded Thomas Cochran of the NRDC.[75]

Through foreign investment, Western firms can provide many of the technologies and skills essential to modernizing the region's antiquated and inefficient economies, just as U.S. investment in Germany and Japan after World War II helped these countries undertake the rebuilding process. U.S. drilling technology, for example, could yield access to oil reserves hitherto inaccessible with local technology that dates back to the early twentieth century. Western turbine technology could increase the efficiency and throughput of oil and gas pipelines and decrease transmission costs, and imported monitoring and repair equipment could reduce the rate of leakage and accidents. In the end, not only would the environment be better safeguarded, but the oil and gas conserved could be exported to earn much-needed hard currency. Finally, Western entrepreneurs familiar with ex-Soviet design bureaus speak highly of innovative technologies with potential application for pollution abatement and environmental cleanup, which have never been developed because of the obstacles of the Soviet economy. The application of Western capital, production methods, and business know-how could bring many of these technologies to fruition for the benefit of all.

Rendering direct financial and technological assistance to the states of the former Soviet Union is as economically sound as it is ecologically beneficial. Russia has already taken significant steps to reduce domestic sulfur emissions; paying the country to reduce emissions at its metallurgical plants on the Kola Peninsula presents the least-cost means of controlling air pollution in Finland. Helping St. Petersburg and the Baltic states treat their sewage helps Sweden clean up its beaches at home. Western aid to seal methane leaks in gas pipelines and coal mines could reduce the potential for global warming with less expense and disruption than curtailing carbon emissions elsewhere in the world.

Nevertheless, international investment and aid must be rendered in an ecologically sound manner and with extra care taken not to worsen an already tenuous situation. Environmentalism in the former Soviet Union has been strongly associated with national and ethnic awareness, and environmental degradation proved an effective vehicle for promoting pronationalist sentiments, be it in Lithuania or Russia. A perception that the West has contributed to the devastation only has reinforced the environmentalist-nationalist nexus. To many, like Russian social commentator Valentin Katasonov, Western cooperation often has abetted environmental destruction and threatens to turn the region into "an ecological colony."[76] The reputation is not entirely unfounded. Environmentalists point out that logging enterprises level entire expanses of Siberian taiga to feed raw wood stock to Japan and Korea.[77] Pipelines, often built with imported material, carry Siberian oil and gas to customers in Western Europe but spill or leak up to 20 percent of their throughput in the process. Writing in *Pravda*, an economist accused an Odessa ammonia plant built with the assistance of a U.S. firm of turning the northwestern region of the Black Sea into "an ecological disaster area."[78]

The experience of the infamous Astrakhan natural gas condensate processing complex is exemplary. The plant was built with the assistance of foreign firms and was supposed to be equipped with French-made pollution control equipment: "[T]here is no more modern technology in the world today," proclaimed General Director V. Shchugorev. But the construction of the 15-billion-ruble plant was rushed, and by the time its first capacity came on line in 1987, only 14 of 42 pollution control features were installed. Moreover, a belated environmental impact study conducted by the Russian environmental agency found in the plant's construction almost 1,000 defects, the majority of which involved pollution abatement. The results were tragic: On March 1, 1987, four people died and others fell ill as a result of a gas leak. In 1988, the first full year of operation, the plant belched forth 400,000 tons of highly toxic pollutants; that year ambient levels of highly poisonous hydrogen sulfide exceeded air quality standards 243 times. Children in nearby towns were issued gas masks to use when walking to school, and villages inside a 25-kilometer "exclusion zone" had to be permanently evacuated. Production eventually had to be scaled back by up to two-thirds until the proper repairs could be effected, making the plant a chronic money loser.[79] Although fault for the plant's poor management rests with the Russian side, opposition to the enterprise nevertheless has focused on the facts that imported technology was used and that the enterprise's output is sold on international markets.

Astrakhan is but one example of how the environmental impact of Western businesses will only increase as the Soviet successor states seek to integrate into the world economy and to attract foreign investment. In 1989, a group of academics wrote to *Izvestiya* protesting a Western-backed plan to build five mammoth petrochemical plants to process natural gas coming out of western Siberia. Government assurances that the 31-billion-ruble joint venture was "absolutely ecology-safe," they warned, were "intentional lies."[80] Lambasting a deal with Chevron Corporation to develop the Tengiz oil field in western Kazakhstan, the usually pro-Western newspaper *Moscow News* asserted, "The contract has been drawn up in such a manner that the corporation can get more than $100 billion. This country does not get anything like this. Chevron does not take on any serious ecological obligations."[81] "We are being plainly tricked. We are being robbed through joint ventures," decried Aleksei Yablokov to Western reporters in 1989. "We have to set up legal barriers. We are not ready for cooperation."[82]

In the wake of the collapse of the Soviet regime came announcement of a flurry of new raw materials extraction and processing projects, leading many to believe that a new "Klondike" was about to ensue. "For a long time [Siberian] forests have been locked up because of the political system," warned Russell Mittermeier, president of Conservation International. "What's happening is that you're going to see the Americans, the Japanese—everyone else who needs timber—moving in there like crazy."[83] "The terrifying efficiency of the Japanese and Koreans will devastate our forests and watersheds far more effectively than we Russians are capable of," asserted Yablokov.[84] For many regions of the former Soviet Union, the only hindrance to rapid development remains a lack of transport.[85] A sense that the West is profiteering from the exploitation of the region's wealth of natural resources while causing irreparable environmental damage could turn public sentiment away from cooperation with and integration into the global community, especially in Russia where attitudes toward the West are particularly fickle. The implications for international politics and security, in turn, could be enormous.

Popular attitudes toward the West and multinational firms often belie a poor understanding of the nature of foreign investment and reveal expectations of international ventures that are patently unrealistic. In 1991, the Russian government passed a law requiring environmental impact studies of development projects involving foreign investment, yet the legislation failed to specify with which regulations investors must comply.[86] In deference to the evolving ethic of international accountability, many multinational firms, particularly those from the United States, earnestly would like to adhere to local environmental regulations, but these are rarely standardized or transparent. As a result, agreements specifying international firms' environmental responsibilities must be hammered out in lengthy and arduous negotiations for every project.[87] As stated in Chapter 5, up to 80 percent of hazardous wastes produced during the Soviet era were disposed of on the premises of the enterprises that produced them, leading to the potential need for large-scale and expensive cleanups. In such cases, foreign investors simply will shy away from the region unless they are granted indemnity for environmental damage caused by prior management.[88]

Despite these caveats, the West bears responsibility, when possible, not to violate the good faith and hopes of the emerging societies in the region. Pressure must be exerted in the West, therefore, to ensure that all Western firms doing business in the former Soviet Union follow a basic code of environmental ethics. In Europe, this is already beginning to happen: At the June 1990 European Community (EC) environment meeting in Dublin, the EC signed a joint communiqué with the USSR and six East European countries calling for the creation of an EC environmental agency that would be open to non-EC members in order to facilitate cleanup efforts.[89]

Nongovernmental organizations also can play a vital role in monitoring economic development. In 1990, Occidental Petroleum Corporation agreed to postpone plans for a $200-million polyvinyl chloride plant in Ukraine because of local concerns over the environment. Occidental had planned to use feedstock from an existing Soviet-built plant in the western Ukrainian city of Kalush, but the NRDC in conjunction with Moscow's Social-Ecological Union and Ukraine's Zelenyi Svit conducted an environmental study of the region and found that air pollution emissions from the existing plant exceeded Soviet norms by up to 9 times, while the volume of petrochemicals in a river downstream from the facility exceeded the norm by 6 times. "We're not opposed to the Occidental plant," said Kristen Suokko, the NRDC's program coordinator for the former Soviet Union. "We just think it's a perfect opportunity for [Occidental] to set a model for corporate behavior abroad by helping to solve the environmental problems caused by the existing plant."[90]

For Soviet society, the state of the environment, in physical terms, epitomized the state of the Union. Environmental destruction, added to social, economic, and political stresses, compounded the people's anger and ultimately undermined the Soviet regime. The Soviet Union can be relegated to history, but its *dostizheniya* (achievements), manifest in the legacy of widespread environmental destruction, cannot be easily erased. Will the emerging post-Soviet societies cope with the challenge?

The possibility of a praetorian, reactionary swing driven by hypernationalism is real, given that the nascent post-Soviet states remain highly polarized and volatile and democratic political institutions have yet to be consolidated. Ongoing environmental crises like Chernobyl, Chelyabinsk, Astrakhan, and Aral would only fuel the anger. Jack Snyder, a specialist in international relations and Soviet politics, argues that the best way to prevent the rise of mass praetorianism and the threat to peace is for the West to create strong political, institutional, and economic ties with the Soviet successor states in order to promote stability and security.[91] The scale of the post-Soviet environmental challenge, in terms of global interdependence, mandates cooperation to support the democratic alternative.

Notes

1. "Gosudarstvennaya programma okhrany okruzhayushchei sredy . . . ," *Ekonomika i zhizn'*, No. 41, 1990, insert page 6; V. V. Prokhorov, "Ekologicheskaya programma—vozmozhny varianty," *Energiya: Ekonomika, tekhnika, ekologiya*, No. 3, 1990, p. 2.

2. N. V. Uspenskaya, "Nuzhna polnaya ekologicheskaya glasnost'," *Priroda*, No. 11, 1989, p. 5.

3. Radio Moscow, May 3, 1990.

4. Stanislav Shatalin et al., *Perekhod k rynku: Kontseptsiya i programma* (Moscow: Arkhangel'skoe, 1990), p. 182.

5. According to USSR Deputy Minister for Labor and Social Affairs Nikolai Cheshenko, nearly 80 million people in the USSR "live close to or below the poverty line." TASS, April 2, 1991. Cheshenko's comments were made at the time of the government's first across-the-board price hikes, and it was not clear if he was referring to conditions before or after the increase. His comments nevertheless reveal the scale of poverty. By 1992, many observers claimed that up to one half of the Russian population lived in poverty.

6. Radio Moscow, July 30, 1990.

7. *Economist*, October 19, 1991, p. 57. In early May, the Kyrgyzstan government asked Russia for 1.5 billion rubles to meet its budget for the second quarter of 1992 alone. Interfax, May 11, 1992, as reported by Radio Free Europe/Radio Liberty (RFE/RL) Daily Report, May 12, 1992.

8. TadzhikTA-TASS, December 18, 1991.

9. *Kuranty*, March 12, 1992, p. 4.

10. Belarus Radio, January 17, 1992, cited in RFE/RL Daily Report, January 21, 1992.

11. Steve Raymer, "Cash Needs Precede Forests in Poverty-Stricken Russia," *National Geographic News Feature*, April 1992, pp. 2–3.

12. Associated Press (AP), May 2, 1990; Reuter, May 2, 1990; RFE/RL Special Report, May 12, 1990.

13. AP, June 18, 1990.

14. *Izvestiya*, October 15, 1990, p. 2.

15. Philip Hanson, "The Dimensions of the Monopoly Problem," *Report on the USSR*, No. 17, 1991, p. 6.

16. *Kazakhstanskaya pravda*, September 22, 1990, p. 3; *Pravda*, August 28, 1990, p. 2.

17. *Izvestiya*, November 4, 1990, p. 2.

18. Ibid.

19. Personal communication with Vyacheslav Vashanov, Moscow, August 1991.

20. If they were to have traded with each other at world prices in 1988, all of the Soviet republics with the exception of the Russian Federation and Turkmenistan would have had a trade deficit. *Economist*, October 20, 1990, p. 9. See also *Ekonomika i zhizn'*, No. 10, 1990.

21. *Izvestiya*, July 18, 1990, p. 2.

22. Raymer, "Cash Needs," p. 2.

23. *Economist*, October 5, 1991, p. 74.

24. Raymer, "Cash Needs," p. 1.

25. Kaunas Economics Institute, "Urgent Ecological Problems in Lithuania," briefing submitted to the Lithuanian Council of Ministers, November 1988, pp. 16–20.

26. *Moscow News*, No. 13, 1991, p. 5.

27. *Los Angeles Times*, October 2, 1991, p. A1.

28. Ukrainian Prime Minister Vitold Fokin, cited by TASS, February 13, 1991, translated in JPRS–TEN–91–005, p. 33. In 1989, coal accounted for over 76 percent of primary energy production in terms of energy equivalents. Natural gas and crude oil accounted for 19 and 4 percent of energy production, respectively. Ukrainian SSR State Committee for Statistics, *Narodnoe khozyaistvo Ukrainskoi SSR v 1989 godu* (Kiev: Tekhnika, 1990), p. 295.

29. *Pravda*, December 3, 1991, p. 2.

30. R. Caron Cooper, University of California, Berkeley, Energy and Resources Group, personal communication, Los Angeles, May 1992.

31. Radio Kiev, February 18, 1991. In 1991, Ukraine exported 16 billion kilowatt-hours of electricity to Eastern Europe. *Times* (London), March 25, 1992.

32. David Marples, "Future of Donbass Coal Field Reviewed," *Report on the USSR*, No. 18, 1990, p. 18.

33. *Pravda Ukrainy*, April 26, 1991, p. 2; *Financial Times*, October 18, 1991, p. 2. In many ways, the situation in Ukraine is similar to that in neighboring Czechoslovakia. In 1990–1991, Czechoslovakia faced a steep drop in oil imports from the USSR as the result of a decrease in Soviet production. Czechoslovakia's supply problems were compounded by the fact that prices shot up when a new trade agreement forced Czechoslovakia to buy Soviet oil and gas at world market prices using hard currency. As a result, Czechoslovak power plants increased their burning of low-quality brown coal obtained domestically. Meanwhile, the Czechoslovak government has pressed on with its ambitious nuclear power program (based on Soviet technology) despite the misgivings of neighboring countries. Unlike Ukraine on the eve of its independence, the Czechs, and environmentalists in particular, have supported nuclear power as the only viable solution to the widespread environmental devastation in their country caused by a heavy reliance on dirty coal.

34. USSR Goskomstat, *Okhrana okruzhayushchei sredy i ratsional'noe ispol'zovanie prirodnykh resursov v SSSR* (Moscow: Finansy i statistika, 1989), p. 28; USSR

Goskompriroda, *Sostoyanie prirodnoi sredy v SSSR v 1988 g.* (Moscow: VINITI, 1989), p. 15.

35. Elizabeth Fuller, "Mass Demonstration in Armenia Against Environmental Pollution," *Radio Liberty Research* (RL) 421/87, October 18, 1987, p. 2; Agence France Presse, October 17, 1987, translated in FBIS–SOV–87–203, p. 63.

36. Valerii Papanian, consultant to Union of Greens of Armenia, personal communication, Kiev, July 1991. See also *Izvestiya,* February 7, 1991, p. 2.

37. *Golos Armenii,* April 23, 1991, p. 1.

38. *Golos Armenii,* April 27, 1991, p. 1.

39. Papanian, personal communication, July 1991.

40. See, for example, *Izvestiya,* February 5, 1991, p. 1, and October 7, 1991, p. 2.

41. *Golos Armenii,* July 11, 1991, p. 3.

42. *Golos Armenii,* April 23, 1991, p. 1.

43. *Pravitel'stvennyi vestnik,* No. 24, 1991, p. 6.

44. TASS, December 31, 1991.

45. The figures are 1987 estimates converted at U.S. purchasing-power equivalents by the Central Intelligence Agency, *Handbook of Economic Statistics, 1989* (Washington, DC : Government Printing Office, 1989).

46. The low overall energy efficiency was in part the result of the relatively large share of the Soviet economy devoted to heavy industry. Nevertheless, as illustrated with a few sectors in Chapter 5, the sectors' efficiency, in terms of various inputs, remained substantially below that of other countries.

47. Christopher Flavin, vice-president, WorldWatch Institute, telephone communication, January 1992. The higher estimates of Soviet energy intensiveness were based in part on downward revisions of estimates on the size of the Soviet economy.

48. USSR Goskomstat, *Narodnoe khozyaistvo SSSR v 1989 g.* (Moscow: Finansy i statistika, 1990), p. 690.

49. Ministerstvo Vneshikh Ekonomicheskikh Svyazei SSSR, *Vneshnie ekonomicheskie svyazi SSSR v 1989 g.* (Moscow: Finansy i statistika, 1990), p. 47.

50. Jan Winiecki, "Large Industrial Enterprises in Soviet-type Economies: The Ruling Stratum's Main Rent-Seeking Area," *Communist Economies,* Vol. 1, No. 4, 1989.

51. Central Television, "TSN," November 22, 1991, cited by RFE/RL *Daily Report,* November 26, 1991; Radio Moscow, December 3, 1991, cited by RFE/RL *Daily Report,* December 4, 1991.

52. Postfactum, cited by RFE/RL *Daily Report,* May 13, 1992.

53. Lester Brown and John Young argue that the revival of agriculture in the ex-Soviet world is likely to be slow, given the demise of a family-based farming culture. "Feeding the World in the Nineties," in Lester R. Brown et al., *State of the World, 1990* (New York: W. W. Norton, 1990).

54. Dr. Hartmut Walter, Department of Geography, University of California, Los Angeles, personal communication, February 1991.

55. V. G. Glushkova, "Vazhnye napravleniya ekologicheskoi situatsii v Moskve," in E. M. Pospenov et al., eds., *Problemy uluchsheniya ekologicheskoi*

situatsii i ratsional'nogo prirodopol'zovaniya v Moskovskom regione (Moscow: Moskovskii filial Geograficheskogo Obshchestva SSSR, 1989), p. 72.

56. Robert K. Watson and David B. Goldstein, "The National Resources Defense Council/USSR Academy of Sciences Joint Program on Energy Conservation," *Soviet Geography*, November 1989, p. 731.

57. See, for example, Barry Commoner, "The Environment," *New Yorker*, June 15, 1987.

58. *Molodezh Moldavii*, August 2, 1990, translated in JPRS-UPA-90-056, p. 69.

59. Personal communication with Sheryl Belcher, Kiev, July 1991.

60. Of citizens polled in Russia in the summer of 1991, one-fifth said they would like to change their place of residence because of pollution problems. Radio Rossii, July 1, 1991, translated in JPRS–TEN–91–015, p. 63.

61. *Sovetskaya Rossiya*, November 10, 1988, p. 4; *Rabochaya gazeta*, December 5, 1988, p. 3.

62. Central Television, June 23, 1989.

63. Tom Lane, "Scientists Probe Puzzling Childhood Illness," *Healthpro*, Fall/Winter 1991, p. 11.

64. Foreign advice does not always help. Having rendered a judgment on the state of affairs, foreign visitors have reported that their Soviet hosts may disagree, demanding that they be "more frank" and deliver more critical assessments.

65. RFE/RL Special, February 1, 1990. According to Lithuanian environment minister Julius Sabaliuaskas, the study found "no deviations from global construction standards."

66. RFE/RL Special, June 23, 1989. Yeremy noted that the heating plant was of a "very forgiving" design and "basically sound" conceptually, but said that the group did not address the quality of construction, though they made some recommendations for improvement.

67. Comments made at a press conference chaired by Sergei Zalygin and featured in *Izvestiya*, February 9, 1991, p. 3.

68. Reuter, March 7 and May 10, 1990. For a report on the initiation of the project, see *Pravda*, August 3, 1990. As an advocate of nuclear power, the IAEA also had a compelling interest in assuaging the public's fear.

69. *Wall Street Journal*, May 21, 1991, p. A19.

70. Green World, "Ukrainian Greens Outraged over IAEA Report on Chernobyl," press release, Kiev, June 23, 1991. In the study, the IAEA did not examine an estimated 600,000 persons who participated in the cleanup operation or the more than 100,000 people permanently evacuated from contaminated villages.

71. V. Baryaktar, vice-president, Ukrainian Academy of Sciences, and chair, Ukrainian Chernobyl Commission, cited in RFE/RL Special, May 23, 1991.

72. Interfax, May 29, 1991, translated in JPRS–TEN–91–012, p. 60.

73. *New York Times*, February 15, 1992, pp. 1, 4; *Los Angeles Times*, February 18, 1992, p. A1.

74. *Financial Times*, February 18, 1992, p. 1.

75. Reuter, August 17, 1990.

76. Valentin Katasonov, *Velikaya derzhava ili ekologicheskaya koloniya?* (Moscow: Molodaya gvardiya, 1991).

77. The criticism has not been limited to Western capitalists. For a critique of North Korean logging practices in the Russian Far East, see *Komsomol'skaya pravda,* October 21, 1990, p. 3.

78. *Pravda,* March 20, 1990, p. 5. For a report about an Italian leather factory built in Minsk, see *Rabochaya tribuna,* February 1, 1990, p. 2.

79. For reporting on the Astrakhan complex, see *Pravda,* June 17, 1989, p. 1; *Kuranty,* March 12, 1992, p. 4; *Sovetskaya Rossiya,* May 24, 1989, p. 4, March 24, 1989, p. 3, and May 28, 1989, p. 3; *Sovetskaya kul'tura,* March 10, 1990, p. 5; William Freeman, "Environmental Opposition to Foreign Investment in the USSR," U.S. Information Agency Research Memorandum, November 22, 1989, p. 3; Fedor Morgun, "Ekologiya v sisteme planirovaniya," *Planovoe khozyaistvo,* No. 2, 1989, p. 54. See also Boris Yermolaev, "Gazovaya ataka," *Energiya: Ekonomika, tekhnika, ekologiya,* No. 7, 1990.

80. *Izvestiya,* April 3, 1989, p. 2. For more details of the projects and opposition to them, consult Matthew J. Sagers, "News Notes," *Soviet Geography,* No. 3, 1990, pp. 224–227.

81. *Moscow News,* No. 25, 1991, p. 10. A commission assembled by Kazakh President Nursultan Nazabayev to review the project subsequently gave a favorable review of the environmental impact. *Rabochaya tribuna,* July 6, 1991, p. 3. For more coverage of the debate, see *Nezavisimaya gazeta,* June 4, 1991, p. 4, and June 27, 1991, p. 1; *Rossiskaya gazeta,* August 14, 1991, p. 2; *Argumenty i fakty,* No. 25, 1991, p. 1.

82. Reuter, September 15, 1989. For more on the joint venture debate, see *Argumenty i fakty,* No. 32, 1989, p. 2; *Literaturnaya gazeta,* No. 27, 1989, p. 10; and Freeman, "Environmental Opposition."

83. AP, February 14, 1991.

84. Raymer, "Cash Needs," p. 1.

85. For example, in January 1992, Kazakhstan's deputy minister for foreign economic relations, Bolaton Taiyanov, told a group of visiting German industrialists that his government hoped to boost its export earnings quickly to pay off its share of the Soviet debt by exploiting its wealth of natural resources. A lack of transport was the main obstacle, however. *Handelsblatt,* January 24, 1992, cited in RFE/RL Daily Report, January 24, 1992.

86. See the RSFSR law "Ob inostrannykh investitsiyakh v RSFSR," *Ekonomika i zhizn',* No. 34, 1991, insert p. 7.

87. Kristen Suokko, National Resources Defense Council, telephone communication, July 1991.

88. Writing on the situation in the Czech republic, the country's deputy environment minister noted that the value of an enterprise up for privatization often is established by its "ecological debt." Dr. Pavel Trpak, "Problems of the Ecological Policy of the Ministry of Environment of the Czech Republic," typescript, 1991.

89. Reuter, April 22, 1990.

90. Reuter, May 3, 1990; *Journal of Commerce*, May 4, 1990.

91. Jack Snyder, "Averting Anarchy in the New Europe," *International Security*, Spring 1990.

Acronyms and Abbreviations

CIS	Commonwealth of Independent States
CPSU	Communist Party of the Soviet Union
Donbass	Donets Basin, complex of heavy industries based in eastern Ukraine
FBIS	Foreign Broadcast Information Service
Goskomgidromet	State Committee for Hydrometeorology, the Soviet meteorological service
Goskompriroda	State Committee for the Protection of Nature, the Soviet environmental protection agency
Gosplan	State Committee for Planning, the state's central planning agency
IZA	*Indeks zagryazneniya atmosfera* (Index of Atmospheric Pollution)
JPRS	Joint Publications Research Service
Kuzbass	Kusnetsk Basin, complex of heavy industries based on coal deposits in central Siberia, centered in Kemerovo
NGO	nongovernmental organization
NRDC	National Resources Defense Council
PDK	*predel'no dopustimaya kontsentratsiya* (maximum permissible concentrations)

PDV	*predel'no dopustimyi vybros* (maximum permissible emission)
RFE/RL	Radio Free Europe/Radio Liberty
RSFSR	Russian Soviet Federated Socialist Republic
SSR	Soviet Socialist Republic
VINITI	All-Union Institute of Scientific and Technical Information

Selected Bibliography

Barr, Brenton and Braden, Kathleen. *The Disappearing Russian Forest.* Totowa, NJ: Rowman and Littlefield, 1988.

Brown, Lester E. et al. *State of the World 1990.* New York: Norton, 1990.

Central Intelligence Agency. *Handbook of Economic Statistics, 1989.* Washington, DC: Government Printing Office, 1989.

Chandler, William, ed. *Carbon Emissions Control Strategies: Executive Summary.* Washington, DC: Conservation Foundation, 1990.

Darst, Robert G. Jr. "Environmentalism in the USSR: The Opposition to the River Diversion Projects." *Soviet Economy,* July-September 1988, pp. 223-252.

DeBardeleben, Joan. *The Environment and Marxism-Leninsm.* Boulder: Westview Press, 1985.

Feshbach, Murray and Friendly, Alfred Jr. *Ecocide in the USSR.* New York: Basic Books, 1992.

French, Hilary F. *Clearing the Air: A Global Agenda.* WorldWatch Institute Paper No. 94, Washington, DC, January 1990

French, Hilary F. *Green Revolutions: Environmental Reconstruction in Eastern Europe and the Soviet Union.* WorldWatch Institute Paper No. 99, Washington, DC, November 1990.

Green, Eric. *Ecology and Perestroika.* Washington, DC: American Committee on U.S.-Soviet Relations, 1990.

Jancar, Barbara. *Environmental Management in the Soviet Union and Yugoslavia.* Durham, NC: Duke University Press, 1987.

Komarov, Boris. *The Destruction of Nature in the Soviet Union.* White Plains: M. E. Sharpe, 1980.

Micklin, Philip P. *The Water Management Crisis in Soviet Central Asia.* Carl Beck Paper No. 905, University of Pittsburgh Center for Russian and East European Studies, August 1991.

Natural Resources Defense Council. *Nuclear Weapons Databook,* Vol. 4 (Soviet Nuclear Weapons). New York: Harper & Row, 1989.

Pryde, Philip R. *Environmental Management in the Soviet Union.* New York: Cambridge University Press, 1991.

Rozengurt, Michael A. *Water Policy Mismanagement in the Southern USSR: The Ecological and Economical Impact.* Report to the National Council for Soviet and East European Studies, November 1989.

Singleton, Fred, ed. *Environmental Problems in the Soviet Union & Eastern Europe.* Boulder: Lynne Rienner, 1987.

U.S. Bureau of the Census. *Statistical Abstract of the United States: 1991.* Washington, DC: Government Printing Office, 1991.

United Nations Environment Programme. *Environmental Data Report.* Oxford: Blackwell, 1991.

Volgyes, Ivan, ed. *Environmental Deterioration in the Soviet Union and Eastern Europe.* New York: Praeger, 1974.

Weiner, Douglas R. *Models of Nature: Ecology, Conservation, and Cultural Revolution in Soviet Russia.* Bloomington: Indiana University Press, 1988.

World Resources Institute. *World Resources 1992–93.* New York: Oxford University Press, 1992.

Ziegler, Charles E. *Environmental Policy in the USSR.* Amherst: University of Massachusetts Press, 1987.

About the Book and Author

The dramatic revelations of environmental catastrophe in the Soviet Union made during the late 1980s and early 1990s were a driving force behind reform in, and later the demise of the communist party-state. But while the Union no longer exists, the independent republics confront the same dilemmas that plagued the Soviet state: Will the goal of economic growth continue to take priority over that of environmental quality?

Making good use of personal contacts and the latest official as well as unofficial data to compellingly illustrate the challenges posed in people's daily lives by contaminated food, drinking water, and air, the book also explores developments in environmental policy and politics in recent years and assesses the likely long-term effects of the dramatic economic and political trends in the post-Soviet era. Parallel data on environmental conditions in other regions around the world will assist the student and generalist to view developments in the states of the former Soviet Union in a broader, comparative perspective. The result is a well-balanced, accessible, and engrossing account.

DJ Peterson is a Graduate Fellow at the RAND/UCLA Center for Soviet Studies in Santa Monica, California, and a PhD candidate in Political Science at UCLA. In 1989–1990, Mr. Peterson worked as a research analyst at Radio Liberty in Munich, Germany, where he specialized in Soviet domestic affairs.

Index